Beyond
Superfailure
America's Toxics Policy
for the 1990s

Beyond Superfailure
America's Toxics Policy for the 1990s

Daniel Mazmanian
David Morell

Westview Press
BOULDER • SAN FRANCISCO • OXFORD

Copyright © 1992 by Westview Press, Inc.

Published in 1992 in the United States of America by Westview Press, Inc., 5500 Central Avenue, Boulder, Colorado 80301-2847, and in the United Kingdom by Westview Press, 36 Lonsdale Road, Summertown, Oxford OX2 7EW

Library of Congress Cataloging-in-Publication Data
Mazmanian, Daniel A., 1945–
  Beyond superfailure : America's toxics policy for the 1990s /
Daniel Mazmanian, David Morell.
    p. cm.
  Includes index.
  ISBN 0-8133-1466-6. — ISBN 0-8133-1467-4 (pbk.)
  1. Pollution—Government policy—United States. 2. Hazardous wastes—Government policy—United States. 3. Environmental policy—United States. I. Morell, David. II. Title.
HC110.P55M39 1992
363.72'8756'0973—dc20

91-40094
CIP

Printed and bound in the United States of America

The paper used in this publication meets the requirements of the American National Standard for Permanence of Paper for Printed Library Materials Z39.48-1984.

10   9   8   7   6   5   4   3   2   1

Contents

Boxes

Preface and Acknowledgments

This book emerged from our desire to solve a puzzle. America had undertaken an ambitious, indeed, in some respects valiant effort to address the leading environmental issue of the 1980s: what to do about toxic wastes and the safe management of toxic materials that are pervasive throughout society. Yet by most accounts this effort seems to have failed. Why?

Actually, pronouncing the effort a complete failure is an overstatement, as we show. Some important successes are apparent. With 10-plus years of effort now behind us, however, the attempt as a whole has clearly fallen far short of the mark by virtually all measures.

Why has this occurred? How best to remedy the situation in the years ahead? The answers to this puzzle struck us as in many ways a parable of environmental policy as the United States stands on the threshold of the twenty-first century. The problems and the possibilities evident in toxics policy are beginning more and more to mirror those of air, water, resources, and other environmental policy domains. For this reason we felt compelled not only to solve the immediate puzzle but to seek out an alternative, better course for America's second toxics decade.

Our conclusions from the experience with toxics policy in many ways run contrary to today's conventional wisdom, which for understandable reasons dwells mostly on the shortcomings apparent in toxics management. Therefore, we need to offer a perspective seen in the simplest terms in the contradiction between microsuccesses and macrofailures. The first toxics decade began from ground zero, without any real appreciation by the general public of the scope or severity of hazardous waste and toxics problems facing American society. No well-grounded public policy was available to address the issue. From this bleak beginning, it is noteworthy that the decade had several appreciable successes, documented in this book. A number of major pieces of new hazardous waste and toxics legislation have been enacted; a good deal of data gathering and scientific and policy learning by government, industry, and the public has occurred; there has been a profound national awakening to the overall hazardous wastes and toxics problem; and a growing appreciation exists that any solution will need to satisfy not only scientific, technical, and economic considerations but social and democratic ones as well. In this vein, we can indeed speak of successes. Yet each is on the "micro" level when viewed from the enormity of toxics problems as a whole.

Somewhat paradoxically, though the point is equally valid, our efforts to deal with hazardous wastes and hazardous materials during the first decade have come almost to naught. Thousands of old and abandoned waste sites have been uncovered, but only a handful have been adequately cleaned up after more than 10 years of effort and the expenditure of literally billions of both public and private dollars. Public pressures to act have been enormous; both Congress and state legislatures have responded admirably, passing numerous new laws. Yet the enactment of law after law in pursuit of toxics management has resulted in a nightmarish web of federal, state, and local regulations that seem to impede as much as facilitate the cleanup effort and to confuse further the picture. Litigation dominates over remediation.

Well before America could make significant progress in the cleanup task, which we are now told may take 50 years or more and cost up to $750 billion, the focus of toxics policy was extended to the far more sweeping domain of the safe management by business and industry of hazardous materials per se. All of this occurred with little to show where it most counts. Given the ambitious goals of dramatically changing how business and industry and individual citizens use and dispose of toxic materials and squarely facing the ramification of these issues in all facets of our modern lives, we (and many others) judge the effort to have been a macrofailure. In the vernacular of policy analysis, America's first toxics decade witnessed a substantial flurry of activity in terms of policy output but very little in terms of policy impact. We have coined the term *superfailure* to capture this situation.

This book addresses two questions. First, what went wrong such that the first toxics decade resulted in microsuccesses but macrofailure? No single or simple explanation exists for the failure of policy, as we illustrate through countless examples in our review of the first decade. Most attention has been paid to the effort to clean up old and abandoned hazardous waste sites. The effort to monitor and dispose safely of the ever-flowing stream of new hazardous wastes is another, perhaps equally important part of the picture, one in which macrofailure has received much less public attention. These two topics alone raise a host of questions of technical feasibility, costs, implementation constraints, and how to cope with myriad uncertainties within the framework of existing toxics policy.

The debates have often centered on notions of risk: What is the actual extent of health risk (and financial risk) in doing "a" versus "b," and who is to bear those risks? These questions are inherently difficult to answer. Complexity is only compounded when business, regulatory agencies, and scientists focus primarily on "technical risk" assessment and management, while the other side focuses on "culturally based risks" that stress social, political, and cultural concerns—the more normative dimensions—of risk assessment and management.

We lay to rest concern for availability of technologies for improved toxics management. Adequate technologies do exist, as we show. What keeps them from being rapidly introduced and broadly used? Constraints are evident. This leads back to the problem of designing new approaches to taking action in the thousands of communities across the nation where decisions on hazardous wastes and toxics policy matter most.

How can the lessons of America's first toxics decade be used to improve the situation significantly in the second decade we are now entering? Given the mismatch between promise and performance, it will come as no surprise that the solutions we arrive at involve far more than simply tinkering with existing laws and practices. They involve rethinking the fundamental strategy of toxics policy; redefining the proper roles of government regulatory bodies, especially those of the U.S. Environmental Protection Agency and of state environmental agencies in carrying out that policy; internalizing within businesses the costs of toxics management; and seeking out better methods of democratic governance at the community level.

In trying to solve for ourselves the toxics policy puzzle, we have come to the conclusion that the quickest and most effective way to reach viable solutions for hazardous wastes and toxics management problems is not by piling on more and more microsuccesses in hopes of eventually achieving macrosuccess. Instead, we need to approach the whole issue anew. The shortest path to successful dispute resolution and policy implementation in this contentious field is through what may seem to be the most cumbersome and time-consuming approach of all: a participatory democratic process.

In our view, this is one of the most important lessons of the first toxics decade. Few viable technical solutions will be implemented without the public trust and confidence in the experts and the business and government leaders who are responsible for carrying out our environmental policies. Similarly, without public trust "acceptable" levels of risk for each community directly affected will never emerge. This became apparent time and again throughout the first decade. Government officials and business people who so often ignored this truth inevitably suffered the consequences. For both philosophical and pragmatic reasons, the burgeoning democratic imperative driving contemporary American politics needs to be recognized as we move into the future on even the most seemingly technical dimensions of toxics policy, if not on all environmental policies.

This book was written in an attempt to tell the full story of America's experience in developing its policies for hazardous wastes and toxics. It presumes little prior knowledge by the reader; certainly no particular technical expertise is required. The only prerequisite is a willingness to glean from the past what is worth keeping and that which needs to be changed, with the objective being to chart a more viable course. Our intended audience? Surely included are the hazardous wastes and toxics policy experts, affected government officials, and business managers and planners—virtually all of whom are affected whether they know it or not. The book is of equal value, we believe, to community and environmental activists concerned with how environmental policy in one of its most controversial arenas emerged in the 1980s, and what this foretells for the 1990s and beyond. America's experience with toxics policy will also intrigue scholars and students of policy design and implementation. It compels the policy analyst to reach beyond the usual framework of looking at one statute or case at a time. Instead, here one must view the complex web created in a rapidly unfolding policy domain, with the unavoidable entanglements that occur when several major pieces of legislation are enacted, then modified in relatively rapid succession, each ostensibly addressing a different slice of the same policy pie; thus, policymakers are constantly changing the rules and sometimes operating at cross-purposes. Finally, we write for those who look to the future and ask not what is foreordained but how can the experience in toxics policy best inform the fashioning of a better and more democratically grounded policy for tomorrow.

The idea for this book and the work that it took to make it a reality could not have been possible without the help of many others. To the literally hundreds of people with whom we have had conversations or formal interviews, and those whose writings on the subject of toxics policy we have used liberally, we owe an enormous debt of gratitude. The project would simply have been impossible without them. Little progress would have been made on the manuscript save for our research assistants, first Miriam Green and Michael Stanley-Jones, followed by Daniel Press; they kept to the grindstone when we would become distracted with other tasks. Michael's work on Chapter Two and Daniel's on Chapter Five deserve special recognition. Michael Kraft's critique of the full manuscript resulted, we believe, in a better book and we thank him.

Ted Trzyna, president of the California Institute of Public Affairs (CIPA), deserves particular recognition. Early on he called upon us to explore the toxics policy story, and through CIPA he supported the initial phase of the project. We might not have come together as coauthors nor have undertaken the project but for Ted. The entire staff of EPICS International has contributed immeasurably to our knowledge, our insights, and our commitment to explaining toxics policy in all its complexity. Alison Bronstein's production support was invaluable.

For generous financial support, we thank the Randolph and Dora Haynes Foundation for helping to fund our efforts, first through a grant to CIPA and then with a summer research grant to Mazmanian to see the project through to fruition. A manuscript does not become a book, of course, without an editor and publisher. We had the good fortune to work with Jennifer Knerr at Westview Press, and she is wonderful—responsive, enthusiastic throughout, insightful, and professional in all respects. Authors can ask for no more.

Although there is joy in writing a book, there are many hectic and crazy moments along the way. We deeply appreciate the understanding and forbearance of Andy and Mary throughout.

Daniel Mazmanian
Claremont, California

David Morell
Oakland, California

Acronyms

AHM	acutely hazardous material (California term for EHSs)
ARAR	applicable or relevant and appropriate requirement (of other statutes)
ATSDR	Agency for Toxic Substances and Disease Registry
BCEE	bis (2-chlorethyl) ether
BTU	British thermal unit
CAA	Clean Air Act (amended 1990)
CAS	Chemical Abstracts Service
CBO	Congressional Budget Office
CCHW	Citizens Clearinghouse for Hazardous Waste
CDC	Centers for Disease Control
CERCLA	Comprehensive Environmental Response, Compensation, and Liability Act (1980)
CFCs	chlorofluorocarbons
CSAC	County Supervisors Association of California
DDT	dichloro-diphenyl-trichloroethane
DEP	Department of Environmental Protection (New Jersey)
DHS	Department of Health Services (California)
DOT	Department of Transportation (U.S.)
ECRA	Environmental Compensation Responsibility Act (New Jersey)
EDF	Environmental Defense Fund
EHS	extremely hazardous substance (see AHM)
EPA	Environmental Protection Agency
FEMA	Federal Emergency Management Agency
GAO	General Accounting Office
GOOMBY	get out of my backyard
HAPs	hazardous air pollutants
HMTA	Hazardous Materials Transportation Act (1980)
HRS	hazard ranking system
HSWA	Hazardous and Solid Waste Amendments (1984)
LEPCs	local emergency planning committees
LUSTs	leaking underground storage tanks
MACT	maximum achievable control technology
MSDSs	material safety data sheets
NACEPT	National Advisory Committee for Environmental Policy and Technology
NESHAPS	national emission standards for hazardous air pollutants
NGA	National Governors Association
NIMBY	not in my backyard
NPDES	National Pollutant Discharge Elimination System
NPL	National Priority List

NSPSs	new source performance standards
NTC	National Toxics Campaign
OES	Office of Emergency Services
OTA	Office of Technology Assessment
PALLCA	Pitman–Alcyon Lake–Lipari Landfill Community Association (New Jersey)
PCBs	polychlorinated biphenyls
PPA	Pollution Prevention Act (1990)
PRP	potentially responsible party
RAP	remedial action plan
RCRA	Resource Conservation and Recovery Act (1976)
RI/FS	remedial investigation and feasibility study
RMPP	risk management and prevention program
ROD	record of decision
RQ	reportable quantity
SARA	Superfund Amendments and Reauthorization Act (1986)
SCHWMA	Southern California Hazardous Waste Management Authority
SQG	small-quantity generator
TCC	Toxics Coordinating Committee
TCE	trichloroethylene
TCPA	Toxic Catastrophe Prevention Act (New Jersey, 1985)
TPQ	threshold planning quantity
TRI	toxics release inventory
TSCA	Toxic Substances Control Act (1976)
TSD	treatment, storage, and disposal
TTUs	transportable treatment units
USTs	underground storage tanks
YIMBY	yes in many backyards

CHAPTER ONE

Past Lessons and Future Promises

The problem of safely managing hazardous wastes and hazardous materials proved in the 1980s to be an enormous and frustrating environmental challenge to American society. This is true for at least three reasons. To start with, the issue of hazardous waste poses one of the more intractable questions of environmental protection. Dealing with the air and water pollution of the 1970s was challenging and continues to be so, but those kinds of pollution problems have accepted solutions that usually focus on the end of the pipe: add an air scrubber to a utility or industrial smokestack or a catalytic converter to an automobile, treat water at a municipal treatment facility, and so forth. Even though these solutions have costs, effective technologies and know-how are generally available and industry and the public have both been willing to settle for such after-the-fact approaches. Few people ever ask where the pollutants, now quite concentrated and thus often "hazardous wastes," end up after being removed from air and water emissions. This topic is left to others. The answer is that these concentrated pollutants have typically been transported out of sight rather than being chemically or biologically transformed into harmless substances. Along with the rest of the nation's enormous flow of industrial, commercial, and municipal hazardous wastes, residues from our air and water pollution control devices end up dumped on the land, pumped into wells deep into the earth, or left to evaporate in holding ponds at industrial sites.[1]

But what to do when we finally discovered that there is no "there" there—that the end of the line for America's industrial wastes is only the beginning of the next environmental catastrophe? All landfills eventually leak, not only contaminating the soil around them but all too often seeping into adjacent aquifers and despoiling water used for drinking, recreation, irrigation, and commerce. This dirty backside of industrial activity produced the challenge of toxic wastes management, though it took quite a while for people to realize it.

Second, the health benefits of water and air pollution control are widespread, and the costs are relatively hidden from public view. Although costs involved are often high, they can frequently be passed along by industry to consumers by way of higher prices for electricity, automobiles, water, and so forth. Financial risks of air and water pollution control can be understood, measured, planned for in advance. Not the same with hazardous wastes. Although the beneficiaries of safer management of hazardous wastes are equally widespread, the wastes still head for landfills that have neighbors who typically believe they are unjustly being asked to shoulder the health and environmental burdens associated. These people came in the 1980s to resist mightily. For them, the costs and risks are seen explicitly in terms of human health, especially cancer, rather than dollars and cents.

Third, America's hazardous waste and toxics issues surfaced during a time of deepening public skepticism and distrust of corporate, political, and scientific authority. The causes are many, but the mood is captured in the rhetoric of "chemophobia" (at heart, a fear of cancer), "empowerment," and "local control." Trust in expert judgments made by outsiders is at an all-time low. The solution to our hazardous wastes and toxics problems became, and remains, bound up in how society addresses the pervasive fear of chemicals and the growing demand by citizens for greater control over their individual lives and their community's destiny.

The search for solutions has not been aided by the inflated rhetoric on all sides, which early on found its way into the discourse of hazardous waste and toxics policy. Legislative promises of a "super" fund for cleanup, of "permanent" remedies, of prompt action, of bans on land disposal—all these set us up for comparative failure as statutes were actually implemented. People were promised much; then government and business gave them too little. In response, frustration rose notch by notch. The ultimate rhetorical inflation is seen in the liability scheme of Superfund (the now-common name of the program created by the 1980 Comprehensive Environmental Response, Compensation, and Liability Act, or CERCLA), under which anyone who had contributed to the hazardous waste problem that had been percolating in waste sites for decades could be made to pay.

This chapter sets the context for discussion of these issues, beginning at the point at which hazardous wastes first became a major issue on the nation's policy agenda. The body of the chapter provides an overview—a preview—of how far we have traveled in the first toxics decade (roughly from the late 1970s through the end of the 1980s) and of the new directions imperative if we are to achieve greater success in the second toxics decade now under way.

THE LEGACY OF LOVE CANAL

In 1977 the tragedy of Love Canal startled the American public into an awareness of the devastating consequences of the mismanagement of our hazardous wastes and toxic materials.[2] Thirty-five years earlier, Occidental Petroleum's Hooker Chemical and Plastics Corporation began burying more than 20,000 tons of chemical waste in an abandoned waterway ironically named for its former owner, William Love.

In 1953 the landfill was covered with topsoil and the property sold to the Niagara Falls (New York) Board of Education for a token one dollar. Later the school district parceled out lots to developers. Homebuilding in the neighborhood moved at a rapid pace throughout the 1950s, prompting the school district to build an elementary school and playing field on its remaining parcel.

By the conventional rules of that day, this procedure was a common occurrence in thousands of locations across the nation: Fill a pit or ravine with industrial or household garbage, cover it, level it, and build on it, because towns and cities were pushing ever outward amid the burgeoning prosperity of the post–World War II American industrial boom and suburban expansion.

The toxics time bomb exploded when the Niagara River overflowed its banks and flooded the buried canal a quarter mile away. Floodwaters pushed contaminated groundwater into the basements of residents. What had been suspected all along by a few could no longer be ignored by the many. Over 200 dangerous chemical compounds were eventually identified in that waste pile, including benzene, trichloroethylene, and most potent of all, dioxin.

President Jimmy Carter stepped in to declare Love Canal an emergency disaster area, with all the attendant federal government activities that status brought, including the evacuation of 1,004 households and a $30 million government buyout for those living closest to the old canal/dump. By the end of a decade, $150 million had been spent on the cleanup effort.

After having for years resisted all local calls for action, New York state placed a clay cap over the canal's most severely contaminated 16 acres, eventually extending the cover to more than 40 surrounding acres. The title of a 1978 report by the New York commissioner of health said it all: "Love Canal: Public Health Time Bomb."

Biochemist Dr. Beverly Paigan's study of some 900 children from this area counted seizures, learning problems, eye and skin irritations, incontinence, and severe abdominal pains and found these problems much more prevalent among the children of Love Canal than those from nearby neighborhoods. Although questions were subsequently raised by respected scientists about Paigan's methodology and conclusions, the impact of her study on public fears and perceptions remained largely unchanged. In truth, "Accurately describing the risks from exposure to the Love Canal site may require decades, or generations; it may never happen."[3]

The media were quick to take up the cause, playing on the fear of widespread chemical poisoning that had been creeping slowly into the gradually awakening American psyche. The tragedy at Love Canal was symptomatic, *Newsweek* said in 1978, of America's "Faustian" bargain: "The products and by-products of industrial efforts to improve consumers' standards of living are threatening those same people with disease and death." Love Canal was featured on the "Today Show," "The MacNeil-Lehrer Report," "Sixty Minutes," and "Good Morning America"; Phil Donahue brought in residents from Love Canal and devoted an entire program to their plight.[4]

Clearly, Love Canal was a tragedy of significant human and environmental proportions. However, it was not the first such event; nor would it be the last or even the most dramatic revelation of toxics contamination from the largely forgotten landfills and industrial sites scattered across the American landscape. Yet this case remains outstanding in almost everyone's mind.

That flood of 1977, so calamitous to nearby residents, was by no means the first signal that a serious hazardous waste problem existed at Love Canal. People living nearby had been complaining as far back as the 1940s about nauseating vapors, black sludge seeping into their basements, and sometimes burns and blisters from contact with contaminated soil and residues. In 1976, a local reporter brought to the attention of anyone who wanted to listen the growing body of evidence about the health threats to the community posed by the chemicals buried beneath it. But few people listened. Psychologically, the Love Canal residents were no different from many other people across the country at this time, who seemed to block out what was simply inconceivable: that they and their children were sometimes at fatal risk from exposure to hidden toxic chemicals.

This episode clearly set the tone of the debate that would ensue over what to do about hazardous wastes and toxic materials. However, and contrary to popular belief, Love Canal was not the episode that first alerted Congress to the potential dangers of hazardous waste in the environment. Important laws had already been passed. The Resource Conservation and Recovery Act (RCRA) enacted in 1976 (see Box 1.1) established a national system to collect data and track industry's toxic wastes from "cradle to grave," in the hope that this tracking system would ensure their safe disposal. Nevertheless, hazardous waste

BOX 1.1 Selected Major Laws and Events

Date	Laws and Events
1976	RCRA (Resource Conservation and Recovery Act): Defines national policy for management of hazardous wastes (and of municipal solid wastes); focus on treatment, storage, and disposal facilities
1976	TSCA (Toxic Substances Control Act): Declares a national policy that adequate data should be developed regarding the effects of chemical substances on human and environmental health
1978 on	Several states enact early hazardous waste facility siting laws (e.g., Massachusetts, Minnesota, Rhode Island)
1978	Love Canal, New York, declared a federal disaster area by President Carter
1980	CERCLA (Comprehensive Environmental Response, Compensation, and Liability Act): Superfund—sets out hazardous waste site cleanup program; defines new liability scheme; allocates $1.6 billion to cleanup
1983	New Jersey Worker and Community Right-to-Know Act: Businesses required to disclose hazardous substances onsite; precursor to federal SARA Title III
1983	Federal government buys and evacuates Times Beach, Missouri, for $33 million
1984	HSWA (Hazardous and Solid Waste Amendments): Modifies RCRA to require corrective action at hazardous waste facilities; bans land disposal of selected hazardous wastes
1984	Leak of methyl isocyanate at Union Carbide in Bhopal, India, kills at least 2,000 and injures many more
1984	Hazardous waste facility planning law enacted in California (AB 2948): Involves counties and cities in siting
1985	New Jersey Toxic Catastrophe Prevention Act: Pre-SARA, covers 11 extremely hazardous substances (EHSs)
1986	SARA (Superfund Amendments and Reauthorization Act): Amends 1980 Superfund, increases fund to $8.5 billion, adds community right-to-know (Title III)
1986	California Safe Drinking Water and Toxics Enforcement Act (Proposition 65)
1990	Clean Air Act amended, adding extensive requirements for management of air toxics
1991	19,000 gallons of metam sodium herbicide spilled into Sacramento River, northern California

management was the hidden step child, merely one component of a revised solid waste management law focused on household garbage. Furthermore, the federal rules implementing RCRA did not emerge until 1980, after the furor of Love Canal.

On the books, too, was the Toxic Substances Control Act (TSCA), also adopted in 1976. The goal of its authors was to test the safety of all chemicals introduced into industrial and commercial use in the United States; polychlorinated biphenyls (PCBs) were high on the list for TSCA attention. In signing this bill, President Ford referred to TSCA as "one of the most important pieces of environmental legislation that has been enacted by the Congress."[5] The wheels of the legislative process were turning. Yet TSCA would not be used as a powerful tool to address effective management of hazardous wastes.

Why was Love Canal accorded such attention, and why has it since been generally regarded as the starting point for America's intensifying concern with toxic wastes and hazardous materials? Timing![6] Love Canal was one of those rare catalytic events, one of those seemingly isolated incidents that so often throws an entire nation into turmoil. This unpredictable turning point in the late 1970s bared both the sensitive chemophobic nerve lurking just below the surface of American public consciousness and the growing lack of trust in both business and government expertise. Love Canal was to the toxics issue what the 1969 Santa Barbara oil well blowout represented for overall U.S. environmental policy; what Three Mile Island in 1979 became for domestic nuclear power; what the 1973 and 1979 OPEC oil embargos had been for energy policy; and what the *Exxon Valdez* later came to mean for oil spills. And at Love Canal, as with all the other incidents, the public's perceptions of the problem were far more important politically than can be deduced by any reading of the "facts" of these cases.

What followed Love Canal was tantamount to a public confessional. America really did have a serious problem with hazardous wastes. Even the president had now openly proclaimed that the problem was all too real, quite serious, and pervasive. Headline-hungry media amplified Carter's warning in frightening detail. Confirming evidence (real and exaggerated) appeared almost overnight from every corner of the nation.

Horror stories soon abounded, from spots with such interesting names as the Valley of the Drums (Kentucky), Price's Pit (New Jersey), and the Stringfellow Acid Pits (California) and from so many other now-discovered toxic dumps. Throughout the avalanche of publicity, Love Canal remained the primary symbol for the nation in its concern about the crisis of coping with the hazardous wastes it had been producing at an accelerating rate for half a century. There the issue remained through what we term "America's first toxics decade."

RESPONDING TO LOVE CANAL

A political response was unavoidable—indeed it represented the first microsuccess as public outcry led to congressional action. It was no surprise that Congress swiftly enacted a "Superfund" program calling for cleanup of abandoned and other dangerous hazardous waste dumps across the land. Most of the states followed suit, passing their own cleanup laws. But the legislation has not worked, at least not sufficiently. And to this day, it is inexplicable to many that hazardous waste management has remained so vexing a problem despite the continuing flurry of federal, state, and even local legislation.

Implementing Superfund and all the other laws has proved so much more difficult than passing them that we term this phenomenon superfailure! This debilitating if exhilarating cycle moved at a rapid pace during America's first toxics decade, creating a policy arena plagued with multiple contradictions. Each onslaught of new rules and regulations was designed to address a particular element of the problem but never the whole. This pattern has been identified in other rapidly evolving major policy arenas, but in toxics management the problem has become acute.

Through the decade, public attention moved markedly beyond how to manage old hazardous wastes on to a panoply of other toxics issues (see Box 1.2). These issues include (1) reassessing the rights and responsibilities of business manufacturers and producers in their handling of hazardous materials; (2) reducing the flow of hazardous wastes at their source; (3) banning altogether certain highly toxic materials; (4) trying to coordinate local, state, and federal layers of government; and (5) searching for new forms of public-private governance to assuage public suspicion that neither usual business practices nor traditional government agencies are structurally capable of remedying public concerns. These developments are as important to achieving a successful toxics policy in the 1990s as they are unprecedented—but more on all this later.

LESSONS OF AMERICA'S FIRST TOXICS DECADE

For anyone reviewing the first toxics decade, hindsight emphasizes several notable phenomena. Clearly, such a large, complex, chemically based economy can modify its ways in the face of the mounting health and safety risks it has caused. Many significant changes in toxics management have in fact occurred. In several cases, industries have shown a remarkable willingness to reduce their waste streams, which they had simply been dumping into landfills, toxic pits, or lagoons.

BOX 1.2 Evolution of Hazardous Waste and Toxics Policy Options

SITING
- Potential conflict with source reduction since TSD facilities need guaranteed waste stream
- NIMBY still prevalent

HAZARDOUS MATERIALS MANAGEMENT
- Potential Chronic Hazards: Underground liquid storage (mostly gasoline); aboveground tanks (gases and liquids); dry solid chemicals
- Potential Acute Hazards: Gases or liquids that gasify; transportation spills; pipe or tank ruptures

SOURCE REDUCTION
- Many businesses reducing their wastes to capture economic benefits, but many more are unconvinced or uninformed about savings
- Future emphasis on pushing industry beyond "easy" economics to process changes

TREATMENT
- Growing preference for onsite treatment over offsite disposal
- Resistance to siting and development of treatment facilities, especially incineration

CLEANUP
- Little real cleanup actually performed at many Superfund sites (less than 6% of sites fully cleaned)
- Several sites have been excavated; soils and wastes sent to other landfills

LAND DISPOSAL
- Land bans effective soon but most wastes still sent to land disposal untreated
- In the second toxics decade, push toward physical stabilization and residuals repositories

Technologies new and old and some new hazardous waste management practices have been introduced to reduce waste flows: separating water from oils; lessening use of solvents in cleaning; sorting and recycling; incinerating; and even adopting substitute feedstocks.

Unfortunately, not everyone moves at the same pace. Despite all the recent attention given by government, the media, and industrial associations to hazardous wastes and to the management of hazardous materials, by the end of the first toxics decade, the vast majority of affected businesses still remained basically outside this changing system. Remedial cleanups were generally stymied. Most new wastes were still being dumped—untreated—onto the land or into sewers. Ignorance and the high cost of converting to new hazardous waste management practices were the usual excuses. Even when facing criminal sanctions and growing fines, many businesses flatly defied the law. Incidents of illegal disposal and midnight dumping were far too numerous to be dismissed as the practices of a few outlaws. The combination of limited enforcement and high costs of compliance proved too powerful for many to resist.

At the same time, local citizens and environmental groups showed an extraordinary capacity to use the apparatus of government to discourage development even of modern new hazardous waste management facilities. American-style popular democracy gave ordinary people tremendous power, especially to say "Stop!" both to business and government. Unless facility proponents could present a strong case for the safety of what was being proposed, such opposition—just say "No!"—almost always prevailed.

The clever catch-phrase acronym NIMBY (not in my backyard) became the label for the commonplace occurrence of local resistance to any siting proposals. Even states have tried, with some success, to ban entry of hazardous wastes coming from other states. The tactics used to convey the NIMBY message were seldom genteel, and they have left festering wounds on individuals, communities, and businesses. While the system of political checks and balances and electoral accountability worked well to compel policymakers at every level of government to reassess their toxics policy—so far, sufficient progress remains an unmet aspiration.

The experience of the decade also points to the limitations of the U.S. political process. Although basic rights can be protected and the voices of citizens heard, few mechanisms exist through which consensus can be formed within a broader community adequate to allow positive action to be taken. Parochial fears dominate over the desire of the community at large for better toxics management. Equity demands assume the lowest common denominator. Yet if new facilities to treat wastes cannot be sited, careless land disposal and sewering practices continue far longer than necessary, and longer than was contemplated in the new laws. Thus, America remains dependent on leaky landfills because hazardous wastes cannot and do not simply disappear.

Mutually beneficial forums have rarely emerged through which antagonistic groups such as industry, environmentalists, local citizens, and governments can work together toward an economically productive and safe common future. At the same time, the experience of the decade shows that cooperative decisions can sometimes emerge out of policy gridlock; building consensus is possible (a point we address at length in Chapters Seven and Eight). Though these experiences are too few in number, we hope they will find broader acceptance during America's second toxics decade.

Throughout the first decade, the constitutional separation of local, state, and federal administrative powers complicated implementation of toxics programs. Every major federal effort at cleaning up sites, monitoring hazardous waste movement, regulating hazardous waste generators and landfills, and getting businesses to develop better hazardous materials practices was carried out in part or whole by state and local governments. Federal legislation set broad policy goals for the nation, but in practice state and local officials often responded more to local political and economic pressures (for the good or ill) in implementing toxics policy. As a result, some states and localities were far ahead of the federal government, others fell far behind. But overall, the sheer complexity of intergovernmental coordination required under the American federal system severely impeded effective program starts, especially in the early period of trying to carry out each new law.

The first decade laid bare the limits of narrowly construed techniques of policy analysis. This was revealed most vividly when time and again the analysts' basic tool, benefit-cost analysis, provided little direction for decisionmakers and found little acceptance from the general public. Policy choices based on the economics of a particular situation (a new treatment facility, for example) failed in any significant way to capture public concerns about toxics safety and made no allowance for public skepticism about the motives and trustworthiness of both business and government decisionmakers.

The first decade also revealed the significance of *risk perception*. Public attitudes can indeed drive the policy process, a concept perhaps not new to elected politicians but certainly a shock to technical specialists in and out of government. Failures in discourse were enormous, as "experts" and citizens talked past and around one another. The immediate interpretation by many in business and government was that ordinary people were simply selfish (or irrational); all opponents were accused of having a NIMBY mentality. More accurately, the assessments of "technical" risk by business and regulatory bodies proved to be of little avail in addressing "culturally" based concerns of citizens: About their health and safety, and about whom they should trust. These clearly differing perceptions of risk actually showed that when people were asked to bear the brunt of health and safety risks created by wastes being generated by others, their answer was a resounding "no." Fear and outrage made a potent combination. Each backyard defended its parochial interests, as local equity concerns overwhelmed the experts' efficiency calculations.

Selfish? Maybe, but most citizens found attempts to impose unspecified and uncertain health risks upon them both unreasonable and unfair. The public demanded that risks be reduced by spreading them across all of the communities that stood to benefit, rather than trying to concentrate the risks in a single community.

The efforts to implement the new hazardous wastes and toxics policies also saw a constant tug-of-war between those who wanted to remedy the problem by working within current policies and state-of-the-art knowledge and those who wanted first to establish long-term goals and the interconnectedness of the pieces before acting. These tensions made surpassing the status quo difficult at best and often impossible. Each issue, with all of its attendant debate and lawmaking, piled atop the previous issue before any one had been effectively addressed. No wonder the whole process appeared chaotic. It was. And the chaos only increased as the decade progressed.

For example, policy called for accelerated transition away from landfilling of hazardous wastes; wastes were to be treated instead. This goal was sought through banning land disposal of the most problematic toxic substances. Short of courting illegal disposal or closing down the industries generating these hazardous wastes, officials had to know that adequate treatment facilities were available before they could phase out dumping. The legislative bans could not go into effect, therefore, until adequate treatment capacity existed. When needed treatment facilities were not built, partly because of local opposition and partly because lower-priced landfills remained open as attractive marketplace alternatives to treatment, the policy stumbled badly in implementation.

One more example of policy failure: Laws enacted at the outset of the first toxics decade aimed at ensuring that those who had sent their wastes to the thousands of abandoned hazardous waste sites would actually pay for their cleanup. This was done mainly by adopting a combination of two legal principles—strict liability and joint and several liability—to create strict joint and several liability. In essence, negligence was no longer relevant. If you generated the hazardous wastes, you could be asked to fund the cleanup . . . even if you had done nothing wrong.

However, these very features of the 1980 Superfund law had the inescapable effect of discouraging waste management entrepreneurs from stepping in with innovative new waste treatment techniques. Under these new liability laws, the only way to remain clear of responsibility for any harm (or alleged harm) resulting anywhere along the life path of a hazardous waste was to avoid it entirely. Inevitably, this policy discouraged private development of a marketplace in hazardous waste treatment.

By the end of the first decade, an appreciation of such inter-connectedness proved crucial to making significant headway on almost any front. That sensitivity will surely need to be a hallmark if overall success is to be achieved in the second toxics decade.

THE FOUR STAGES OF THE FIRST TOXICS DECADE

Hazardous waste and hazardous materials policy evolved through a sequence of stages in the first decade. Once these phases are recognized, it is easier to appreciate how and why policymakers found themselves slipping deeper and deeper into the frustrating morass.

At first, policymakers sought to compartmentalize the problem into three distinct issues—hazardous wastes past, present, and future—with the "sins of the past" dominant. That was an understandable conclusion considering the notoriety of Love Canal and similar examples of the unacceptability of past practices of land disposal of hazardous wastes.

Hazardous Waste Cleanup:
The Superfund Dilemma

As the problem of past practices of dumping untreated hazardous wastes on the ground was addressed, three issues predominated:

- To what sites are these wastes to be moved? Typically, excavation and redisposal were chosen as the cheapest short-term option, even though it soon posed new cleanup problems at the new locations.
- Who will pay the expensive bill for cleanup? This is the liability and cost-allocation question.
- What standards are to be applied? That is, "how clean is clean?" and "how safe is safe enough?"

Almost everyone seemed preoccupied by the liability and funding question: Who pays? By the early 1980s, the Office of Technology Assessment estimated that total long-term national cleanup costs would reach $100 billion, drawn out over several decades. This sum far exceeded the $1.6 billion allocated in the original 1980 Superfund (the Comprehensive Environmental Response, Compensation, and Liability Act, or CERCLA) or even the $9 billion in the 1986 Superfund Amendments and Reauthorization Act (SARA). A 1991 study by a University of Tennessee research team estimated total public and private cleanup costs at a staggering $750 billion over the next 30 years.[7] In view of this immense funding gap, litigation and debate over financial responsibility often overshadowed the search for enduring cleanup solutions.

Moreover, the formula for allocating money to cleanup efforts under the 1980 law skewed spending in favor of excavation and redisposal of the hazardous wastes and surrounding soil because this cleanup method was often presented as the cheapest. In effect, hazardous wastes from one site were hauled to a second presumably "safe" site, where they were again dumped, untreated, onto the land. Wastes from cleanup of the Chemical Control Corporation facility in Elizabeth, New Jersey, went to landfills—later closed—in upstate New York. Wastes from Stringfellow in Riverside County, California, were redumped at the later-closed BKK landfill in Los Angeles County. Shortsightedness and narrow economics prevailed over environmental and public health goals.

The 1986 Superfund amendments adopted a vastly different approach, one that reflected substantial learning in just six years about the political and economic realities of cleanup. Under SARA, "permanent remedies" are now supposed to prevail over redisposal. Unfortunately, how that will be accomplished on a nationwide scale has yet to be determined.

The amended Superfund law also sets out a strong preference for onsite remedial treatment of wastes instead of carrying them elsewhere either for treatment or redisposal. This approach assumes that local demands for effective remedial action will balance local acceptance of (or at least a begrudging tolerance of) operation of the necessary treatment technologies at the cleanup site. But onsite incineration is often not accepted by the neighboring community. And local residents fear that encapsulation of the wastes will degrade property values. Basic remedial action policy has become far more reasonable, but shows little sign of becoming much more successful in leading to widespread cleanup of the country's thousands of contaminated sites.

Today's Wastes: Transition from Land Disposal to Treatment

While public attention was riveted on Superfund, some policymakers and community leaders began to appreciate the broader implications of the hazardous waste management problem facing the entire industrial system. Besides the cleanup legislation, a second set of laws began to focus on prevention of further contamination, first through tighter land disposal standards and later through phasing out the land disposal of hazardous wastes. This reflected a growing appreciation of the problem posed by generation of more than 200 million tons of hazardous wastes every year—about six pounds a day for every American. How should these vasts flows be managed to keep from adding to an already unmanageable hazardous waste legacy?

The 1976 Resource Conservation and Recovery Act (RCRA) emphasized safer, better methods of land disposal. New rules called for standards for liners, leak detection systems, leachate collection, and so on. Major regulations from the Environmental Protection Agency (EPA) were delayed for four years, however, and then emerged only in response to growing public concerns over the many Love Canals spewing poisons across the land. By the time EPA's landfill regulations appeared in 1980, initiatives in several states had already begun to shift focus away from landfilling of this continuing flow of huge volumes of new hazardous wastes.

As the federal government was dragging many states into the modern hazardous waste management era, in turn several of the more innovative and aggressive states were leading EPA farther and faster than the always-cautious federal agency was prepared to go. That effect became evident as early as 1981–1982, when California banned future land disposal of six categories of hazardous wastes. Within the next several years, solvents, strong acids, PCBs, and other dangerous wastes were to be banned from land disposal and treated instead. Unfortunately, California's actions could not match its rhetoric. For the several reasons already mentioned, more than a decade later adequate treatment capacity has yet to come on line. Across the nation, the vast proportion of hazardous wastes is still being placed in landfills and surface impoundments or injected into wells.

As more information became available on the dangerous environmental consequences of relying on land disposal for these wastes, Congress took steps to redress the balance in favor of treatment. In late 1984, the Hazardous and Solid Waste Amendments (HSWA) to RCRA set a new tone for national hazardous waste policy. Strict congressional guidelines called on EPA to ban land disposal nationwide of most hazardous wastes, including the entire "California list." Federal bans were to take effect between 1989 and 1992. Illinois adopted similar restrictions, though on a faster schedule; California accelerated its phase out program.

Despite popular misconceptions, most prescribed hazardous waste treatment is neither exotic nor exorbitantly expensive. Perhaps 80 to 90 percent of all the hazardous wastes being generated in the United States could be treated by modern variants of 1930s-era wastewater treatment technologies.

Acids can be neutralized while held in steel tanks; metals can readily be removed from liquid waste streams. In both cases, the remaining liquids can then be discharged safely into sewers available in every industrial area. Waste oils and solvents can be recycled through traditional separation and distillation techniques (akin to small refinery operations). Another 10 percent of today's hazardous wastes probably require thermal destruction in a rotary-kiln or fluidized-bed incinerator, which can be equipped to function safely using the latest air pollution control technology.

But the problem of hazardous waste management does not end with treatment alone. All these treatment methods leave residues requiring land disposal: sludge, ash, and typical residuals from pollution control equipment. Heavy metals, in particular, are ultimately amenable only to land disposal. Dried and stabilized, they can be stored safely in a new kind of landfill—a "residuals repository"—that uses a permanent cover to protect them from rain or snow. Such facilities already exist in Europe but not yet in the United States. With no liquids in the waste residues allowed for disposal in the residuals repository, and none entering from precipitation, no leachate can be formed to threaten nearby groundwater. Several decades hence, perhaps we can even reclaim the metals economically from carefully managed hazardous waste repositories.

Treating hazardous wastes instead of dumping them on the ground obviously requires new treatment facilities. Within the context of the widespread fear of toxics, few communities will consider siting such facilities, even those employing the newest and most advanced treatment facilities. People do not want someone else's wastes brought into their community for treatment, irrespective of purported treatment facility safety. Consequently, during the first toxics decade, siting new treatment facilities proved to be one of the major stumbling blocks to realizing the treatment "solution" to hazardous waste management. By the mid-1980s, a few communities were beginning to see treatment facilities as an integral part of their overall waste management strategy, but it would take even more effort in these communities to accomplish siting of these facilities; elsewhere, successful siting seemed a virtual impossibility.

The Source Reduction Imperative

Before new siting processes had really been tried as a way to locate new hazardous waste treatment facilities and residuals repositories, an entirely new and seemingly obvious perspective joined the equation: "source reduction." That is, why not produce less waste in the first place? Source reduction was an early theme of the environmentalists, and both government and industry officials soon came to appreciate the wisdom of this approach as a major component of any successful long-range hazardous waste management strategy.

By the end of the first toxics decade, the increasing costs of waste management and of liability insurance had already begun to move many larger firms toward source reduction. The 3M Corporation based in Minnesota is a classic instance of a company that drew economic benefit from pollution prevention (including hazardous waste source reduction). A community wide effort in Ventura County, California, was equally impressive. Ventura focused on the 75 local businesses responsible for generating 90 percent of the area's entire hazardous waste volume. Through aggressively promoting source reduction and better onsite treatment, in only two years these firms reduced by 70 percent their wastes headed for land disposal. North Carolina early on made source reduction the hallmark of its state hazardous waste management strategy.[8]

Most small and medium-sized businesses around the country have proved to be a far greater challenge, however. They lack the capital, technical support, and awareness of the numerous new toxics waste laws now evident in the larger firms. And they fear (as do the larger and wealthier firms) they will become the target of environmental groups, local enforcement officers, or local district attorneys. Reaching these small-quantity hazardous waste generators with effective techniques for source reduction (and treatment), therefore, remains one of the greatest challenges in the second toxics decade.

Beyond Hazardous Wastes: Regulating Hazardous Chemicals

Unfortunately, as promising as the source reduction approach to the problem may seem, controlling hazardous wastes represents only a small portion of what is now becoming viewed as the "real" problem. As was learned so tragically in late 1984 at Bhopal, India—and in several U.S. and European industrial accidents—the storage and handling of hazardous chemicals poses grave dangers to public safety, probably even more serious than safe hazardous waste management. After Bhopal, several states took the lead in mounting new planning and regulatory programs for their industries' use of hazardous materials, with several states continuing to exceed federal regulations.

When the Superfund Act was amended by SARA in 1986, an entirely new section, Title III, was added that has little to do with abandoned waste sites. Rather, it sets out a national program of hazardous materials management. The law includes new reporting and inspection requirements and requires a plan for all firms using acutely hazardous materials. The intent is to prevent dangerous releases of toxic materials by implementing strict prior reporting and emergency planning regulations. These provisions were expanded by Congress in the Clean Air Act of 1990 to cover situations in which air emissions are involved.

A radically new approach to the toxic materials issue is being tried in California. This effort was begun directly by the citizens in 1986 through the ballot initiative process when Proposition 65, the Safe Drinking Water and Toxics Initiative, was approved by over 60 percent of the state's voters. Under its provisions, no business with 10 or more employees can knowingly discharge into sources of drinking water even minute quantities of any chemicals known to the state to cause cancer or birth defects. The burden of proof rests with these firms to show that any such discharges pose "no significant risk." Strict warning requirements also apply for all exposures to these chemicals. Citizens can sue to enforce the law, which can only be modified by a two-thirds vote of the legislature and then only "in furtherance of the purposes of the initiative." Implementation of all these stringent new hazardous materials storage and use requirements is fundamentally the responsibility of the often understaffed local governments (fire and health departments, in particular) and, of course, of the private industry whose facilities must comply with the law.

In short, the challenge of effective *hazardous waste* management by the end of the first toxics decade had already been eclipsed in importance by the need to regulate *hazardous materials*, even before hazardous waste management was well under way. If not carefully orchestrated locally, multiple reporting requirements for industry, different inspections of the same facilities, and the numerous fees collected by different agencies to pay for these programs all were sure to cause enormous disruption. Already, government agencies are finding the maze of different laws nearly impossible to implement and to enforce; industry finds it difficult to comply with all of them; and the general public finds the whole process largely incomprehensible. Consequently, government's credibility and the public's trust continue to remain low and public fear high, despite all the policymaking and learning throughout the decade and despite all the new laws that themselves have been the very responses to demands for action from concerned citizens.

THE TRANSFORMATION TO
THE SECOND TOXICS DECADE

This dramatic decade-long evolution in policy and law amounts to a major reorientation from dumping of hazardous wastes carelessly across the landscape to not only regulating tightly hazardous waste disposal but also requiring treatment, encouraging source reduction, and controlling the use of hazardous materials. This restructuring is clearly one of the most important hallmarks of America's first toxics decade. At first, policymakers were confronted with the significant but fairly narrow issue of what to do about old hazardous waste dumps. Yet today, despite the creation of a multi billion-dollar public works program and an awesome new overarching approach to hazardous waste liability, the Superfund solution has become an implementation nightmare: Superfailure.

That result triggered even more stringent controls over hazardous waste landfills in general and sparked a major push for treatment in sharp preference to continued landfilling. Policy momentum shifted rapidly from land disposal to treatment, on the assumption that, eventually, every landfill will leak. Permanent remedies were called for in place of excavation and redisposal. In practice, however, by the late 1980s, little actual progress had been made.

The second major shift in policy and law came about when source reduction was added to the hazardous waste management equation (see Box 1.2). Not only were wastes to be treated, but the entire waste stream coming from business and industry was to be reduced considerably. A common estimate is that reductions of 50 percent or more can be realized through existing technology, at least by the larger companies. Policy shifted toward shrinking the waste stream, and then treating what remained. As noted, however, these two goals were to some extent mutually exclusive. As programs to lessen the waste stream were actually adopted, market incentives to develop additional treatment capacity began to disappear.

How successful source reduction has been is difficult to estimate precisely, but the continued flow of hazardous wastes into landfills and injection wells suggests that progress has been slow. Overall, by the end of the 1980s, the total hazardous waste stream had declined by perhaps 10 percent, though that is admittedly only an informed guess. It is clear that many large firms applied their technical knowledge and capital resources to reduce their waste generation significantly; small ones, having neither, accomplished little. Economic considerations predominated in industry's calculus of the value of source reduction. Because land disposal has remained cheaper than either treatment or many of the process changes needed for source reduction, land disposal is still preferred by the hazardous waste generators. Some states began to mandate source reduction planning; the federal government followed suit.

Moreover, before either the conversion from land disposal to treatment or to source reduction had become a reality, the universe of concern had multiplied 20-fold, as policymakers brought into the picture all of industry's hazardous materials. The initial concern—simply the safe management of hazardous wastes—had expanded by the end of the first toxics decade to encompass all hazardous materials. The overriding theme was to minimize their use and minimize the dangers involved. In this broadly expanded universe, as we move into the second toxics decade, hazardous wastes may increasingly be viewed as only the tip (or tail end) of the iceberg.

The Two Faces of Risk

One of the oddities of the experience during America's first toxics decade was the vastly different ways in which people evaluated and responded to two different kinds of risk: public health/environmental/toxics risk on the one hand, economic/financial/commercial risk on the other. These differences resound through all the different phases of toxics policy, from cleanup and management of new hazardous wastes to management of hazardous materials and facility siting.

America's political economy is rooted strongly in the philosophy of risk taking. Business entrepreneurs have always received high prestige and unusual recognition—from Thomas Edison and Henry Ford to Donald Trump and Steven Jobs. Scholars over several generations, from Joseph Schumpeter to Peter Drucker to Thomas Peters, point to the ability to seek out economic risks, grasp them, and even revel in them as essential to the health and viability of our economic life.

Moreover, our system is designed to encourage economic risk-taking: witness such special tax provisions as oil depletion allowances, "S" corporations, depreciation schedules. And when the assumption of economic risks results in failure, an all too common occurrence, we have structures specifically designed to provide a soft landing in the safety net: Chapter 11 bankruptcy rules, for example. Not only is the assumption of economic risk recognized and applauded, but many vehicles have been created to spread out risks. The entire insurance industry is based on this notion, pooling literally thousands of individual risks and using statistically based underwriting precepts to set annual premiums for such coverage.

Contrast this quite positive approach to economic risk-taking with the flat rejection of risks of any kind involving toxics and hazardous wastes.

Thousands of tons of hazardous materials are used every day by U.S. industries, and vast volumes of hazardous wastes are being generated all the time, but the risks of all this activity are either ignored or disdained. Such risks are simply not perceived as "legitimate." Conceptually, risks of this kind are to be avoided at any cost rather than assumed, managed, and shared. Local residents clamor "not in my backyard," and local activists demand "zero toxics risk." In the face of such opposition, Schumpeter's entrepreneur runs from the opportunity to invest in a new hazardous waste treatment facility.

Throughout this book, the reader will observe numerous aspects of this vast difference between how Americans approach economic and business risk versus toxics risk. We suggest ways in which the accepted methods of coping with economic risks can be translated during America's second toxics decade into improved techniques for managing toxics risk as well.

FROM IDEAS TO ACTION: THE SECOND TOXICS DECADE

So we come to the present. What are the options for the 1990s and the second toxics decade? Do we accept the status quo of impressive laws and implementation failures? Do we increase government monitoring, rulemaking, taxation, fees, and surveillance to the point that the masses of toxics laws will actually be followed (an option for which there will surely be enormous pressures)? Or do we find some other way to achieve a less toxic, safer society?

By all accounts, the status quo is unacceptable. Public pressures to act intensify; politicians respond with more laws; problematic citizen initiatives proliferate. The public is uncomfortable with dramatically enhancing the conventional powers of government, a concern those closely associated with toxics policymaking share. Even if government were granted all-encompassing police powers, it is unlikely elected officials would be willing to override public opposition to the siting of needed new facilities. To encourage siting, we need greater public acceptance, not more government firepower.

Instead, a dramatic transformation is called for in the ways we govern toxics and hazardous materials issues. This transformation would be based on the successes and, yes, the failures of the first toxics decade. A substantial shift toward much greater and more effective participation by all affected interests is needed in the political process and in modes of public-private interaction. These profound changes in action in the 1990s would parallel the revolution in analysis of toxics management that occurred in the 1980s. Unfortunately, to accomplish that result may require a shock to the system similar to the one Three Mile Island caused in nuclear power. More optimistically, maybe we can learn the lessons from the past decade well enough to overcome the inevitable political and economic barriers to making any serious changes at all.

The New Imperatives of Toxics Policymaking

The broad outlines of more comprehensive and effective yet flexible approaches to policymaking—in the broadest sense, more democratic governance—are becoming apparent. Taken alone, each feature may seem merely an extension of an existing orientation or approach. But these features are too interrelated to be viewed in isolation. In their amalgamation they represent a dramatic change in political power and decision making, with radical implications for the behavior of business, government, and the public.

Toxics policy in the 1990s will need to build on the appreciation by everyone concerned of the unacceptable costs—to industry, to public health, to the environment—of continuing policy gridlock and minimal implementation of major existing statutory initiatives. No single interest can expect to dictate policy in the second decade.

The most potent political power demonstrated in the first toxics decade was negative. Even the promises of equity, compensation, and state-level control and coordination tried in several states did little to change that. It is clear that genuine progress will be made only with the concurrence of business, environmental groups, and health and local community interests. This will require a new democratic discourse within a framework that takes into account both the economic and political dimensions of our lives.

The second toxics decade will need to be guided by the broad principles of source reduction, efficiency, and equity. Also, it became clear in decade one that the U.S. industrial system is too diverse and dynamic to be directed by a centralized command-and-control government along the lines of conventional environmental or health and safety regulatory control; that too will need to be recognized in decade two.

These are formidable objectives. In terms of decisionmaking, the cooperative business, governmental, environmental, and community forums that began to emerge tentatively at the close of the first toxics decade must become far more prevalent. Collaborative community-management plant oversight is one possible strategy shown to have a number of attractive features for both industry and the community. For example, to be decentralized and responsive to local concerns and to gain public trust and confidence, the resolution of siting controversies during decade two may take the form of specific performance contracts between businesses and the local community. These agreements would cover allowable emissions to air and water, placement of treatment residues onto the land, hours and modes of operation, and similar aspects of facility operations after its siting has been approved. No matter how interventionist that may seem to private businesses, local communities can reply simply: "No contract, no siting approval." Enforceable contracts between businesses and their host communities would spell out the toxic materials to be used, source reduction objectives to be met, and a public reporting system. The contract would be enforceable in local courts instead of citizens having to rely as at present solely on uncertain state or federal regulatory enforcement.

On a more comprehensive level, the development of public-private partnerships in regional treatment, transfer, and residuals repository systems—approaches already in use in Europe—may also work in certain circumstances in the United States. Areawide risk management planning and priority setting along the lines of EPA's integrated environmental management projects in Baltimore, Denver, Philadelphia, and Santa Clara County (California) may become the common framework for balancing growth and economic development with public health and environmental goals.

One idea just beginning to receive attention is the "bottle bill" analogy for hazardous waste management. Suppose all generation of hazardous waste were taxed, with the monies rebated to those firms demonstrating successful movement toward source reduction and waste treatment. Designed correctly, a deposit-and-return system would ensure safe disposal of all hazardous wastes. It would eliminate the specter of illegal dumping, which would lose its economic appeal.

This approach provides clear incentives for business to reduce wastes in all production stages, to recycle, and constantly to develop more efficient methods of treatment. All of this would be accomplished with the least governmental intrusion into the operations of thousands of firms, which would each be affected somewhat differently. Instead of a command-and-control bureaucracy issuing permits and conducting sporadic enforcement visits (or failing to do either), price incentives would stimulate firms to pursue source reduction, waste minimization, and appropriate onsite and offsite treatment of their hazardous wastes. Although no panacea, tax-and-rebate schemes for hazardous waste management certainly offer huge advantages over the present confusion.

The analysis presented here of the second toxics decade focuses on where we are headed in hazardous waste and toxics policy rather than on the terrain already covered and thus is inherently prescriptive and speculative. Nonetheless, we firmly believe there are some definite signs of the needed new directions that, taken together, make feasible an entirely new regime of toxics policy. Given the seriousness of the issues, it is disheartening to contemplate the future if toxics policy does not move more rapidly in these positive directions.

WHAT IS TO FOLLOW

In the chapters that follow, we detail the key elements of America's hazardous waste and toxics policy. In Chapter Two, "Cleanup: Superfund or Superfailure?" the cleanup effort under Superfund is addressed: what the law calls for, experience with its implementation to date, and the status of cleanup at the threshold of the second toxics decade. The complexity, frustrations, and cross-cutting concerns of cleanup at the nation's Superfund sites are put in bold relief in the illustrative case of New Jersey's Lipari Superfund site in Chapter Three, "How Clean Is Clean?"

Although most media attention has gone to Superfund, the directive in the Resource Conservation and Recovery Act to monitor today's hazardous wastes from cradle to grave is as critical to the nation's overall hazardous waste policy. Its implementation is assessed in Chapter Four, "An Ounce of Prevention."

Chapter Five, "Engineering, Economics, and Politics," moves from the questions of the implementation of the legal policy guidelines to the technical dimensions of safer, more efficient, and more economical management of hazardous wastes and hazardous materials. This topic is always a backdrop to policy discussions, but has seldom been fully understood or made accessible to the nontechnical audience. The reader interested only in the analysis of the relevant public policy can bypass this chapter, however.

Chapter Six, "Beyond Hazardous Waste," moves to the issue of the need for safer hazardous materials management throughout business and industry and examines how toxics policy is being extended to engulf this ever-growing domain.

Chapter Seven, "Just Say 'No,'" brings all the elements of the issue together in a discussion of the thousands of industrial locations and communities across the nation where decisions about specific facilities to manage hazardous wastes and to use hazardous materials must be made. The experiences of the first decade have proved frustrating at best. They most vividly underscore that toxics policy cannot and will not be implemented in a vacuum but in the context of broader social, cultural, and political considerations.

Chapter Eight, "Looking Forward," is our window into the future. Here we attempt to lay out a blueprint for accomplishing through dramatically different approaches the goals of the hazardous waste and toxics policy generally articulated in the first decade.

NOTES

Some of the ideas presented in this chapter appeared earlier in print in "The Elusive Pursuit of Toxics Management," *The Public Interest*, #90 (Winter 1988), 81–98; as "The 'NIMBY' Syndrome: Facility Siting and the Failure of Democratic Discourse," in Norman J. Vig and Michael E. Kraft, eds., *Environmental Policy in the 1990s* (Washington D.C.: Congressional Quarterly Press, 1990), pp. 125-143.

1. As an example, smokestack scrubbers used to reduce sulfur dioxide emissions into the air from coal-fired power plants produce 3 pounds of sludge for every pound of sulfur dioxide removed. The sludge must then be deposited somewhere, and it is usually in a landfill. See Paul R. Portney, "Environmental Evolution," *Resources*, #85 (Fall 1986), 2.

2. The Love Canal story has been told, retold, and debated more than any other episode of the hazardous wastes saga. It is presented most fully by Michael Brown, who wrote over 100 stories about Love Canal as a reporter for the *Niagara Gazette* and two books on toxics and hazardous waste in the United States. The Love Canal story is summarized in his two retrospectives following the tenth anniversary of the incident: "Love Canal Revisited," *The Amicus Journal*, 10, #3 (Summer 1988), 37–44; "A Toxic Ghost Town," Sierra, 74, #4 (July 1989), 23–28.

3. Walter A. Rosenbaum, *Environmental Politics and Policy*, 2d ed. (Washington, D.C.: Congressional Quarterly Press, 1991), 221. Paigan is cited in Brown, "A Toxic Ghost Town," 24.

4. Marc Landy, "Cleaning Up Superfund," *The Public Interest*, #85 (Fall 1986), 61. The *Newsweek* story is cited in Robert W. Crandall, "Learning the Lessons," *Wilson Quarterly*, #4 (Fall 1987), 78.

5. Richard Riley, "Toxics Substances, Hazardous Wastes, and Public Policy: Problems in Implementation," in James P. Lester and Ann O'M. Bowman, eds., *The Politics of Hazardous Waste Management* (Durham, N.C.: Duke University Press, 1983), 24.

6. John Kingdon identifies timing—"the window of opportunity"—as a crucial ingredient in understanding why out of the competition of many, a particular issue moves center stage on the political agenda. *Agendas, Alternatives, and Public Policy* (Boston: Little, Brown & Co., 1984).

7. Rudy Abramson, "U.S. Waste Cleanup Bill Put at $750 Billion," *Los Angeles Times*, December 10, 1991, A-29.

8. The transition in energy policy from consumption to conservation in the 1970s presents an interesting analogy to the evolution of toxics policy in its first decade. Despite warning signs, seemingly out of nowhere the nation was in each instance hit by a major jolt. In energy, the impetus to action came from the OPEC oil embargo and the long lines at gasoline stations.

Just as American society was asked to respond impressively to the energy crisis by reducing demand for electricity and fossil fuels in homes, factories, and cars—thus lowering the need for ever more power plants, OPEC oil, and offshore drilling—large corporations and small businesses are now being asked to make their production processes more efficient, thereby producing fewer hazardous wastes. Energy conservation and hazardous waste source reduction have much in common.

It was clear that application of imagination and some retooling could produce energy savings sufficient for the nation to afford to curtail dramatically its growing dependence on nuclear power. For many who may have had second thoughts about that policy shift, Three Mile Island and Chernobyl quickly silenced them. That same thinking is being applied to the use of hazardous materials: Converting to a less-toxic substance whenever possible has the twofold benefit of reducing health threats to workers and to society in the first instance, and in the second, of simply reducing the amount of toxic substances to be dealt with eventually as wastes.

CHAPTER TWO

Cleanup: Superfund
or Superfailure?

Congress responded swiftly to Love Canal and to the specter of thousands of similarly abandoned hazardous waste dumps corroding the nation's landscape. The public was frightened of unsuspected cancer-causing chemicals that might affect water supplies, homes, children, and communities as well as the natural environment. The effects of these chemicals might at times be obvious and immediate. But even more frightening for some people, the toxins could be slow to appear, long after the time when anything could be done to prevent trouble.

The real fear was enhanced because no one knew for sure about any of the ignored dumps: how many there were, the levels of contamination they held, and what risks they posed to human health and the environment. The public mood was a mixture of anger, fear, confusion, apprehension, and a deep sense of betrayal by business and by government. On balance, the public's outrage was expressed more commonly, and often more strongly, than its fear. The one clear message was "take action now." Legislative bodies quickly responded.

Like so many other flash points that ignite the political arena one day only to fizzle the next, at the outset there was no accurate way to gauge just how deeply the hazardous waste issue was felt, nor how enduring would be the public concern. Conventional thinking suggested the hazardous waste scare would take its place alongside so many other emotionally charged public issues, especially those dealing with environmental protection, that followed the fairly predictable "issue-attention cycle" outlined by Anthony Downs.[1]

In this cycle of concern and response, an issue begins with the pre-problem stage, in which a "highly undesirable social condition exists but has not captured much public attention." Experts begin to write about the problem; their work is read almost exclusively by other experts. Then comes the alarmed discovery of the issue by the public, often precipitated by some dramatic event such as an accident at a nuclear power plant or discovery of groundwater contamination near a drinking-water well, or discovery of a Love Canal.

The next step in the issue-attention cycle is accompanied by "euphoric enthusiasm about society's ability to 'solve the problem' or to 'do something effective' within a relatively short period of time." Soon "answers" appear, typically in the form of new legislation. Unfortunately, for most problems, solutions are seldom easily attained. Over the course of several years, this realization breeds policy frustration and public disillusionment, which in turn typically lead to a decline in public interest and lowered support for strong government action. Meanwhile, other compelling issues come to the fore, capturing the public limelight as well as the energy of policymakers.

Uncharacteristically, the public's concern with hazardous wastes and hazardous materials in America has not followed Downs's cycle of enthusiasm, disillusionment, and diversion over the course of the first toxics decade.[2] New laws—"answers"—were indeed passed. But instead of the typical decline in public interest in the topic, intense frustration over failures in implementation of these laws has been evident. Public frustration here combined with growing public interest in toxics policy to intensify escalating demands for more and more "answers." In turn, new laws have been passed, one after the next, only to lead to more implementation failures. This has kept toxics near the top of the public agenda for an unusually long time.

Somehow, frustration and disappointment with slow progress on this issue have not desensitized the public. Instead, citizens' demands for efforts to combat risks from hazardous wastes and hazardous materials have steadily increased. Rather than an ebbing of public concern, there has been an ever-louder crescendo. Other superseding issues simply have not come to the fore—at least not yet.

In the early 1980s, all that was known for sure was that the hazardous waste issue had reached extraordinary heights in public awareness. According to a CBS News–Harris national poll, fully 86 percent of the U.S. public supported "giving the problem of toxic chemical dumps and spills very high priority for federal action."[3] This intensity was not missed by elected officials. A review of public opinion across the 1980s shows that hazardous waste remained a major and enduring dimension of the public's concern with environmental pollution.[4]

Thus, instead of following the typical issue-attention cycle, overall the public steadfastly placed environmental protection high on its agenda, and toxics were at the top of the environmental list. This was so even in the face of competing claims made on behalf of the need to develop and produce energy, the threat presumably posed to economic growth by environmental regulation, and the assault on stringent environmental regulations by the Reagan administration throughout the 1980s.[5]

The attention paid to Love Canal and other early contamination sites produced a highly charged atmosphere. Members of Congress were not willing to gamble their political futures on predictions that the hazardous waste issue would go away anytime soon or that they could rely on the private sector to provide a full remedy. Fearing the directions the newly-elected Reagan administration would take, the Democratic Congress passed and President Jimmy Carter promptly signed in December 1980 the Comprehensive Environmental Response, Compensation, and Liability Act of 1980 (CERCLA), better known as Superfund. The title of the law suggested that strong and decisive action would be taken. This certainly helped lead people to expect a great deal of actual cleanup, far more than would actually ensue.

CERCLA directed the federal Environmental Protection Agency (EPA) promptly to clean up old and abandoned hazardous waste sites; to remove leaking waste barrels and hazardous materials from dumps and industrial sites; to drain old holding ponds and lagoons filled with hazardous liquid wastes; to purify contaminated groundwater; and to remove and neutralize toxics-laden soil. With its sweeping provisions, the new Act was indeed unprecedented federal legislation. It covered virtually any release of hazardous wastes and pollutants into the environment whether by spilling, pumping, pouring, emitting, discharging, injecting, escaping, leaking, dumping, or disposing. The only exclusions were for hazards that might result from use of petroleum and natural gas (the result of intense industry lobbying), nuclear materials or by-products (covered under existing law), and the normal agricultural application of fertilizers and pesticides.

CERCLA was supposed to be action-oriented: "shovels first and lawyers later"[6]—indeed, a *super* fund! Cleanups were to be swift so as to avoid the kinds of delay typified by the experience at Love Canal. With well over $1 billion in the fund, the question of "who pays" presumably was to be left for later resolution: "Clean up now, send invoices later."

Congress sent a strong message to those responsible for generating toxic wastes in the first place by making the new law retroactive and by removing nearly all traditional legal immunities. Strict joint and several liability gave maximum reach into the "deep pockets" of industry needed to pay for all these cleanups, the total cost of which would vastly exceed the money allocated to the federal fund. Negligence—the conventional legal doctrine applicable to business operations—was swept aside; the only questions asked were "Did you generate or handle these wastes or own the property?" and "Can you afford to pay for their cleanup?"

A number of states followed this legislative lead, developing their own programs to clean up the many hazardous waste sites not likely to be covered under the federal legislation. These states created their own administrative mechanisms to carry out their new federal and state responsibilities.

How Superfund and parallel state laws came to be implemented across the country is a far more complicated and disheartening tale. Tragically, just as Love Canal became synonymous with the problem of hazardous wastes, a decade later the consensus of many observers was that Superfund had come to symbolize frustration over government's failure to cope adequately not only with old waste sites but with the entire hazardous waste problem.

Ten years after implementation of CERCLA, some successes were apparent: thousands of potential Superfund sites had been identified, hundreds were singled out for action, and dozens of cleanups were actually under way. But only a relative handful of sites have been decontaminated. Why this state of affairs has been allowed to persist is a significant element of the tragedy of America's toxics policy. At the end of the first toxics decade, too few shovels had been turned, too few sites cleaned, too few communities placated—Superfund had become a superfailure.[7]

THE CERCLA PROCESS

By 1980, most Americans and virtually every public official had heard about Love Canal and other hazardous waste horror stories. No one, however, had good answers to fundamental questions: How many leaking and dangerous sites actually were polluting the American landscape? What wastes were involved? How frequently and to what extent were they released into the environment? What was their actual effect on human health and the environment? Who should be held responsible? How much cleanup was needed to protect people? How should these cleanups be managed? At what cost? To get answers, CERCLA called for substantial data gathering and scientific analysis by EPA—just when EPA's budget and staff were being cut significantly by the White House.

At the heart of the CERCLA process is the requirement that EPA develop a National Priority List (NPL) of those sites in need of prompt cleanup; a designation that made them eligible for federal Superfund attention. The NPL was to begin with 400 entries and build from year to year based on information gathered by EPA and its state-level counterparts. The many sites less seriously contaminated would then fall to the states, local communities, and private parties to clean up as best they could. The steps in the cleanup process are summarized in Box 2.1.

The Act specified the number of sites to be identified, but failed to spell out selection criteria. Would the Superfund program be restricted to cleaning waste sites abandoned because bankrupt companies were responsible? Should it be extended to cover the worst and most dangerous sites, abandoned or otherwise? Should it cover the politically most visible sites?[8] If the largest, costliest sites were listed, would enough money remain in the fund to allow cleanup of other sites added to the NPL over time?

To be systematic and consistent in its site listing, EPA developed a numerical rating scheme known as the hazard ranking system (HRS). This process weighed seven factors:

1. Relative hazard to public health or the environment, taking into account the population at risk;
2. Hazardous potential of the substances at the site;
3. Potential for contamination of drinking water supplies;
4. Direct contact with or destruction of sensitive ecosystems;
5. Damage to natural resources that may affect the human food chain;
6. Ambient air pollution; and
7. Preparedness of the state involved to assume its share (typically 10 percent) of the total costs and responsibilities for the cleanup.[9]

Because no two contaminated sites were exactly alike, scoring and remedial analysis became a matter of judgment on the part of EPA project officers and their technical consultants in the field, with these criteria serving only as a general guide. Sites receiving a score of 28.5 or more on a scale from 1 to 100 were placed on the NPL. This score, with no intrinsic value, initially was chosen simply to ensure that at least 400 sites nationwide made the NPL. Subsequently, however, the figure became embedded in EPA procedures,[10] even as many more NPL sites were added. Up to the time of CERCLA's renewal in 1986, EPA had amassed information on nearly 25,000 potential Superfund sites and had placed more than 1,200 on the NPL.[11]

EPA's ranking system came under strong criticism from both industry and environmentalists. A 1988 study by the Office of Technology Assessment (OTA) found EPA's scoring procedure to be far from infallible, with serious errors of both inclusion and exclusion.[12]

BOX 2.1 The Cleanup Process at a Glance

Step 1   Determine the necessity for immediate control or removal of contaminants posing imminent and substantial danger to health and environment. Such a *removal action* (RA) decision can be made during the initial investigation of a site, or at any time thereafter should it appear that the threat posed could get much worse before more permanent action can be taken.

Step 2   Estimate the site's relative danger through a *preliminary assessment* (PA).

Step 3   Based on the results of the PA, either terminate the investigation or move to the full analysis stage: the *site inspection* (SI). If an SI is conducted, follow the guidelines of the *hazard ranking system* (HRS) to score the site for possible inclusion on the National Priority List (NPL).

Step 4   Determine who are the potentially responsible parties (PRPs) or parties involved at the site, and thus ultimately who should pay for the cleanup.

Step 5   Conduct a *remedial investigation and feasibility study* (RI/FS) to define the site's contamination and environmental problems in detail, and tentatively determine the most appropriate long-term cleanup methods for the site. These usually fall into one of three categories:

(a) containment of contaminated materials at the site;
(b) excavation of contaminated materials for redisposal elsewhere;
(c) permanent treatment of contaminated materials, onsite or offsite.

Identify the recommended cleanup alternative.

Step 6   Allow a two-month period for public comment on the recommended cleanup approach by the affected community, environmentalists, industry, and others.

Step 7   Set forth a *record of decision* (ROD) on the preferred cleanup alternative. This includes detailed cleanup goals and the rationale for choosing a particular cleanup approach or technology for the site. The ROD must be prepared by EPA, even when the PRPs have the lead at a particular site.

Step 8   Design specific steps for the cleanup and arrange for the work: the *remedial design* (RD) stage. This can be done by EPA or the PRPs.

Step 9   Implement the *remedial action plan* (RAP), which may include long-term monitoring to determine whether the cleanup effectively addresses all site concerns.

Step 10   Determine final approval of the cleanup, and remove the site from the NPL.

Sources: Julie L. Edelson, "Superfund: Still in the Dumps," *Technology Review* 91 (November/December 1988), 27–28; Office of Technology Assessment, U.S. Congress, "Are We Cleaning Up? 10 Superfund Case Studies—Special Report" (Washington, D.C.: Government Printing Office, 1988), 3.

IDENTIFYING EFFECTS ON HUMAN HEALTH

Under CERCLA, Congress established the Agency for Toxic Substances and Disease Registry (ATSDR) within the Public Health Service, under the administration of the U.S. Surgeon General. The ATSDR was directed to gather scientific information on the health effects of hazardous wastes by conducting periodic surveys and screening persons exposed at Superfund sites and to develop in one location an inventory of scientific research on the effects of toxics contamination and exposure. The goal was to trace scientifically the link between hazardous waste exposure and both acute and chronic health problems. Whenever hazardous waste emergencies occurred, facilities of the Public Health Service were to be made available to exposed persons.[13]

Commencement of these tasks was delayed for six years, however. As a result, none of the all-important inventories and tracking studies got under way until 1986—and even then only after intense prodding from Congress. Not until 1988, and then at only two Superfund sites, were surrounding residents fully identified and incorporated into a tracking study.[14] A decade has been lost and a second will probably pass before the kind of data gathering and scientific analysis Congress called for will be available.

WHO PAYS?

The liability reach of Superfund is extremely wide. The basic philosophy guiding the drafters of CERCLA was that those who had contributed in any of a number of ways to the contamination of a site should pay for its cleanup, either directly or by reimbursing the government. The law is designed to find some party (other than the federal government) able to pay for almost every conceivable cleanup. Parties found responsible for cleanup include any individual, corporation, or other entity that is a present or even past owner or operator of the now-contaminated site; any generator or transporter who contributed any hazardous substances to the site; land owners; or even under some circumstances, a bank that loaned money to the site owner/operator or the insurance company that covered operations there.[15] When no *potentially responsible party* (PRP) can be located with the ability to pay for the cleanup, then the cost is borne by the revolving Hazardous Substances Response Trust Fund established by CERCLA.

This fund was set up in 1980 with $1.6 billion and in 1986 it was increased to $8.5 billion. The bulk of this money—87.5 percent—comes from a tax on chemical feedstocks, the balance from the public treasury.[16] With only a few petroleum and chemical companies from which to collect, the administrative task was made easy. The prevailing argument at the time was that taxing only the large corporations was justifiable on the grounds that most hazardous substances found at Superfund sites could be traced to their petrochemical lineage.[17]

An understandable but ultimately counterproductive provision of CERCLA was "fund balancing." This required EPA to make certain that expenditures from the trust fund at any one site would not be so large as to affect drastically EPA's ability to foster cleanups at all the other sites. Although seemingly logical, this provision had the effect of almost no cleanups being carried out at all. Emergency removal actions were completed; full site cleanups were not. Because the funds were inadequate to do a good cleanup job at any major site without drawing down money potentially available to clean up another site, well into the 1980s little funding was released for actual cleanup anywhere. Fund balancing became an excuse for delay, particularly at an EPA under intense pressure from the White House and the Office of Management and Budget to curtail overall federal expenditures.

To ensure that EPA exercised prudence in spending limited Superfund dollars on any particular site, Congress also added the proviso that the cleanup strategy chosen at every site must be "cost-effective." Cleanup strategies would have to balance the need to protect public health and welfare and the environment against the availability of dollars.

With strictures to be penny-wise and to balance expenditures across sites, the antienvironmentalists in the Reagan administration easily justified their go-slow approach. Add to that the heated debates among public officials and affected communities about the right kind of treatment for each contaminated site and about the level of cleanup that would be deemed acceptable, then add litigation initiated by PRPs who were resisting paying for the cleanup and by residents around certain sites, and even a novice observer can easily see why so little progress was made at most of the Superfund sites throughout the 1980s. It was no surprise that EPA came under sharp criticism from an increasingly agitated and outraged public. Inexorably, the gap between expectations and reality grew as time dragged on.

Strict Joint and Several Liability

It is one thing to declare flatly that the "polluter pays"—that those responsible should bear the cost of cleanup. It is quite another matter to define that responsibility, to locate responsible parties, and actually to collect money from them. Over 200 generators, for example, had sent their hazardous wastes to the Stringfellow Acid Pits, near Riverside,

California, because the state agency responsible at the time had told them to do so; now these 200 were to pay for the cleanup. Was it fair to identify as responsible those original waste generators who had done nothing wrong? They had complied fully with the mandates of the responsible state agency. Why should an absentee landowner, for another example, be forced to pay? Such apparent inequity induced further litigation.

Another dilemma was how to allocate cleanup costs to all the businesses and communities that for years had contributed to now-contaminated municipal landfills. Too often, EPA sought to identify a single "deep pocket" that could be made to pay for the whole cleanup, even if that company's contribution to the site had been minimal. Adding to the problem is the fact that most Superfund sites are old industrial or municipal landfills or ponds and lagoons adjacent to industrial facilities. Many sites had changed hands; some sites' owners had gone bankrupt even before listing of the sites under Superfund. As such, under traditional tort law, any liability associated with these sites had presumably disappeared as well. After all, "let the buyer beware!" was an established principle of law.

The issue of fairness produced intense reaction. Were those who had acted completely within the law as it existed before Superfund really going to be held financially responsible after the fact? Were they to be required to pay for the dumping of others? Were states and local governments going to be able to evade all responsibility for their earlier regulatory decisions (and regulatory failures)?

Although the $1.6 billion fund might cover costs at a good number of truly abandoned sites, no one believed it could possibly pay the cost (estimated at $100-plus billion by OTA) for the 50-year cleanup task at the 20,000 to 30,000 hazardous waste sites across the nation. As the federal budget deficit grew in the 1980s, the administration pressed EPA to "go slow" with Superfund spending; private parties were to pay whenever possible. Consequently, EPA's response was frequently to slow down the costly cleanup process and to accelerate other delaying tactics.

Even the $8.5 billion infusion from Congress in 1986 was already known to be insufficient compared with estimated cleanup costs. Clearly, significant sources of funding had to be found elsewhere. With the stakes so enormous, stiff resistance from potentially responsible parties was hardly surprising. Litigation and further delay were the obvious results.

In CERCLA, Congress had spoken to these issues. The law defined broadly those who could potentially be held responsible for cleanup: All were PRPs. The only exceptions in CERCLA were for residents whose homes had been erected atop contaminated land and for public agencies.[18] Without that exception, the hundreds of homeowners at Love Canal and elsewhere would have had to pay—and that was politically unthinkable.

To overcome traditional legal protections available to responsible parties, especially the hurdle that negligence must be proved, the first version of CERCLA passed by the House of Representatives had included a "strict liability" clause. This voided any "hold harmless" or indemnification portions of a sales agreement or any statutes of limitation that might otherwise shield parties from paying for cleanup. With strict liability, the government would not have to prove negligence or intent on the part of the waste generators and landfill operators in order to bill them for the cost of cleanup; they had only to fall into the category of PRPs so broadly defined by the new Act.

The House version of CERCLA also included provisions for "joint and several" liability, a legal concept under which the government would not have to establish the extent to which any particular party had contributed to a hazardous site, only that it had done so. Each PRP could legally be held accountable for 100 percent of the costs of cleanup, no matter what its actual contribution to the problem.[19] Thus, the government could assess one (presumably well financed and readily accessible) party for all cleanup costs at that site. It would be up to that party later to recover some of the cleanup costs from others who also had been responsible.

These provisions for strict liability and joint and several liability were deleted from CERCLA in a last-minute compromise between the House and Senate over several issues in the bill. However, in a striking example of judicial activism immediately after CERCLA was passed, the courts reinstated those provisions on the grounds that they were integral to the national cleanup program and to what Congress had intended.[20]

In truth, it is difficult to imagine how most past owners of and contributors to Superfund sites could have been drawn into the picture without adoption of these broad liability provisions. In their absence, Superfund cleanups would have had to be funded almost entirely from the federal treasury. Of course, that was unacceptable politically in the 1980s.

Even with this court intervention, few companies and individuals faced with enormous potential cleanup charges have been in a mood to act swiftly. Indeed, most initially have found it cheaper to pay lawyers to litigate and engineers and geologists to study than to pay for any actual cleanups.[21] Even those few firms willing to step forward voluntarily with a "fair-share" contribution were deterred from doing so for fear that once involved, they would inherit the entire cleanup cost.[22] For big business especially, Superfund had become "the legal equivalent of a 'survivor-pays-all' game of roulette."[23] This led one state official to observe that "listing a site on the Superfund National Priority List can actually be counterproductive in achieving cleanup of the site."[24]

Corporate inaction matched EPA inaction. The sure and swift cleanups envisioned by the authors of Superfund and expected by the general public failed to materialize. Paralyzed by the "who's responsible" thus "who pays" dilemma in an era of American tax phobia, cleanup foundered.

Settlements (Though Not Yet Cleanups)

It would be several years before many of America's leading industries accepted that public concern was not going away—and neither was the EPA or Superfund. EPA was learning too. After a half decade of nearly total ineffectiveness, it began to adopt a more flexible stick-and-carrot approach to cleanup. New EPA enforcement and funding guidelines became central to the evolving federal Superfund strategy.[25] The stick: In negotiations, responsible parties are now given a specific date by which to agree on a cleanup strategy or the agency takes them to court. The carrot: When direct negotiations are successful, EPA is prepared to release the settling party from full financial responsibility for the cleanup and will even contribute Superfund assets to the cleanup task.[26]

The first real signs that this strategy was having an effect came in a series of major settlements. In early 1986, for example, EPA and the Justice Department reached agreement with Aerojet-General Corporation and its subsidiary, Cordova Chemical Company, to clean up soil and groundwater contamination at an 8,500-acre waste site in Rancho Cordova, California. The $82 million price tag marked the first time a major company had agreed to clean up an entire site and to reimburse federal and state government agencies for their investigative and oversight costs.[27]

Another agreement covered cleanup by a single firm at multiple sites. Westinghouse Electric agreed to spend between $75 million and $100 million to clean up six hazardous waste sites in Bloomington, Indiana. However, later local resistance to the proposed siting of a hazardous waste incinerator needed for this cleanup has stalled any action. A settlement was also reached in a suit brought by EPA and the State of Colorado against Shell Oil Company to force the Dutch multinational firm to pay a portion of Superfund cleanup costs at the Rocky Mountain Arsenal, outside Denver. In January 1988, Shell assumed responsibility for up to $580 million of what could eventually prove to be a $2 billion cleanup. Once again, however, actual cleanup has lagged behind this legal settlement.[28]

Even though the dollar amounts of these settlements at over 200 different sites have been large,[29] they remain dwarfed by the magnitude of the costs for actual cleanups. For example, at the Stringfellow Acid Pits, which accepted 35 million gallons of hazardous waste before its 1972 closing, 16 firms agreed in June 1988 to contribute a total of $6 million to cover future cleanup costs. However, costs there may ultimately reach $880 million. The firms also agreed to reimburse the Superfund program for $1.4 million in costs already incurred, though combined federal and state expenses had already reached $43 million. Nevertheless, these settlements are a step forward.

EPA has pursued multiple settlements with responsible parties to cover different aspects of a cleanup. In December 1988 and January 1989, EPA announced two agreements for the Operating Industries, Inc. (OII) NPL site near Los Angeles. A $21.3 million settlement under which 51 companies and the Los Angeles Department of Water and Power would begin initial cleanup of a closed dump in Monterey Park, California, was accompanied by a separate consent decree (for $35.9 million) with 60 companies and one regional transit agency to develop and manage an environmental control system at that same site. OII began accepting various industrial wastes in 1948; operations ceased there in 1984 when it was placed on the NPL. Together, these agreements cover about two-thirds of the 189 companies responsible for 80 percent of the 230 million gallons of hazardous waste dumped there between 1976 and 1984. Perhaps as many as 4,000 companies might eventually be forced by EPA to contribute to this cleanup; that many firms have been identified as sources of all the waste deposited there.[30] In December 1991, EPA announced further progress in financing cleanup at the OII site: a consent agreement with 170 parties who will spend $130 million to clean up the site. This settlement was deemed "the largest private party settlement ever under the federal Superfund program,"[31] bringing to $200 million total cleanup expenditures at this site.

By 1991, estimates of total cleanup costs nationally had soared to the unfathomable sum of $750 billion. This includes both public and private expenditures over the next 30 years. The estimate resulted from a 3-year study by a University of Tennessee research team headed by former EPA Assistant Administrator Milton Russell. Costs to clean up NPL sites alone would range from $106 billion to $302 billion; the lower figure assumes containment of hazardous wastes, the higher one anticipates their destruction.[32]

Who will pay all the costs of America's full hazardous wastes bill? Contradictions have constantly emerged between the total cost of cleanup and Superfund or PRP money available. Indeed, the largest and most contaminated sites may never be cleaned adequately because of the enormous costs involved. These examples include Calumet Industrial Disposal in Illinois, Kin Buc in New Jersey, and BKK and Benicia in California. For cost reasons alone, regardless of their impacts, these immense sites may well be ignored forever or merely capped and declared "safe."

FEDERALISM IN ACTION

CERCLA delegates to the various states substantial responsibilities for a major role in cleanups, an important but all too easily overlooked aspect of the overall effort. Cleanup is not just a federal program. Many states have adopted hazardous waste cleanup programs designed to deal with the next tier of sites below those on the federal NPL. Illinois has a research and development program for its cleanup sites; California has in effect a $100 million bond issue to pay for state-level cleanups; Texas has a special program to cover cleanups of leaking underground gasoline tanks.

CERCLA itself calls for extensive federal-state interaction. It requires EPA to involve the states in beginning negotiations with PRPs over cleanup alternatives. When federal agencies and the parties agree on a cleanup action, the state must be notified formally and given 30 days to review the proposal before it is signed. A state may challenge specific cleanup actions proposed by EPA. Even if its challenge is overruled, the state can still press for an alternative—so long as the state is prepared to pay any additional costs.

A state agency may be designated as responsible for overseeing a particular cleanup at a federal Superfund site, or EPA may take this responsibility. (Criteria for deciding whether federal or state officials will lead remain ambiguous, with politics interwoven with considerations of respective EPA/state workloads. Often, the same engineering contract firms work for both EPA and the state.) Regardless of which government level has the leadership role, states are required to make significant, long-term commitments to safe hazardous waste cleanup of Superfund sites. Before initiating a cleanup action, the federal government must reach a cooperative agreement with the state to guarantee proper long-term maintenance at that site. Further, states must cover 10 percent of the cleanup costs if the site was privately owned and operated, 50 percent if it was publicly owned and operated.[33]

These requirements can result in substantial commitments of state resources. Florida officials have calculated that monitoring and flushing contaminated groundwater at the Whitehouse Oil Pits Superfund site near Jacksonville could extend "for as long as 50 years" in order to prevent contamination of wells in the neighborhood; costs to the state are estimated at $3 million.[34]   As site cleanups increase, so too will long-term state obligations like these. Finally, although state involvement in these arrangements is understandable and politically desirable, at many sites state participation has simply added further delay to actual cleanup.

States also share with the federal government the right to recover the cost of repairing damage to the environment at Superfund sites.[35] Collecting from the parties involved has often proved difficult, though. A court awarded $12 million in recovery costs to the Florida Department of Environmental Resources from Sapp Battery Salvage, a firm that had discharged heavy metals into a swamp that drained into a pristine estuary, but the state's actual recovery was only $30,000—from the sale of that bankrupt firm's last tangible asset, a repossessed truck.[36]

Not all states are affected equally by the Superfund program. Federal Superfund sites tend to be clustered in the north-central industrial corridor, from Minnesota in the west to the mid-Atlantic states in the east. Washington, California, Texas, and Florida also have significant numbers of Superfund sites.[37]

At the same time, all 50 states and many thousands of local governments have a responsibility to clean up the vast numbers of contaminated sites not included on the federal NPL. This responsibility was expanded significantly under provisions added to Superfund in 1986, when new legislation extended coverage to the hundreds of thousands of episodes of contamination from leaks or spills from underground storage tanks across the nation. Because Congress recognized the crucial role local and state governments need to play to accomplish the federal program's complex goals, other Superfund provisions call for early and continuous consultation, federal funding of cleanups and technical assistance, legal assistance, and overall state coordination and oversight.

Even without the aid of federal and state cleanup dollars, private owners of contaminated sites face pressures from states and localities to begin their own cleanup efforts. But can they? Even something so straightforward and promising a solution as voluntary cleanup at a Superfund site by the responsible parties was stalled in EPA's bureaucratic maze for years. Only recently, under pressure from EPA Administrator William Reilly and several court rulings on the meaning of SARA's language, has the EPA issued guidelines under which it will sanction voluntary cleanups worked out between the states and the PRPs.[38]

How successful all this federal-state cooperation has been remains problematic. If experience is any guide, some degree of tension and conflict among local, state, and federal officials is inevitable, despite the most astute legislative drafting and the best intentions on the part of all involved.[39]

To what extent can we expect effective intergovernmental relations among federal, state, and local governments in future cleanup efforts? Drawing on their experience in several areas of environmental policy, Sheldon Kamieniecki, Robert O'Brien, and Michael Clarke identified six factors that influence whether intergovernmental relations will be harmonious in the context of hazardous waste policy:

- perception on the part of public officials of the urgency of a problem and the need to act immediately;
- public and political pressure to act;
- degree to which a specific governmental unit has jurisdiction or responsibility for involvement in the area;
- costs and potential financial and legal liabilities involved in the abatement and cleanup procedure;
- extent to which government agencies must rely on other government agencies at different levels for expertise and financial assistance; and
- degree of openness of communication between government agencies.[40]

The authors studied six case histories of Superfund hazardous waste cleanup efforts: Alkali Lake in south-central Oregon; the Denver-area radium sites in Colorado; Jackson Township, New Jersey; Stringfellow in southern California; Valley of the Drums near Louisville, Kentucky; and Woburn, Massachusetts. The results reveal a great deal about the difficulties in translating swiftly into actual cleanup the promises of Superfund, such as rapid federal action and the availability of money and technical assistance for local efforts.

In all six cases, a perception of urgency if not crisis at first tended to trigger intergovernmental cooperation. With one exception, however, extensive wrangling ensued over who would pay and how much as well as who was legally liable. (The one exception was at the Denver radium sites, for which the federal government agreed early on to provide substantial funding.) These disputes were clearly not conducive to effective intergovernmental relations.[41]

Any cleanup of significance requires scientific analysis, site assessment, engineering, and planning well beyond what local communities and even most states can afford to provide. Therefore, the more technical assistance the federal government provided in the cases studied, the better the atmosphere of intergovernmental relations. In this respect, the federal government performed reasonably well in all six cases.

At four of the six sites, citizen groups had organized and were pressuring local officials. Despite previous experience to suggest this would bring public officials from all levels closer together, these results were not always present in the Superfund cleanups studied. At times community pressures resulted in local officials taking positions contrary to those of state and EPA administrators; such divergence occurred over the Valley of the Drums when local officials opposed installation of an incinerator.

Frequent and open communications between policymakers usually provide a catalyst to cooperation, and this was the experience at most of the six waste sites. The importance of communication was most vividly seen in its absence. In one case, federal and state officials resorted to communicating mainly through the local press, an approach that did not build trust or good working relations and indeed hindered the cleanup effort.

According to the team, designating a single agency with "clear jurisdiction over and responsibility for the abatement of a given toxic waste site is likely to facilitate intergovernmental relations." Otherwise, time and energy can be wasted when some agencies shirk responsibilities while others are busy building bureaucratic empires. That was the bitter lesson of Love Canal; the same pattern could be seen in the jockeying for position and the efforts at "blame avoidance" by local, state, and federal officials at most of the six sites studied. The implication is that effective program implementation calls for a single lead agency, empowered to coordinate the actions of all the agencies and to manage a successful cleanup effort from beginning to end.

Even without federal guidance, some states have devised effective procedures for communicating with responsible parties, local governments, local citizens, and—at Superfund sites—even EPA. New Jersey has a particularly impressive community relations effort under way at its hundreds of state Superfund sites. However, most federal Superfund sites still have no clearly defined lead agency.

CRITERIA FOR CLEANUP

One of the most hotly contested issues in Superfund implementation is the standard for cleanup: "How clean is clean?" or "Just how much cleanup is enough?" If the contamination risks from a site cannot be eliminated completely, then how much of the residual risk is acceptable? And to whom?

Surprisingly, CERCLA was silent on these points. Part of the omission no doubt stemmed from the implicit recognition in the Act that precise quantitative risk assessments were often impossible given the complex and differing circumstances at each waste site. Congress addressed two cleanup criteria explicitly, but only in the negative: Superfund sites did not have to be restored to pristine or even background levels, and cleanups did not have to rely on the "best available technology" (a highly ambiguous standard at best) if that would be more costly.[42] In 1980, CERCLA cleanup actions were to be "consistent with [a] permanent remedy . . . to prevent or minimize the release of hazardous substances so that they do not migrate to cause substantial danger to present or future public health or welfare or the environment."[43]

In effect, Congress granted EPA vast discretion in determining how thorough cleanup would need to be at any particular site. This discretion, combined with contradictory pressures from responsible parties concerned about cleanup costs and from local residents wanting absolute cleanup ("zero risk"), served to encourage delays in the cleanup process and reinforced pressures from the Office of Management and Budget to constrain Superfund expenditures.

As much as anything, this focus on cost rather than health risks led EPA to choose redisposal of cleanup wastes as its preferred cleanup strategy. In most cleanups, contaminated materials and soils were excavated and removed from a Superfund cleanup site only to be redeposited, untreated, at some still-operating landfill elsewhere. The fundamental problem with redisposal was obvious, however, because no landfill in the nation could be called leak-proof. By the mid-1980s, many landfills holding EPA permits under the Resource Conservation and Recovery Act (see Chapter Four) were found to be leaking and were closed to further hazardous wastes; some of these secondary locations later became Superfund sites.[44] Carting toxics from site to site appeared to most observers outside of EPA to be barely penny-wise and certainly pound-foolish. This toxics "shell game" served to intensify public skepticism about the environmental value of EPA's handling of Superfund. The agency's credibility declined another notch.

In 1986, Congress restated and clarified the principal criteria for evaluating proposed remedial actions, calling for "permanent remedies" instead of excavation and redisposal. According to the Superfund Amendments and Reauthorization Act (SARA),[45] a remedy must not only protect human health and environment and be cost-effective, it must also incorporate state-of-the-art treatment technologies and be designed as a permanent solution. Also, Superfund cleanups now must meet all other "legally applicable or relevant and appropriate" federal or state environmental standards. At the federal level, these include standards set under the Toxic Substances Control Act; Safe Drinking Water Act; Clean Air Act; Clean Water Act; Marine Protection, Research, and

Sanctuaries Act; and Solid Waste Disposal Act. More stringent state standards must also be applied to cleanups conducted under federal aegis. Although SARA did not remove EPA's discretionary authority to select the specific cleanup strategy at a given site, it underlined congressional impatience with the agency's failure to implement a clear and consistent treatment policy weighed in favor of permanent remedies. The message seemed clear on the face of it: Health and environmental risks were to take precedence over costs.

Even so, for several years after the passage of SARA, EPA continued to rely mostly on short-term economic criteria in selecting remedial strategies based on excavation and redisposal.[46] Cost remained the agency's dominant concern, the language of SARA notwithstanding. In 1988, EPA finally responded to criticisms of its policy by issuing new cleanup guidelines. Although retaining the general concept that each site is unique, EPA directed its staff to select whatever remedy "provides the best balance of tradeoffs with respect to . . . nine criteria" (see Box 2.2).

Critics contend that EPA's remedy-selection process still fails to clarify how tradeoffs are to be made among these nine points. Leaving that to

BOX 2.2 Nine Principal Criteria in Selecting Remedial Actions

---

- Overall protection of human health and the environment;

- Compliance with applicable or relevant and appropriate requirements of other statutes;

- Long-term effectiveness;

- Reduction of toxicity, mobility, or volume;

- Short-term effectiveness;

- Implementability;

- Cost;

- State acceptance;

- Community acceptance

Source: EPA, *A Guide to Developing Superfund Proposed Plans* (Washington, D.C.: EPA, July 1988).

the discretion of EPA (which, in practice, usually means leaving the decision to EPA's engineering consultants) unquestionably reflects the unique nature of each different Superfund site. However, the ambiguity only serves to compound the delays created by the wrangling over the "who pays" side of the equation. Without specific guidance as to remedies, those PRPs wishing to settle in advance of EPA's selection of a remedy have no reliable way to evaluate their financial exposure. Thus, PRPs, EPA, and state and local agencies continue to engage in study after study at a site, with each participant often trying to amass new data to buttress its claims regarding the extent of cleanup desired (and the costs incurred). Any hope for remediation gets pushed aside while debates rage, seemingly without end, over how much cleanup is necessary to protect health and how much cost can be justified to clean the site.

VICTIM COMPENSATION

CERCLA has at least one glaring omission: it has no provision to address the harm done to people in close proximity to Superfund sites or to compensate those who once worked at these sites.[47] The Act focuses solely on cleanup of the site and of any contamination in underground aquifers or the surrounding environment. This was a conscious choice by Congress when it decided to delete from the Act a proposed victim-compensation provision. Apparently, the rationale was to keep EPA focused on cleanup and also to avoid the potential financial drain that would occur if the federal government assumed responsibility for any adverse health effects that might plausibly be linked to specific Superfund sites.

CERCLA's silence on personal injury or adverse health effects has not prevented a number of PRPs at Superfund sites from being sued for health and environmental harms allegedly caused by toxics exposure. The legal precedent for victim compensation was set in the Three Mile Island accident case, when 280 residents sued owners of the nuclear power plant for economic and medical harm. This court action opened the gates to a flood of private and often class-action litigation against polluters. The TMI precedent has been used frequently in cases of hazardous waste pollution.

In the largest settlement with private plaintiffs to date, 1,300 former and current residents of Love Canal reached a $20 million settlement with Hooker Chemical Company and other responsible parties for contamination of soil and water in the township. Smaller settlements began to appear at other sites (see Box 2.3).

BOX 2.3 Private Settlements

In January 1985, Chevron became the first company at the McColl Superfund site in Fullerton, California, to settle in a dispute with local residents arising out of their claims that health and property values had been damaged by the dump. The McColl site, a rural waste dump opened in the 1940s for oil companies manufacturing wartime aviation fuel, now lies under a portion of a golf course ringed by expensive housing developments. A $26.5 million cleanup, 90 percent to be drawn initially from Superfund monies and then to be repaid by the oil companies, was ordered in 1985. The cleanup plan envisioned removing contaminated soils from the site at a rate of 40 truckloads of waste a day for 18 months. Chevron agreed to pay $400,000 to 78 families in the Meadows neighborhood north of McColl. The settlement, however, did not constitute an admission of liability on the part of the company. Six additional chemical firms followed suit in July 1985, agreeing to pay 121 area families $1 million. (Further litigation and remediation studies have continued to stall the actual cleanup at McColl; in mid-1990 the cleanup had yet to begin.)

Not all out-of-court waste case settlements involve designated Superfund sites. A settlement between BKK, formerly a major southern California hazardous waste disposal firm, and 508 persons living in the vicinity of the company's West Covina landfill was reached in December 1986. The amount of the settlement, $43 million, was the largest ever in a toxic waste case. This facility accepted more than 3.4 million tons of hazardous waste between 1968 and 1984 (by contrast, Hooker Chemical Company had dumped a scant 21,000 tons of hazardous substances into its landfill at Love Canal). After a five-year battle with area residents, including a narrowly defeated municipal ballot initiative to close the site and a belated city ordinance revoking the firm's 30-year waste disposal permit, the company ceased accepting toxic wastes at the site in November 1984. (In June 1984, EPA regional officials recommended BKK be placed on the Superfund list immediately after its closure. The site scored 48.24 on the EPA's hazard ranking system, high enough to place it in the top 50 percent of (then) 536 Superfund sites. However, because BKK remained open as a commercial municipal solid waste landfill, EPA rules precluded adding it to the NPL.)

TOWARD IMPROVED
IMPLEMENTATION OF SUPERFUND

When Congress passed SARA in 1986, it was responding to the enormous gap between the promise and the performance of the original Superfund act. In an effort to remedy some of the problems it had identified, Congress specified that sites must be listed in order of priority, depending upon which posed the greatest threat to human health. Leaving as little as possible to chance (or to EPA's shaky administrative discretion under the Reagan administration), Congress in SARA required that within two years, no fewer than 100 additional hazardous substances be listed as such by the EPA, and thereafter no fewer than 25 annually. A toxicological profile of each substance is now required, with the information then carried over to the health assessment required in every Superfund site analysis.[48] Congress ordered the Agency for Toxic Substances and Disease Registry to work with EPA to conduct health studies and prepare a list of substances commonly found at Superfund sites. SARA required that more potential Superfund sites be inventoried, preliminary studies undertaken, and cleanups begun. EPA can claim significant progress in meeting all these goals, and by the year 2000, it even expects to have added a thousand more entries to the Superfund list.[49] Yet as late as 1991, the bottom line was still that EPA had fully cleaned only 63 sites on the NPL.

The overall trend of settlements by responsible parties since passage of SARA shows a quickening of the pace and an increase in their size. SARA's new mandate to focus on "permanent remedies" provided an incentive for companies to settle, and the go-slow pace of Superfund action in general at EPA has begun to fade into the past. The Bush administration accelerated enforcement efforts, and EPA is arriving at ever more settlements with responsible parties.

As noted earlier, Congress in SARA clarified its intentions about the extent and quality of cleanup it wanted. In selecting a remedial action, now EPA is supposed to select not just the most expedient and cost-conscious method of cleanup but one that permanently and significantly reduces the volume, toxicity, or mobility of the hazardous substances present. Moreover, redisposal of wastes to another site is not to be selected if other treatment methods are available. Although the costs involved in this kind of cleanup may be higher, Congress said EPA should "determine an adequate level of protection of human health and the environment, and then, afterwards and secondarily, select a cost-effective means to achieve the adequate level of protection."[50]

The old question still remained, however: At any particular site, "how clean is clean?" Instead of giving a clear answer, Congress incorporated as standards "relevant" and "appropriate" for SARA cleanups all those environmental protection standards already on the books!

Near-term evidence suggests SARA accomplished its goals of invigorating EPA and the administrative processes of Superfund. Moreover, the new EPA team appointed by President Bush, headed by environmentalist William Reilly, began to move more forcefully on Superfund activities. Reilly's first major policy assessment of Superfund called for strengthening enforcement efforts, accelerating cleanups, applying innovative technologies, and involving affected communities far more closely,[51] and for that he has won wide praise. In July 1991, EPA's Assistant Administrator for Solid Waste and Emergency Response, Don Clay, reported to Reilly that EPA had several options to reduce substantially the average time for completion of cleanups: partly by setting firm annual targets, partly by standardizing the remedy selection process, and partly by increased consistency in risk management decisions.[52]

At the end of the decade, EPA adopted a new position on recovering voluntary cleanup costs. CERCLA was ambiguous on this point; after SARA's passage in 1986, EPA's informal position was that private cleanups were not sanctioned. However, the agency later came to accept that voluntary cleanup costs—including attorney fees—could be recovered from responsible parties under CERCLA provisions for a "private right of action." EPA in its March 1990 revised National Contingency Plan for Superfund clarified procedures required for cost recovery,[53] thereby encouraging private parties to proceed with cleanups at an accelerated pace.

With all this activity, however, calling for action in Washington, then delivering it at the thousands of Superfund sites across the land are quite different matters. As noted, in the five years since SARA was passed, the basic controversies remain over the extent to which a site must be cleaned.[54] And for all the publicity about permanent remedies, they are hard to come by and they can be costly. Reflecting on these realities after two years of following the new administration, one important member of Congress has reluctantly concluded that at least "from a qualitative perspective, remedy selection, in some degree, the 'guts' of the Superfund process, has not achieved the law's potential."[55]

It should not come as a surprise that several groups have begun to call for a major overhaul of Superfund's fundamental philosophy. One such example focused on "no fault" is described in Box 2.4. In May 1991, another industry grouping formed a coalition "aimed at amending Superfund to set up a new system of funding the cleanup of past pollution. . . . the present operation of CERCLA is not working. . . . The problem lies in the fact that most responsible parties would be blameless

BOX 2.4

America Needs a New System to Achieve Fast and Effective Cleanup of Our Environment

An Alarming Lack of Progress in Cleanup.

When Congress enacted the Federal Superfund program in 1980, the goal was to quickly clean up America's most dangerous hazardous waste sites. Congress and many others assumed there would be only a relatively few such sites and that cleanup costs would be limited.

Now after a decade of trying to make Superfund work, it's clear these assumptions were wrong and that a quick fix was never possible. What's wrong with Superfund and why has so little been accomplished?

The problem is twofold. First, the real scope of our nation's hazardous waste situation is far greater than Congress anticipated. With 1,200 priority sites already identified, growing numbers of sites are being found in every state. The Environmental Protection Agency expects that by the year 2000, there may be as many as 2,000 priority sites.

With rapidly rising cleanup costs, which now average about $25 million per site, the eventual price tag is staggering. According to a top government agency, cleaning up all of America's hazardous waste sites could take from 30 to 60 years and cost up to $500 billion!

A second problem is Superfund's alarming lack of progress in cleanup. A decade and billions of dollars later, fewer than 60 out of the 1,200 sites have actually been cleaned up.

Why? One major reason is Superfund's liability system. It requires that cleanup be paid for by establishing liability—who sent what waste, how much and where—and then negotiating or litigating with those believed to be responsible. While this sounds good in theory, it hasn't worked in practice. Instead, the result has been delayed cleanup and enormous legal, consulting and other costs unrelated to cleanup.

Compounding the Problems Instead of Solving Them.

This is because working out who pays and how much for cleanup is very difficult. Under Superfund, anyone who simply used or owned the site at any time could be liable for the entire cleanup bill. Users can include major corporations, small businesses, local governments, hospitals, nursing homes, schools, even individuals. And it does not matter who caused the harm or whether they did anything wrong. Superfund's retroactive liability provision makes parties pay for past actions based on today's standards.

For example, at 422 sites almost 14,000 parties have been notified that they could be liable. In turn, many of them are identifying still others who contributed in some way to the presence of waste at each site. And since Superfund liability deals with past waste disposal, the record of users can go back 25, 30 or even 40 years and can number in the hundreds.

(continues)

BOX 2.4 *(continued)*

The result? The focus on cleanup has been lost as private and public parties spend years in difficult but unavoidable negotiations and litigation, trying to work out agreements that would provide funds for cleanup. At some sites, more money has been spent resolving complex factual issues than on cleanup itself. This does a lot for lawyers and consultants, but very little for the environment. And of course, these costs are eventually passed on to all of us as consumers in higher prices for goods and services. Isn't it time to stop this wasteful process and get on with cleaning up our environment?

At AIG, we think so. There is little to be gained by arguing over waste disposal that happened long ago. America needs a system that will promote fast and effective cleanup, reduce unnecessary legal fees, spread the cost of cleanup broadly, and encourage responsible waste management practices today.

A Proposed Solution:
The National Environmental Trust Fund.

To accomplish this, we have proposed creating a National Environmental Trust Fund, similar to the National Highway Trust Fund. Its resources would be used exclusively for cleaning up old hazardous waste sites. Superfund's tough liability provisions would still apply for future pollution, as would all other state and federal environmental laws designed to promote responsible waste management.

One way this fund could be financed would be by adding a separate fee to commercial and industrial insurance premiums in the United States. Even a modest assessment, say 2% of premiums and an equivalent amount for self-insureds, would provide about $40 billion over the next decade—more than enough to clean up the 1,200 highest-priority sites. Without endless time and money spent on legal debates about liability.

A national advisory board consisting of private individuals, industry and public officials could be charged with overseeing the program. We also suggest giving consideration to establishing local technical monitoring committees in each community. These groups of local citizens, representatives of industry and others would work with the Environmental Protection Agency and their own state on the particular cleanup site—from the very beginning of the cleanup effort.

You Can Help.

We've waited long enough and spent enough money in the courtrooms. Now it's time for action. A cleaner America should be all Americans' shared goal and shared responsibility.

To express your views, or if you would like further information about AIG's proposed National Environmental Trust Fund, write to Mr. M.R. Greenberg, Chairman, American International Group, Inc., 70 Pine Street, New York, NY 10270.

Source: Reprinted with permission from American International Group, Inc.

under traditional theories of tort liability . . . . The preoccupation with pinpointing responsibility for past pollution has prevented us from achieving the primary purpose for which Superfund was enacted—the cleanup of hazardous waste sites." The fundamental actions recommended by this group involved refocus on Superfund's highest priority sites, and a shift from pursuing PRPs to pay for cleanups to having EPA use Superfund monies for this purpose. The coalition pointed to three new sources for replenishing Superfund's coffers: (1) a fee as a percentage of premiums paid for industrial property casualty insurance; (2) an excise levy on all industrial concerns; or (3) the "peace dividend."[56] We give our recommendations in Chapter Eight.

In sum, there is good news to report. SARA has improved the design of the Superfund program. The vigorous Bush team at EPA, and its removal of several key legal roadblocks to reaching accord with the responsible parties—indicated by the recent trend in settlements—are pushing implementation forward. Nevertheless, many more years will pass before these administrative actions are translated into many actual cleanups. For all the policy learning and especially the recent microsuccesses in implementation, it remains the case that superfailure in the cleanup of Superfund sites will come to an end neither easily nor soon.

NOTES

1. Anthony Downs, "Up and Down with Ecology—The Issue-Attention Cycle," *The Public Interest* 28 (Summer 1972), 38–50.

2. For an interesting recasting of Downs's thesis in light of the environmental movement in general, see Riley E. Dunlap, "Public Opinion and Environmental Policy," in James P. Lester, ed., *Environmental Politics and Policy: Theories and Evidence* (Durham, N.C.: Duke University Press, 1989), esp. 118–121.

3. Steven Cohen and Marc Tipermas, "Superfund: Preimplementation Planning and Bureaucratic Politics," in James P. Lester and Ann O'M. Bowman, eds., *The Politics of Hazardous Waste Management* (Durham, N.C.: Duke University Press, 1983), 41.

4. Riley E. Dunlap, "Polls, Pollution, and Politics Revisited: Public Opinion on the Environment in the Reagan Era," *Environment* 29 (July/August 1987), 6–11, 32–37. A Roper poll of March 1990 found the two most pressing environmental concerns in the public's mind to be actively used hazardous waste sites and abandoned hazardous waste sites. See Howard Kunreuther, "Managing Hazardous Waste: Past, Present, and Future," *Risk Analysis* 11 (March 1991), 19.

5. Norman J. Vig, "Presidential Leadership: From the Reagan to the Bush Administration," in Norman J. Vig and Michael E. Kraft, eds., *Environmental Policy in the 1990s* (Washington, D.C.: Congressional Quarterly Press, 1990), 33–58, and

app. 2, "Spending on Natural Resources and the Environment, Fiscal Years 1980–90."

6. Quoted by Ann O'M. Bowman, "Superfund Implementation: Five Years and How Many Cleanups?" in Charles E. Davis and James P. Lester, eds., *Dimensions of Hazardous Waste Politics and Policy*, (Westport, Conn.: Greenwood Press, 1988), 129. Bowman goes on to say that within four short years, critics had begun to characterize the implementation process as "lunch now, lawyers maybe, but shovels never."

7. This is the conclusion reached by most observers. In reviewing the broad range of environmental policies in the 1980s, Kraft and Vig conclude that "Progress in dealing with hazardous wastes and other toxic chemicals has been the least satisfactory of all pollution control programs." Michael E. Kraft and Norman J. Vig, "Environmental Policy from the Seventies to the Nineties: Continuity and Change," in Vig and Kraft, *Environmental Policy*, 22. The sentiment is reiterated in the several papers and comments by scholars, attorneys, business managers, and government officials in "Workshop on Hazardous Waste," *Risk Analysis* 11 (March 1991), 19–109; for more of the same, see Hazardous Waste Treatment Council et al. *Right Train, Wrong Track: Failed Leadership in the Superfund Cleanup Program* (Washington, D.C.: June 20, 1988); Office of Technology Assessment (OTA), U.S. Congress, "Are We Cleaning Up? 10 Superfund Case Studies—Special Report" (Washington, D.C.: Government Printing Office, June 1988); and Andrew Danzo, "The Big Sleazy: Love Canal Ten Years Later," *The Washington Monthly* (September 1988), 11–17.

8. Congress appears to have had this partly in mind in specifying that "[a]mong the top 100 priority sites, at least one must be designated by each state." Sidney M. Wolf, *Pollution Law Handbook: A Guide To Federal Environmental Laws* (Westport, Conn.: Quorum Books, 1988), 237.

9. Wolf, *Pollution Law Handbook*, 237.

10. This is a classic example of becoming preoccupied with "golden numbers" rather than what they stand for. See Robert Socolow, "Failures of Discourse: Obstacles to the Integration of Environmental Values into Natural Resource Policy," in Laurence Tribe, Coreen Schelling, and John Voss, eds., *When Values Conflict* (Cambridge, Mass: Ballinger, 1976), 1–33.

11. By 1990, more than 31,000 potential Superfund sites had been inventoried by EPA; see John T. Ronan III, "New Horizons for Superfund Enforcement," *Hazmat World* (February 1990), 43.

12. OTA, "Are We Cleaning Up?" 5.

13. Congressional Research Service, "Summaries of Federal Environmental Laws Administered by the Environmental Protection Agency," CRS, Library of Congress (January 28, 1985), 37–38.

14. Danzo, "Big Sleazy," 16.

15. Most states replicated these provisions, but by the end of the decade it was clear that CERCLA's liability strictures were overly harsh. In 1988, Pennsylvania provided several categories of exemptions from state cleanup liability for those parties truly innocent of any role in causing the contamination: a person who had inherited the contaminated property without knowledge of its

condition, for example. Changes to state liability did not excuse a person from federal CERCLA liability, of course.

16. The tax base was expanded under the 1986 revisions of CERCLA to include a tax on petroleum (8.2 cents per barrel of domestic crude and 11.7 cents per barrel for imported petroleum products), a tax on imported chemical derivatives, and an overall environmental tax of 0.12 percent on every corporation's minimum taxable income over $2 million.

17. At least partly in exchange for these provisions, CERCLA excludes cleanup of petroleum products from federal Superfund liability (numerous states do require petroleum cleanup under their laws).

18. In an unusual exception to the exemption for government agencies, a federal jury in June 1989 found the state of California liable to share in what could amount to a $600 million cleanup at the Stringfellow Acid Pits. The jury found that because the state had encouraged James Stringfellow to open his site to hazardous waste and had certified the dump's operation, it too must contribute to meeting the cost of the cleanup.

19. The 1986 Superfund amendments included a *de minimus* settlements provision under which parties that have contributed only a minor portion of the total wastes at a site can enter into an agreement under which they pay more than their proportional share of the cleanup cost (but much less than 100 percent) in return for early release from further liability. Although this provision has not been used too frequently, it may prove to be of eventual value to many companies. Julie L. Edelson, "Superfund: Still in the Dumps," *Technology Review* 91 (November/December 1988), 32.

20. A review of the courts' handling of the Superfund law is provided by Werner F. Grunbaum, "Judicial Enforcement of Hazardous Waste Liability Law," in Davis and Lester, *Dimensions of Hazardous Waste Politics*, 163–175.

21. An exception may be the collaborative public-private cleanups fostered at some fifty sites by Clean Sites, Inc., a company established by a coalition of environmental and business organizations in 1984 to facilitate waste site cleanups. See Clean Sites, Inc., "Making Superfund Work: Recommendations to Improve Program Implementation" (January 1989). Even here, however, enormous delays have ensued in moving from study to actual cleanup, and Clean Sites fell far short of its initial "every company adopt a site" goal for accelerated nationwide cleanup.

22. In San Jose, California, for example, IBM paid nearly $100 million to pump groundwater contaminated with low concentrations of mildly toxic solvents, whereas the much more hazardous Lorenz Barrel and Drum site nearby (the firm lacked any "deep pocket") remained a serious threat with minimal cleanup.

23. Steven Ferrey, "Toxics Shell Game," *The Amicus Journal* (Summer 1987), 8.

24. Victoria J. Tschinkel, "Economic, Legal, and Practical Problems in Hazardous Waste Cleanup and Management," in National Academy of Engineering, *Hazards: Technology and Fairness* (Washington, D.C.: National Academy Press, 1986), 178. Ms. Tschinkel is former secretary of the Florida

Department of Environmental Regulation.

25. William K. Reilly (EPA Administrator), *A Management Review of the Superfund Program* (Washington, D.C.: EPA, June 1989), 1–6; Ronan, "New Horizons for Superfund Enforcement."

26. Lois Ember, "Review to Call for Revamp of Superfund's Implementation," *Chemical and Engineering News* (May 29, 1989), 19.

27. Aerojet-General was embroiled in the controversy surrounding Reagan administration EPA official Rita M. Lavelle, a former Aerojet employee. Lavelle served four and a half months in prison after lying to Congress about her role in negotiating with her former employer the cleanup of toxic waste.

28. The January 1988 agreement allocated the costs of cleanup between the U.S. Army (site owner) and Shell according to the following formula: Shell and the Army would pay equally for the first $500 million spent on cleaning the site; Shell would pay an additional 35 percent of the next $200 million and 20 percent of remaining costs. See Dan Morain, "Shell Oil to Pay $1 Billion for Toxic Waste Cleanup," *Los Angeles Times* (December 20, 1988). In a related decision, a San Mateo County (California) superior court ruled in December 1988 that Shell rather than its 250 insurance companies was solely responsible for the cleanup costs at the arsenal.

29. Seth Mones, "Capturing Superfund's Potential: Ideas on the Federal Cleanup Program and Environmental Law-Making Generally," *Risk Analysis* 11 (March 1991), 89.

30. Mike Ward, "Cash Flow for OII Cleanup Begins with $21.3 Million," *Los Angeles Times* (January 5, 1989).

31. "EPA Announces Agreement on Operating Industries Superfund Site," *California Environmental Insider* (December 15, 1991), 11.

32. Rudy Abramson, "U.S. Waste Cleanup Bill Put at $750 Billion," *Los Angeles Times* (December 10, 1991), A–29.

33. Wolf, *Pollution Law Handbook*, 238.

34. Tschinkel, "Economic, Legal, and Practical Problems," 173–174.

35. There has been little experience to date with this provision of CERCLA, but it has notable potential for encouraging prudent environmental management by businesses and corporations. See Thomas A. Grigalunas and James J. Opaluch, "Assessing Liability for Damages Under CERCLA: A New Approach for Providing Incentives for Pollution Avoidance?" *Natural Resources Journal* 28 (Summer 1988), 509–533.

36. Tschinkel, "Economic, Legal, and Practical Problems," 171–172.

37. Roger C. Dower, "Hazardous Wastes," in Paul R. Portney, ed., *Public Policies for Environmental Protection* (Washington, D.C.: Resources for the Future, 1990), 171.

38. William H. Bode, "Recovering Voluntary Cleanup Costs," *Hazmat World* (July 1991), 82.

39. For the states, the issue is not simply one of managing the responsibilities placed on them by toxics legislation but also the requirements of federal air, water, and all the other environmental laws adopted over the past two decades.

Their response has been mixed. See James P. Lester, "A New Federalism? Environmental Policy in the States," in Vig and Kraft, *Environmental Policy*, 59–79.

40. Sheldon Kamieniecki, Robert O'Brien, and Michael Clarke, "Environmental Policy and Aspects of Intergovernmental Relations," in J. Edwin Benton and David R. Morgan, eds., *Intergovernmental Relations and Public Policy* (Westport, Conn.: Greenwood Press, 1986), 50.

41. Kamieniecki et al., "Intergovernmental Relations," 52.

42. OTA, "Superfund Strategy, Summary" (1985), 27. Some states have insisted on more stringent cleanups. California has pressed for nondegradation of groundwater (removal of any pollutants added by the waste site) under its Porter-Cologne Water Quality Act. Not even this standard has been applied uniformly, however.

43. Erin Sheridan, "How Clean Is Clean? Standards for Remedial Actions at Hazardous Waste Sites Under CERCLA," *Stanford Law Journal* 6 (1986-87), 18–19.

44. See Environmental Defense Fund, et al., "Nowhere to Go: The Universal Failure of Class I Hazardous Waste Dump Sites in California," Environmental Defense Fund, Inc. (June 1985); Assembly Office of Research, "Today's Toxic Dump Sites: Tomorrow's Toxic Cleanup Sites," California State Assembly (August 1986).

45. These criteria are set forth in section 121 of CERCLA.

46. See Hazardous Waste Treatment Council et al., *Right Train, Wrong Track* (1988).

47. Some states, however, have included such provisions; New Jersey's Spill Compensation and Control Act and California's 1981 State Superfund Act are examples.

48. Wolf, *Pollution Law Handbook*, 259-260.

49. Reilly, *A Management Review*, ch. 1.

50. Wolf, *Pollution Law Handbook*, 233.

51. Reilly, *A Management Review*.

52. "Reilly Considers Major Program Changes to Accelerate Site Cleanups, Define Risks," *Environment Reporter* (August 30, 1991), 1187–1188.

53. 55 *Federal Register* 46 (March 8, 1990), 8666–8865.

54. Sheridan, "How Clean is Clean?" 39.

55. Mones, "Capturing Superfund's Potential," 91.

56. Kimberly A. Roy, "Environmental Business Group Targets Superfund Reform, Liability Reduction," *Hazmat World* (July 1991), 19.

CHAPTER THREE

How Clean Is Clean?
A Case Study of the Nation's
No. 1 Superfund Toxic Dump

The failure to date to implement Superfund adequately by any imaginable standard spelled out in the previous chapter lends itself to many differing explanations. In overview fashion, we have tried to shed light on each one. Some of these are the way Congress designed the cleanup process in the initial 1980 Superfund legislation and then in its amendments of 1986; the resistance of the Reagan administration throughout the all-important initial years of implementation of the law; the failure of EPA and state administrative agencies to coordinate properly and carry out expeditiously the provisions of CERCLA and SARA; and the recalcitrance on the part both of those responsible for the hazardous wastes in the first place and of those who owned and operated the hazardous waste landfills, the parties the legislation said must be made to pay for the cleanups. Another explanation is the ignorance on the part of all about the nature and breadth of the problem of hazardous waste sites and what it would take in both dollars and know-how to clean them up. Still another is the differing expectations of what "cleanup" or "cost-effective" meant to responsible public officials who were trying faithfully to carry out the law, in contrast to those ordinary citizens who found themselves living adjacent to the now-identified Superfund sites. These were all contributing factors.

Yet, too, beneath the aggregate figures—how many sites are on the National Priority List, the technologies selected for remediation, the dollars spent on settlements (though not as yet on cleanups)—lie hundreds of tales about honest disagreements and misunderstandings over what is best for a given site. These reveal the drama of human lives

---

and people fearful for their health, property, and well-being and are equally important to our understanding.

No two cleanup efforts have ever been the same; thus no single instance can suffice as prototypical. But the detail provided in a case study can be valuable in bringing forward the flavor and complex dynamics of our nation's experience with Superfund. In that respect, no case is more apropos than the tale of the nation's top-ranked Superfund site—Lipari, in New Jersey—as told by Carl E. Van Horn and Yvonne Chilik of Rutgers University. This is no story of good versus evil, or even of good intentions gone astray, but instead of the calamity of doing business as usual in the world of waste disposal in the United States. It is a story of what happens and what can go wrong and how long it can take when even the best intentions and powerful administrative and political pressures are put forth. It is a sobering tale. With their permission, the story as told by Van Horn and Chilik is presented here with only slight editing of and revisions to the original.[1]

A SIMPLE BEGINNING

In 1951, Nick Lipari purchased a 44-acre family farm in Gloucester County, New Jersey, near the town of Pitman. He opened a sand and gravel pit operation on the land. To fill in the trenches left behind by the excavation, he began accepting municipal and household wastes for disposal. Seven years later, Lipari also started accepting liquid chemical wastes. The toxic soup that accumulated in the landfill leaked into the groundwater and a nearby lake. At its peak, the flow of contaminated groundwater into Alcyon Lake reached 90,000 to 110,000 gallons per day. By the time Lipari Landfill was closed by state officials in 1971, nearly three million gallons of dangerous chemicals had been dumped into its pits. Today, more than two decades after the government began to address the problem, and after the expenditure of several million dollars for cleanup activities, the site still contains large amounts of dangerous hazardous wastes.

The story of the Lipari site cleanup is one of delay and frustration in dealing with a problem so large it defies simple solutions. Besides the technical problems involved in cleaning up vast amounts of dangerous chemicals, conflicts over defining the actual problem and over the goals of the cleanup operation have also complicated the project. The cleanup has been hampered further by considerable distrust and by a lack of communication among the principal actors involved, compounded by the difficulty of communicating health risks.

In 1970, the residents of Pitman began to complain to the New Jersey

Department of Environmental Protection (DEP) about Lipari Landfill. They reported that noxious odors and odd-colored streams of liquids were coming from the site. They complained of nausea, headaches, and breathing difficulties. In response, DEP initiated enforcement action later that year, charging that Lipari Landfill was in violation of the federal Clean Water Act. In 1971, the New Jersey Solid Waste Authority closed the landfill. Little more transpired there for almost a decade, despite some minimal enforcement actions by the state.

Nine years later, federal involvement in cleanup efforts at the Lipari site began when congressman (now governor) James Florio of New Jersey, a major proponent of the Superfund bill then pending in Congress, announced a $778,000 grant from the U.S. Environmental Protection Agency (EPA) to begin cleaning up this toxic waste site. By 1983, Lipari ranked number one on the Superfund list. Although EPA had spent $7.3 million there by May 1987, much of the actual cleanup process was and continues to be slow, frustrating both local residents and EPA officials.

This case study examines the controversy surrounding the Lipari project, the cleanup options considered, and the roles played by community groups, government agencies, and legislators. As noted later, cleanup efforts are continuing and progress is gradually taking place. And the controversies of this case continue to be repeated time and again as Superfund implementation proceeds across the country. As New Jersey Assemblyman Gary Stuhltrager said with respect to Lipari:

> America needs to pay more attention to its environment and natural resources. What is happening now in New Jersey is the future for the rest of the United States. It's just that the future has come to New Jersey first.

CREATING A TOXIC SOUP

Longtime residents of Pitman, a small town just south of Camden, remember Alcyon Lake as a favorite recreation spot for local residents and visitors. Alcyon Park, which sat on the banks of the lake, boasted a boardwalk, merry-go-round, roller coaster, and in the early decades of the 1900s, large crowds of sunbathers and picnickers. The lake was popular for swimming, boating, and fishing. Vacationers from Camden and Philadelphia traveled to Pitman to spend their summer breaks at Alcyon Lake. For Pitman's 9,000 residents, Alcyon Lake was an idyllic spot.

Only ducks and geese use the lake now. In place of the boardwalk and the merry-go-round are signs warning against fishing or swimming in the polluted water. The lake's environmental troubles predated Nick

Lipari's landfill operation. Swimming in the lake was banned in 1958 by the New Jersey Department of Health when bacterial contamination was found in the water. Officials suspect the pollution was caused by leakage from a sewage treatment plant that once operated upstream.

Starting in 1951, Lipari began to dig soil, sand, and gravel from a six-acre plot nearby for sale as construction fill and to import garbage to dump into his excavation pits. The trash-filled pits were then covered over with dirt. At first, Lipari accepted only solid wastes, such as household garbage and used washers, refrigerators, and other appliances. But in 1958, the same year Alcyon Lake was closed because of bacterial contamination, Lipari began pouring liquid industrial wastes onto his land.

Owens-Illinois was the first company to dump liquid wastes at Lipari Landfill. The company, a large paint and supplies manufacturer from the nearby town of Glassboro, disposed of an estimated 200 gallons a week of production by-products and paint thinner into Lipari's pits. Lipari expanded his disposal business in 1968 when he began accepting liquid wastes from Rohm and Haas, a Bristol, Pennsylvania, company; and from the Almo division of Owens-Corning Fiberglass, which makes phonograph records for Columbia Records and Tapes. From 1968 to 1970, Rohm and Haas disposed of an estimated 46,000 drums (2.53 million gallons) of waste into Lipari. No accurate estimate exists of the amount of waste deposited by Almo, but it was substantially less than what Rohm and Haas contributed.

A total of 74 chemicals have now been detected at this landfill, including the following toxic materials:

- benzene, known to cause cancer in humans and capable of causing central nervous system disorders;
- bis (2-chlorethyl) ether (BCEE), a suspected carcinogen known to increase significantly the incidence of liver cancer in mice;
- cadmium, suspected of causing cancer and birth defects;
- vinyl chloride, another carcinogen that also might cause birth defects; and
- lead, which has been shown to cause blood chemistry disturbances, brain damage, central nervous system disorders, and cardiovascular damage.

According to EPA documents, the nearly three million gallons of waste dumped at Lipari included solvents, paint thinners, formaldehyde, paints, phenol and amine wastes, dust-collector residues, and resins. During the years the landfill was in operation, at least one explosion and two fires were reported.

Throughout this period, the toxic soup that accumulated on Nick Lipari's property began to leak into the groundwater that eventually drained into Alcyon Lake, about 1,600 feet north of the landfill. The landfill sits atop two sand and gravel formations that compose the Cohansey aquifer, a 9- to 16-foot layer of clay, that in turn sits above the Kirkwood aquifer. Apparently, the chemicals deposited in the landfill seeped easily into the Cohansey aquifer, draining into Rabbit Run and Chestnut Branch creeks and finally flowing into Alcyon Lake.

As early as 1970, residents living along the banks of the lake began noticing discoloration of the water. Orange, purple, and blue rings shimmered on the lake surface. Foul-smelling puddles of red and green liquid began to appear in a marsh area just below the landfill.

Before 1971, waste disposal operations in New Jersey were not subject to state permitting requirements. Until then, Lipari Landfill was inspected periodically by the State Department of Health, which gave the operation "acceptable" ratings. In response to residents' complaints, the New Jersey Solid Waste Authority closed the landfill in May 1971 and ordered Lipari to clean up the site. Lipari dug drainage ditches and sprinkled lime on the landfill in an effort to cope with the stench produced by buried chemicals. But those actions had little effect, and Lipari was sued in 1974 by the state DEP, which charged that his landfill had contaminated Alcyon Lake and the land surrounding it. The court ordered Lipari to implement additional remedial actions, but again those efforts did little to stem the continuing flow of contamination from the site.

BUILDING A BATHTUB

Although state officials prohibited Lipari Landfill from accepting any more wastes after 1971, efforts to contain the toxic contents already deposited there did not begin until 11 years later. There were no federal laws affecting regulation of hazardous waste facilities such as toxic landfills until 1976, when Congress passed the Resource Conservation and Recovery Act (RCRA), designed to establish a cradle-to-grave monitoring system for toxic materials such as those at Lipari. And before 1980, no federal legislation specifically addressed the problem of abandoned hazardous waste sites that threatened the environment and public health.

Just as chemicals from Lipari Landfill continued to leach into groundwater and Alcyon Lake, distressed residents continued their complaints to state and local officials. In 1978, a consultant hired by township officials discovered the lake was contaminated with BCEE, a suspected cancer-causing substance that accumulates in human tissue. On the basis of that report, DEP began testing leachate in the landfill and EPA studied lake water. Test samples from the water, soil, and fish showed high concentrations of carcinogens. In 1980, the Pitman Borough Council ordered Alcyon Lake closed to all recreational use, including fishing.

Under the federal Clean Water Act, EPA in 1979 assumed responsibility for cleaning up Lipari Landfill. Then, in March 1980, the federal agency funded feasibility studies of various containment and cleanup strategies. The results pointed to a strategy of containing the hazardous waste in the landfill by surrounding the landfill with clay barriers, known as slurry walls, then covering it with a thick layer of plastic and dirt.

Throughout 1979 and 1980, congressman Florio gathered support for federal legislation to authorize EPA to clean up abandoned hazardous waste sites such as Lipari. Florio, whose district included Pitman and Lipari Landfill, was a chief sponsor of the Superfund law (the Comprehensive Environmental Response, Compensation, and Liability Act of 1980). After President Carter signed Superfund into law on December 11, 1980, Lipari Landfill was one of the first sites to receive cleanup funds. EPA began studying methods to contain dangerous leaks from the site. To recover the costs of the cleanup, EPA sued the firms that had dumped chemicals at Lipari.

Following the general procedures outlined in the Superfund law, EPA completed a remedial investigation and feasibility study (RI/FS). EPA's selected course of action is documented in its record of decision (ROD) [see Box 2.1]. From September through November 1981, EPA conducted public meetings on potential Lipari cleanup strategies. A formal ROD approving a method for containing the toxic soup within the landfill was issued in late 1982.

EPA authorized construction of a slurry wall encircling both the six-acre landfill and an additional ten acres that had been contaminated. Contractors dug a trench around the tract, inserted a mixture of soil and bentonite (an absorbent clay), and placed over the site a thick plastic cap covered with dirt. The wall and cap were designed to keep leachate in and additional groundwater out of the landfill, an approach that turned the site into a giant bathtub without a drain. The construction phase of the project was estimated to cost nearly $2 million.

Before construction could begin, however, Superfund provisions required EPA to conduct engineering design studies. The agency also convened another round of public meetings. Meanwhile, public access to the contaminated landfill was restricted by a chain-link fence. Lipari paid $75,000 of the $165,000 cost of the fence as part of a court settlement;

EPA covered the rest. In August 1983, the U.S. Army Corps of Engineers began to build the slurry wall and cap, which were completed by the following June. EPA had already spent more than $4 million just to contain the toxic liquids in Lipari Landfill.

DRAINING THE TOXIC BATHTUB

Once the new containment walls were in place, the flow of contaminants into the groundwater, creeks, and Alcyon Lake dropped from 110,000 gallons to 2,500 gallons a day—a 98 percent decrease, according to EPA officials, who then turned their attention to collecting and treating the toxic chemicals sitting in the now-enclosed landfill. This task was divided into two stages. First, another RI/FS evaluated various methods to remove and treat wastes contained within the landfill. Then a third RI/FS would address the cleanup of contamination in areas beyond the landfill, such as pollution of Chestnut Branch and Rabbit Run creeks.

EPA released its study of potential remedies for the polluted landfill in August 1985. Prepared by the engineering firm of Camp, Dresser, and McKee, that study evaluated different cleanup options according to different criteria, including safety, implementability, public health, environmental impact, cost, and reliability. As required under Superfund, EPA considered (1) taking no action at the site, (2) the feasibility and cost of completely removing the toxic contaminants, and (3) a range of options between these two extremes.[2] The options examined by Camp, Dresser, and McKee included the following:

- *Complete excavation.* The landfill would be drained and the soil excavated and taken to a secure landfill. (The study did not name any landfills ready and willing to accept these wastes.) The site would be filled in with clean dirt, graded, and seeded. The estimated cost for excavation and redisposal was $290 million.
- *Enhanced containment.* The landfill would be drained by pumping out the aquifers beneath it. This technique involves reversing the flow of water away from the site by lowering the water table to a level below the contaminated soil and maintaining it there. The estimated cost for this approach ranged from $3.7 million to $6.9 million.
- *Flushing.* EPA's preferred remedy involved installation of groundwater/leachate extraction and injection wells inside the contaminated landfill to drain and flush the site. Contaminated water would be treated, preferably onsite, then discharged into a

sewage treatment plant. Either the treated water or fresh water would then be injected into the soil of the landfill and pumped out again, repeating the entire process—just like repeatedly draining and refilling a bathtub. Initially, EPA estimated that "flushing" would take 15 years to remove 90 percent of the water-soluble contaminants. The estimated cost was $8.9 million.

- *No action.* The landfill would be left in its existing condition. EPA would merely monitor the groundwater to gauge the flow of contaminants from the landfill. Doing nothing would cost at least $1.3 million.

Release of the detailed feasibility study in late 1985, along with realization that EPA was not going to excavate the landfill and take away the contaminated soil, spawned a small but intense community opposition movement. During the early phases of the Lipari cleanup, EPA had worked effectively with the town's environmental commission members and conducted several generally positive community meetings. In June 1985, however, a group of Pitman residents who were frustrated with the prolonged cleanup process banded together to oppose the proposed flushing alternative. They advocated complete removal of all contaminants. The active members of the Pitman–Alcyon Lake–Lipari Landfill Community Association (PALLCA) included several disgruntled lakeside homeowners.

Harry Lindsay, a founder of PALLCA, feared that the health of Pitman residents was endangered by the chemicals found in the landfill, the marsh area, and the lake. He was particularly frightened by the discovery in the lake of BCEE, which an EPA medical adviser said in court records "can be expected to cause cancer in persons who presently show no overt signs of irritation. . . . Exposure to (BCEE) cannot be allowed to continue until human cancer actually occurs." Lindsay, whose home overlooks Alcyon Lake, brought this testimony to the attention of Doug and Pat Stuart, two of his lakeside neighbors. At the time, the Stuarts' two young sons were suffering from severe asthmatic attacks, and they became concerned that the chemicals in the lake were responsible.

PALLCA members were outraged by EPA's endorsement of a cleanup effort they viewed as incomplete, time-consuming, and untested. Flushing the liquid wastes from the soil in the landfill would remove water-soluble chemicals, but PALLCA feared this process would leave behind non-water-soluble chemicals that might endanger residents' health. Also, the group was alarmed to learn that the process had been tested only in laboratory settings and had never been used in any actual toxic waste cleanups. Finally, the 15-year frame for remediation did little to allay residents' fears of negative health effects from long-term exposure to the toxic contaminants.

PALLCA members brought their objections to an August 1985 public meeting conducted by EPA on its feasibility study. The Stuarts called the hearings "meaningless," charging EPA did not listen to their complaints:

> In our comments, we laid out some specific questions. When the EPA came to Pitman a few weeks later, we asked the same questions. They said they would need some time to come up with the answers. If they had already read our response, they would have known how to respond to us. We did our homework—we were prepared. We even rehearsed our questions. . . . We were educated when we went into the meetings with the EPA—they weren't. They've never given us the responses we deserved.

To call attention to its concerns, PALLCA organized a lakeside rally in September 1985, drawing a crowd of about 300 people. During the rally, Doug Stuart called the flushing method a "Band-Aid solution."

> "We have the right to decide our future. If they go through with this Band-Aid solution, what will happen to other hazardous sites? There's no hope for them. We make our stand here. We demand total cleanup," Stuart said.

Seven days after the PALLCA rally, EPA released its ROD, officially announcing its intentions to flush the chemicals from the landfill rather than to excavate and haul away the contaminated soil. The Stuarts believed that EPA officials had chosen the flushing option before the public meeting and had simply ignored PALLCA's complaints. "They make up defenses to protect a position they're not going to bend on," Doug Stuart said later.

DUELING DEFINITIONS

The dispute between EPA and PALLCA over cleanup methods stemmed from a difference in how each group defined a "clean" toxic waste site. To the members of PALLCA, a clean site is one from which all dangerous chemicals have been removed. Any cleanup option that falls short of carting away the contaminated soil and returning the entire area to an untainted state was unacceptable.

To EPA, a "clean" site is a site posing no significant harm. Sal Badalamenti, EPA's Superfund section chief for southern New Jersey, defined cleaning up a toxic waste dump as "leaving the site [in a condition that] does not pose a threat to public health or the

environment." Complete removal of all chemicals is not required, nor
must the land be returned to its previously usable condition. Cleaning
up Lipari under this definition "does not mean that this site can be
returned for future land use, or for any use at all. There will always be
a restricted area," Badalamenti said.

Christopher Daggett, EPA regional administrator for the New
York/New Jersey area, believes that differences in definitions were at the
heart of the dispute over the Lipari cleanup.

> "It was a mistake calling the program the 'Superfund cleanup.' It should
> have been called mitigation, because cleanup means, for most people,
> picking it up and taking it away. But this is not what we are doing. We
> just contain it and watch it for a long time in a number of cases," Daggett
> said.

EPA's choice of cleanup strategies was also affected by statutory
requirements. The ROD on Lipari points out that Superfund requires
specific remedies

> to be appropriate when balanced against the availability of Trust Fund
> monies for use at other sites . . . cost-effective, implementable and
> technically sound when compared to other remedial action alternatives,
> and necessary and adequate to protect public health, welfare and the
> environment.

At least at Lipari, EPA also sought a cleanup strategy that would
contain or treat contaminants where they are found rather than moving
them around to other communities. According to EPA documents:

> It is EPA policy to pursue response actions that use treatment, reuse or
> recycling over land disposal to the greatest extent practicable, consistent
> with CERCLA requirements for cost-effective remedial actions. Because
> of the limited land disposal facilities available and the inherent problems
> with land disposal, it is EPA's policy to use land disposal only when other
> alternatives are impracticable or do not sufficiently safeguard public health
> and the environment.

The flushing method met EPA's requirements at the Lipari site. It
would provide a cost-effective, onsite cleanup that would drain off the
water-soluble chemicals that contaminated the groundwater, and it would
render Lipari Landfill harmless by leaving behind only those
contaminants that would not migrate offsite. That remedial strategy did
not meet PALLCA's definition of "clean," however, because it would not
remove all contaminants from the site.

THE CONFLICT EXPANDS

To bolster its case against the flushing option, PALLCA called on two sources of outside assistance. One was the Citizens Clearinghouse for Hazardous Waste (CCHW), a national environmental interest group founded by Lois Gibbs, the original citizen leader at Love Canal. Four members of Congress were contacted as the second source of assistance. PALLCA asked CCHW to assess the strengths and weaknesses of EPA's flushing plan. When PALLCA asked U.S. Senators Frank Lautenberg and Bill Bradley of New Jersey and House members James Florio and William Hughes for help, they in turn requested the U.S. Office of Technology Assessment (OTA), a congressional research arm, to evaluate the flushing plan. PALLCA asked EPA Administrator Lee Thomas to hold up work at Lipari until OTA reported its findings.

The CCHW Report

CCHW expressed three objections to EPA's cleanup proposal. First, the group charged that the flushing operation would not meet EPA's own objectives—removing all waterborne contaminants from the landfill site. Steve Lester, CCHW science director, said some water-soluble chemicals would inevitably remain in the soil and continue to leach into groundwater.

Second, CCHW argued EPA was using the wrong definition of "cleanup" and therefore chose the wrong alternative. "It's not a cleanup if you leave chemicals in the soil," Lester argued. CCHW urged EPA to pursue permanent removal of the contaminated soil.

Third, CCHW maintained EPA had ruled out the excavation option on the basis of inflated cost estimates. Lester said EPA should consider a partial excavation option to collect and treat contaminated groundwater and store excavated soil at the landfill site.

The OTA Report

The OTA report, released in November 1985, also questioned the effectiveness and feasibility of the flushing plan and said "the actual reduction in contaminants during the flushing operation is unknown." OTA criticized EPA for choosing a remedy that would not remove non-water-soluble chemicals, implying that the flushing option did not constitute a full cleanup:

> Some significant contamination might remain in the soil after flushing. This should serve as a warning not to make premature decisions on what

constitutes a final cleanup, or more important, about future use of the site even if monitoring shows no water contamination onsite or offsite after flushing.

The OTA report included some new criticisms and raised the possibility that flushing could force a larger volume of contaminants to migrate into the soil and water surrounding the landfill. Noting that flushing would take many years, OTA warned that despite the presence of slurry walls, the landfill would presumably continue to leach chemicals. Dr. Joel Hirschhorn, author of the OTA report, echoed some of CCHW's concerns. He emphasized flushing was an unproven remedy that had not been demonstrated on soil with permeability similar to that at Lipari. The OTA report also argued that EPA both overestimated the costs of excavation and underestimated the costs of flushing by failing to consider operations and maintenance costs. Like CCHW, OTA criticized EPA for not considering partial excavation.

OTA presented its report at a November 1985 town meeting/press conference sponsored by Senator Lautenberg, who urged Pitman residents to push EPA for a total cleanup.

> If we can't get an effective cleanup at the No. 1 site, what does that signal for the rest of the Superfund program? . . . If we can't get the adequate and necessary public participation here, what does that say about the federal government's commitment to protecting our citizens from the threat of toxic wastes?

The legislators' concerns about the flushing plan were rooted in a much larger context than the specific cleanup of the Lipari site. Congressional debate over reauthorization of Superfund extended to the issue of cleanup standards. The original Superfund law did not specify the particular standards EPA should achieve in each cleanup operation. CERCLA required that remedial actions be cost-effective and mitigate and minimize damage to and adequately protect public health and the environment.

Members of Congress had become concerned that this lack of specific cleanup standards had allowed cleanup decisions to be made ad hoc. They planned to address this issue in the reauthorization of Superfund. Although the Lipari cleanup would not be affected by any changes in congressional requirements contained in the Superfund amendments of 1986 (SARA), its top NPL status and the timing of EPA's consideration of cleanup action during the SARA debates assured that Lipari would become a forum for the broader national debate on cleanup standards.

EPA's Response

After an extensive analysis of the two reports by Camp, Dresser, and McKee, EPA declined to change its decision on the flushing option. According to Jim Marshall, director of external programs for EPA's New York/New Jersey Region II, "Once we had finished this review, we had satisfied ourselves that our initial decision was correct." In a formal response to the OTA report, EPA argued it would be able to determine the effectiveness of the flushing operation by monitoring the level of contamination found in water drained from the site. EPA dismissed concerns about the inability of flushing to remove non-water-soluble chemicals from the land, claiming that because those chemicals cannot migrate, they pose no health or environmental threat and therefore "their presence at the Lipari Landfill is not of significant concern."

EPA also rejected arguments that it should pursue partial excavation at the site. The agency determined that the risks of such a remedy outweighed any advantages. Even partial excavation would require opening the cap that covered the sealed landfill, exposing workers and area residents to the dangers of fire or explosions caused by volatile gases, including methane, trapped inside. EPA also said that partial excavation was not feasible because liquid contaminants had seeped throughout the landfill site.

EPA conceded that flushing had not been used at sites similar to Lipari, but pointed out that several components of the operation—draining the site, treating contaminated water, and reinjecting treated water—had already been successfully accomplished at Lipari itself. Moreover, EPA maintained that pilot testing was not justified before the design phase of the cleanup. Acknowledging that "flushing has the potential to cause seepage of chemicals offsite," EPA decided to install an offsite collection system. In addition, the agency said it would remain active at Lipari for whatever amount of time was necessary to complete the flushing operation.

EPA did agree to make some modifications at the urging of legislators Lautenberg, Bradley, Florio, and Hughes. EPA officials met with them in December 1985 to review the OTA report. The legislators pressed to have the time span of the flushing operation reduced from 15 to 8 years. EPA was also urged to monitor the flushing process and to try another remedy if flushing proved unsuccessful. EPA agreed to amend its formal ROD to incorporate these changes, and the legislators withdrew their objections, at least until the effectiveness of the flushing process became known.

BITING THE BULLET

The opposition to EPA's flushing plan by PALLCA, CCHW, and members of Congress and the debate over amending the Superfund law delayed commencement of cleanup at Lipari for at least seven months. EPA did not begin designing the project until it had dealt with the CCHW and OTA reports and convinced legislators of the feasibility of its plan. The design of the flushing operation would be completed in 1988. EPA hoped construction could begin that summer. In the meantime, toxic chemicals continued to leach into the groundwater and Alcyon Lake, although at volumes far below those present before EPA had completed its earlier containment project.

EPA Regional Administrator Christopher Daggett expressed concerns over the delay in cleaning up Lipari, noting that PALLCA had contributed to that delay:

> I think in general, to the extent that you involve the public in this process, you are going to stretch it out. That is not to say blaming slowdowns on the public is correct. It is just the fact that the more people you involve, the more opinions you have to take into account; the more time it is going to take to review all these things. I welcome this kind of public involvement, but there is no question that it slows down the process.

EPA's Badalamenti noted that PALLCA's impatience ironically contributed to the delay:

> Their perception is that EPA studies too much and does not start to implement a solution. On the other hand, they ask more and more questions which leads to more and more studies and results in a delay. The delay is caused by the community and their concerns.

Jim Marshall of EPA summed up the difficult nature of hazardous waste cleanups and the rocky relationship between EPA and some communities:

> The public has a right to be involved, consulted and listened to, but the responsibility for making a decision in dealing with the problem lies with the government. There is a ... point in the process where you might have to bite the bullet and make an unpopular decision.

Ironically, PALLCA's reactions to the flushing option probably did not represent the opinions of the community as a whole. A group of Pitman residents who participated in an Eagleton Institute of Politics study of public opinion on hazardous waste problems expressed frustration with the lengthy cleanup delays. This randomly selected group said they would support any kind of program that made progress toward improving environmental conditions in their community. They were relatively unconcerned with the drawbacks of flushing as opposed to excavation. The following comment reveals their impatience with the controversy:

> You can get six experts in here and get six opinions and maybe none of those six are right. I don't think we're going to have anybody be willing to haul the stuff away and put it someplace else.

HEALTH ANXIETIES

Uncertainty about the health effects of the chemicals leaking out of Lipari Landfill has been another source of contention between Pitman residents and federal officials. Despite the discovery of carcinogenic and other toxic chemicals in the landfill and in Alcyon Lake, no known health problems have been linked definitively to the pollution. In fact, the warning signs posted along the lake constitute the only evidence of the presence of dangerous substances in the area. As one local resident commented:

> If we were on Love Canal, where everybody's house was built on the landfill and people were becoming ill as they did there, it would be an entirely different situation. We may be No. 1, but as yet it isn't threatening individual homes.

PALLCA members, however, are very concerned about the health effects of the chemicals and have been trying to collect data on the potential effects and the degree to which residents have been exposed to danger. They have had great difficulty getting information they find suitable. On at least four occasions, government agencies have dealt with Pitman residents' requests for data on health effects, but each time these responses have been criticized by members of the community.

Several factors account for the paucity of information about the impact of Lipari Landfill on human health. First, it is very difficult to isolate the causes of illness and nearly impossible to predict the likelihood that a particular chemical will later cause illness. Therefore, government officials are reluctant to advise citizens about whether or not they should take precautions. Citizens interpret this government hesitation as "stonewalling."

Second, Pitman residents and EPA differ about the type of testing that should be done. To the citizens and environmental groups, a "health assessment" means testing for chemical traces in the body and examining health records to determine if unusual rates of disease exist. To environmental agencies, a "health assessment" involves taking samples of soil, water, and air to determine levels of chemical contamination and evaluating potential pathways to human exposure.

Finally, EPA is mandated to focus on cleaning up wastes at the site and protecting further contamination of the environment. It is not primarily concerned with determining the effects of specific chemical exposures on specific individuals. EPA has the authority to sue polluters to recover cleanup costs but not medical expenses. Its responsibilities under Superfund include cleaning up the site, but not compensating any victims for health damages. Although some legislators had supported a victim-compensation program in both the original Superfund bill and in the 1986 reauthorization of the program, Congress did not accept these provisions. Consequently, EPA has little incentive to collect individual-specific health data.

Health Assessment

In response to PALLCA's requests for information about the health effects of the contamination, EPA asked the Centers for Disease Control (CDC) to assess the health hazards faced by Pitman residents. The CDC study issued in October 1985 reported that the groundwater appeared to be uncontaminated and that no significant chemical contaminants were found in soil samples taken from various spots in the town. This report "suggests that there is no significant public health threat from acute exposure to chemical contaminants by inhalation."

PALLCA asked OTA, CCHW, and the Clean Water Action Project to evaluate the CDC report. These organizations criticized it on several counts. First, the environmental groups pointed out, the report was not by their definition a "health assessment" but rather an "exposure assessment." They also objected to the scarcity of data and the difficult, technical language inhibiting public understanding of CDC's findings. The environmental groups observed that the CDC worked from an inadequate data base because none of the data used covered the early years of Lipari's existence. Finally, the environmentalists suggested that CDC's data collection and analysis procedures were themselves shoddy. The critics' reaction to the CDC report is best summed up by the opening line of OTA's critique: "In general, there is little good information in the Health Assessment." The CDC report did little to allay PALLCA's concerns.

EPA also asked the Agency for Toxic Substances and Disease Registry (ATSDR) to perform a health assessment. That study, released in October 1986, was based on soil samples collected from three park and recreational areas and from six residences in Pitman. It reported that the soil samples did not suggest public health risks from exposure. However, ATSDR did recommend that residents wash all homegrown vegetables before eating them.

Patrick Fitzgerald, a member of the Pitman Environmental Commission, complained the report was apparently written by "personnel with absolutely no familiarity with the situation at Lipari." Fitzgerald said that although the report did a good job of assessing the hazards of pesticides found in the samples, none of the pesticides mentioned had ever been associated with contamination from Lipari. Overall, he and others were extremely disappointed with both health assessments because these reports did not clearly convey the extent of health risks they felt existed at Lipari Landfill and in surrounding areas.

Health Registry

To address further the health issues raised by PALLCA and other Pitman residents, EPA formed a committee that included officials from DEP, the New Jersey Department of Health, the Gloucester County Health Department, the Pitman Health Department, the Pitman Environmental Commission, the Mantua Health Department, and PALLCA. The state Health Department began conducting cancer research and keeping track of spontaneous abortions and birth defects in Pitman and surrounding communities. The committee examined local schools' absentee records and visited hospitals to check death records for patterns of illness.

PALLCA members are not convinced even these efforts will produce an adequate assessment of the health dangers posed by Lipari Landfill. According to Pat Stuart:

> Health officials have been looking back through a cancer registry and have been trying to show birth defects, but it's difficult to show a link because you can't see long-term effects. The cancer registry only goes back so far—five years.

THE CLEANUP CONTINUES

EPA hoped to begin constructing a flushing system at Lipari Landfill in summer 1988—nearly 20 years after state officials first discovered toxic chemicals were leaking into the groundwater. Not until summer 1991 was the system installed; only then did cleanup of the site actually begin.

In the decade after EPA assumed control of the cleanup, a bathtublike containment structure and some fences were installed at a cost of more than $7 million in federal funds. EPA spent two years (1986 to 1988) defending its plan to clean up the toxic wastes confined inside the landfill, which continued to leak an estimated 500 gallons of toxics daily into the groundwater and Alcyon Lake. After expenditures of $20-plus million on construction and other unreported amounts on studies and negotiations, the actual decontamination of Lipari is finally under way. The site will be "batch flushed" and monitored for seven years to achieve removal of 90 percent of the hazardous chemicals buried within. The flushed water will be treated at the Gloucester County wastewater treatment facility and fresh water pumped back into the site.[3]

However, that phase would not conclude EPA's cleanup of the nation's foremost toxic waste dump. In June 1987, EPA completed a remedial investigation of offsite areas adjacent to Lipari. The agency tested soil, water, sediment, and air samples from Alcyon Lake, a nearby pond, an adjacent marsh area, four streams, and three public parks. No contamination associated with the landfill was found in public and private wells or area parks. EPA did, however, find potential sources of long-term health risks in the marsh area, the lake, and one stream. Toxic chemicals, including BCEE, chloroform, 1, 2-dichloroethane, ethylbenzene, toluene, and xylenes, were found in the marsh area lying immediately west of the landfill site. The presence of these volatile chemicals could pose long-term inhalation risks to nearby residents. John Frisco, chief of EPA's New Jersey remedial action branch, told Pitman residents at a public hearing in August 1987 that the chemicals could pose for people a slightly increased risk of developing cancer over a 70-year time span.

Landfill-related contamination also was found in Alcyon Lake and in Rabbit Run, the stream that runs along the northwestern perimeter of the landfill site. The sediment in the stream contains BCEE, arsenic, and mercury. Lake water is contaminated by BCEE, lead, and mercury; lake sediments contain arsenic, chromium, lead, mercury, nickel, and zinc.

The remedial investigation report prepared for EPA by Camp, Dresser, and McKee recommended that EPA undertake remedial actions to clean up the marsh area, Rabbit Run, and the Alcyon Lake sediment. The consultants argued that remediation of the lake water was not necessary because water in the lake is replaced every 10 days. Once the seepage from the landfill site is finally stopped and the lake sediment cleaned, the landfill-related contaminants in the water would dissipate naturally.

The consultants' report stressed that Alcyon Lake will not be usable for fishing or recreation even after remediation of Lipari Landfill is completed:

> It is important to recognize that other sources of contamination have contributed and continue to contribute to the degradation of Alcyon Lake.

Major sources of contamination currently include agricultural runoff and urban storm water runoff. Any remediation efforts associated with Alcyon Lake should not be initiated until such time as these other sources of contamination are remediated.

EPA estimated in 1987 that unless there were unforeseen complications, an offsite remedial project would begin operating by 1988. Such complications did arise, however, and several components of phase three, the offsite part of the overall cleanup effort, are still in the design stage. Planning has been done for the pumping and treatment system for the underground aquifer, though construction of the system will not commence until 1992, and it will not be operational until sometime in 1996. Meanwhile, detailed studies revealed that the low-temperature thermal treatment technology recommended for decontaminating the stream and lake bed sedimentation is not technically feasible at the site, and EPA is currently exploring other options. Overall, only 65 percent of the offsite cleanup design is complete, and it is already clear that the initial $21 million that Congress agreed to spend on this phase of the cleanup back in 1988 is going to fall far short of what will be needed.

In anticipation of the 1986 Superfund amendments, EPA awarded a $50,000 technical-assistance grant to Pitman to help the community hire its own consultant to assess proposed remedies. There are some early signs that this cooperation not only helped improve relationships between the community and EPA, but also led to a more rapid resolution of differences.

The tough challenges posed by the cleanup at Lipari are all too typical. Many aspects of Superfailure were evident there, but at least at Lipari a cleanup process—though not one to everyone's satisfaction—is well under way. But the costs and the time frame—now into the third decade—are the most difficult aspects to comprehend. Thus, even this success in remedial action is symptomatic of the broader story of cleanup failure.

NOTES

1. Carl E. Van Horn and Yvonne Chilik, "How Clean Is Clean? A Case of the Nation's No. 1 Superfund Toxic Dump," *Environmental Impact Assessment Review* 8 (1988), 133–148. All interviews cited in their study were conducted by Van Horn and Chilik or by their research assistants. We present this information in the same form as presented by Van Horn and Chilik.

Other useful Superfund site case studies include, from the perspective of communications theory (and the failure thereof), John Duncan Powell, "A Hazardous Waste Site: The Case of Nyanza," in Sheldon Krimsky and Alonzo

Plough, *Environmental Hazards: Communicating Risks as a Social Process* (Dover, Mass.: Auburn House, 1988), ch. 6, 239–297; and, from the perspective of efforts to assess cleanup technologies, Office of Technology Assessment, U.S. Congress, *Are We Cleaning Up? 10 Superfund Case Studies—A Special Report* (Washington, D.C.: Government Printing Office, June 1988).

2. In this pre-SARA period, no permanent remedies such as incineration were considered.

3. Post-1988 update provided by Michael Hornsby, site manager, New Jersey Department of Environmental Protection (interview, July 29, 1991).

CHAPTER FOUR

An Ounce of Prevention: Managing Today's Wastes Successfully

If creating more Superfund sites was to be avoided, radical changes would be needed in the way America's millions of tons of new hazardous wastes were being managed. The total volumes of these hazardous wastes greatly exceeded the scale of the Superfund site contamination problem.

In the mid-1970s, industry still managed its hazardous wastes in a traditional manner. Most were simply dumped onto the land, particularly into lagoons and ponds onsite at industrial locations. These practices, perhaps because the wastes generally were handled at the industrial sites, had not yet captured the public's imagination so strongly as had the more apparent problems of air and water pollution. Even so, a few environmentalists and legislators could see that inept hazardous waste management practices constituted a potential disaster only waiting to be discovered.[1]

By 1976, the casual if not careless way in which industry's new hazardous wastes were being disposed of gained sufficient attention in Washington to cause Congress to add a separate section (Subtitle C) covering hazardous wastes to the Resource Conservation and Recovery Act (RCRA), a bill focused on municipal solid waste issues. This first federal mandate in the country's attack on hazardous wastes came fully two years before Love Canal caught the public's attention and stoked the political firestorm that led to passage of Superfund in 1980.

The goals of RCRA, as ambitious as they were significant, included

- regulating existing hazardous waste sites;
- building new, safer hazardous waste treatment and disposal facilities, both onsite and offsite;
- creating a cradle-to-grave tracking system to collect accurate data on and thereby to monitor industry's hazardous waste practices, both onsite and offsite;

77

- ending the practice of mixing conventional solid wastes with (mostly liquid) hazardous wastes; and
- introducing overall improved hazardous waste management practices.

This approach, impressive in its concept, was meant to be comprehensive: to anticipate and prevent further harm nationwide to human health and the environment, rather than merely to respond after hazardous wastes had been turned loose to wreak havoc on groundwater and nearby residents.

Responsibility for implementing RCRA was put in the hands of the U.S. Environmental Protection Agency's (EPA) newly established Office of Solid Waste Management Programs. There RCRA sank almost without a trace for half a decade into the mire of the already overworked EPA bureaucracy. The failures of toxics management throughout the 1980s were presaged by EPA's near-total failure to implement RCRA from 1976 to 1980. The political fallout from Love Canal and passage of the Superfund legislation were history before EPA undertook seriously to implement RCRA. Although several states in the 1970s took an early lead in developing their own hazardous waste management programs, for the most part state programs too lay dormant until after the Superfund crisis. Meanwhile, industrial firms continued to dispose of their hazardous wastes, primarily on their own premises, without very much oversight or regulation.

Even after EPA and the states did turn to RCRA-related issues in the early 1980s, effective management of new wastes remained grossly subordinate to the more politically pressing and myopic focus on cleanup. The public was mesmerized by the Superfund genie; so was the nascent but rapidly growing commercial hazardous waste management industry. Regulatory agencies followed suit. Thus, management of the larger millions of tons of hazardous wastes continuously being produced remained almost exclusively the turf of industry.

At the end of America's first toxics decade, the verdict on RCRA implementation was harsh. Analysts found that "RCRA's plodding progress defies the multitude of mandatory program deadlines intended to speed its implementation."[2] Although RCRA held out great hope for America for the safer management of hazardous wastes, it was "quite uncertain" if the safety and health goals of the law were being met, though the cost of compliance to business and industry was already reaching into the several billions of dollars.[3] In short, the current RCRA effort simply "does not score very well when measured against the program goals."[4] The best that can be said is that RCRA to date has been both a "model" and a "muddle":

It is a model for ensuring that the buck stops somewhere, that the ultimate fate of toxics constituents is accounted for and cannot merely be shifted from one medium to the next, and that prevention is given its true and necessary emphasis. It is a muddle in that the definitions that determine who and what is in the system, what practices constitute exempt recycling and which ones are regulated, and what the exact nature of the federal/state relationship is, forces us to muddle through all too many situations.[5]

A flurry of administrative activity and some important RCRA accomplishments resulted, especially in the second half of the 1980s, but implementation of RCRA has left much to be desired. Only now in the early 1990s, 15 years after it was enacted, have EPA and industry finally turned to addressing the root problem at which RCRA is aimed —reducing hazardous wastes at their source, in the production process and through recycling—and in this there is cause for hope that RCRA implementation is turning the corner. But first, we examine the promise and performance of RCRA throughout its first decade and a half. The failures of RCRA implementation so often lamented fall into several categories. First, EPA and the states have taken much longer than Congress intended simply to establish the administrative apparatus to collect data and to monitor the flow of hazardous wastes throughout the nation. The data are still woefully inadequate, 15 years into the effort.

Second, most of the monitoring that does exist under RCRA extends only to the small proportion (10 to 20 percent) of hazardous wastes sent for treatment and disposal away from the industrial facilities where wastes are generated. Most hazardous wastes are still treated and disposed of by their generators and thus lie effectively outside RCRA's regulatory reach, though this is beginning to change.

Third, most hazardous wastes even today are being managed as always: dumped onto the ground or pumped down wells deep into the earth. Effective treatment of these wastes remains the exception rather than the rule.

Fourth, of RCRA's manifold goals, reducing the generation of hazardous wastes in the first place is one of the most important for the long term. Despite modest efforts, spearheaded by some of the states and a few select companies, this goal received almost no attention in RCRA's implementation until the very end of the 1980s. Today source reduction has finally become a major factor in EPA's planning and action and gives cause for renewed hope.

With the ever-increasing RCRA activity—amid the swelling EPA and state bureaucracies created to administer this law—RCRA, just like the Superfund program, provides another dramatic example of numerous microsuccesses. A hazardous waste tracking system has been established nationwide, those landfills that continue to accept hazardous wastes are better managed, and some in industry have taken important lead roles in both the better management and reduction of hazardous wastes. Yet in a more profound sense, the implementation of RCRA to date remains a large part of the more basic failure of America's toxics policy.

The most daunting challenge of the 1990s regarding management of new wastes is clearly to streamline RCRA administrative operations (including permitting); to shift rapidly away from relying on land disposal and toward available recycling and treatment technologies; and most important, to make real the promises of source reduction and waste minimization.

DEFINING HAZARDOUS WASTES

RCRA's scope extends well beyond the problems of cleaning up contaminated soil and groundwater typically found at Superfund sites and other industrial locations. This law attempts to regulate the numerous and diverse hazardous wastes being generated by all of America's industry.

In general, *hazardous waste* may be defined broadly as "any by-product that poses a substantial present or potential threat to plants, animals, or humans because it is harmful or nondegradable, or because it may be biologically magnified."[6] The language in RCRA is equally inclusive, if more complex. The Act identifies as hazardous any waste

> which because of its quantity, concentration, or physical, chemical, or infectious characteristics may (a) cause or significantly contribute to an increase in mortality or an increase in serious irreversible, or incapacitating reversible, illness; or (b) pose a substantial present or potential hazard to human health or the environment when improperly treated, stored, transported, or disposed of, or otherwise managed.[7]

In practice, it is often difficult to identify just which wastes actually qualify as "hazardous." We know from prior experience that several chemicals are well known as especially hazardous substances and automatically fall under the regulatory scheme; these include lead, waste cyanides, strong acids, and many waste solvents. But what of the hundreds of other compounds that find their way into industrial wastes but have less obvious effects—or possibly effects not even presently detectable? Moreover, short of a complete prohibition on any release of industry's wastes, what levels of hazardous contamination and exposure should be tolerated under RCRA? How much should health risks count in the face of economic costs? These questions are vexing, and the controversies surrounding their answers have remained heated (just as have the Superfund debates over "how clean is clean" and the meaning of "cost-effective").

Simply getting EPA to initiate the RCRA process was a challenge. It took prodding by several environmental-group lawsuits, four years of study and testing, negotiation with industry, and internal wrangling before EPA came up with its operational definition of hazardous waste, along with the testing protocol industry was to follow and the first lists of 450 substances and several dozen industrial waste streams that would ultimately fall under the RCRA regulatory umbrella. The broad criteria adopted by EPA included substances that are *ignitable, corrosive, chemically reactive*, or *toxic*, plus substances specifically known by EPA to pose risk of harm. The list covers everything from tank sediments at petroleum refineries, dust from air pollution control equipment, spent cleaning solvents, and compounds from the manufacture of pharmaceuticals to the liquid waste streams from paper mills, metal fabricators, steel mills, print shops, and electroplating operations.

Hazardous wastes are generated across a broad spectrum of American industry. The four largest waste-producing industries, however, account for nearly 90 percent of all the total estimated hazardous wastes generated. In decreasing order, the industries are chemical and allied products, primary metals, petroleum products, and fabricated metals. Fully half of all hazardous wastes are inorganic liquids and sludges, most generated by the chemical industry and by petroleum refineries.[8] Some of these are acid or base solutions used to create complex organic compounds, "pickle liquors" that digest metal impurities, or sulfur and lime sludges left over from industry's use of modern air and water pollution control equipment (see Box 4.1).

By no means are all problems associated with hazardous wastes in the United States the products of big-business activities. Smaller firms contribute to the overall volume a modest 10 percent nationally, but the toxicity of these wastes and the potential harm from their poor management practices make these wastes significant. The California Department of Health Services, for example, estimates that 53,000 small firms account for 88 percent of all the companies producing hazardous wastes in that state. Together, these small firms produce 7 to 10 percent of the state's total waste load. Of some 7,000 generators in Alameda County, California, fully 6,300 were small ones, responsible altogether for 10 percent of the county's waste stream. In Massachusetts, the comparable figure is estimated at 20 percent. Moreover, these smaller firms are often located close to residential areas and produce some of the more highly concentrated and dangerous wastes.[9]

BOX 4.1   Hazardous Waste–Producing Industries

Industry	Typical Wastes
Chemical products	Halogenated and nonhalogenated organic solvents, strong acids, bases
Primary metals and cyanide-fabricated metals	Inorganic liquids and sludges, metal solutions
Petroleum and coal products	Halogenated and nonhalogenated degreasing solvents
Rubber and plastic products	Latex, phenols, epoxies, polyesters
Electrical and electronic machinery	Degreasing solvents, carbon tetrachloride, silicon tetrachloride sludges
Wood preserving	Pentachlorophenol
Drum reconditioning	Miscellaneous wastes: oils, solvents, sludges

Source: Congressional Budget Office, U.S. Congress, "Hazardous Waste Management: Recent Changes and Policy Alternatives" (Washington, D.C.: Government Printing Office, 1985), 18.

Despite its sweeping definition of hazardous wastes, RCRA contained several notable exclusions, including wastes generated by mining, agriculture, and drilling operations for oil, gas, and geothermal energy. Such wastes are generated in large volume. Households too were exempted, though wastes there also pose problems (see Box 4.2).

Further, EPA decided to exempt from federal regulatory coverage the more than 250,000 businesses that generate less than 2,200 pounds (1,000 kilograms) of hazardous wastes per month. These small-quantity generators (SQGs) were left essentially to their own devices, with no regulatory oversight. (Congress extended coverage over SQGs when it revised RCRA in 1984.) EPA decided to allow firms to handle and store their wastes up to 90 days with little if any regulation. And EPA chose to exempt from its scrutiny the vast volumes of liquid hazardous wastes being discharged into industrial sewers.

It took EPA more than five years to establish the annual volume of hazardous waste in the United States to be regulated under RCRA as somewhere in the range of 145–435 million tons—quite a range of unknown even back then. The most likely "guesstimate" was 290 million tons; (because most of these wastes are in liquid form, the comparable annual figure of 71.3 billion gallons is useful).[10] In more comprehensible terms, this amounts to one ton annually per person, or more than 6 pounds of hazardous waste for every U.S. resident every single day! Further data collected in 1983 revealed that Texas led in production of hazardous wastes, with almost twice the amounts generated in Ohio, Pennsylvania, or California, which ranked second through fourth.[11] By 1989 Texas generated perhaps one-fifth of the nation's hazardous wastes—over 54 million tons.[12] These volumes of new hazardous waste dwarf the scale of Superfund cleanups, which nevertheless throughout the 1980s remained the focus of most of the political attention.[13]

What remains unclear is how much of a threat chemicals in general[14] and those contained in these wastes in particular pose to human health and the environment:

> While many chemicals have been tested to determine their hazardousness—it is often relatively easy to decide if a chemical is corrosive, or ignitable, or otherwise clearly dangerous when handled or abandoned in the environment—few have been rigorously tested to determine their toxicity. Testing is particularly difficult and expensive when long-term effects of a chemical are being investigated. Studies may require decades.[15]

What is clear is that RCRA was intended to prevent further Superfund sites from being created. And even without scientific certainty, RCRA was to eliminate the potential health and environmental harms that could reasonably be expected to arise were past waste management practices applied to the ever-increasing volumes of hazardous wastes being generated.

Awesome to say the least are the dimensions of the task of overseeing the safe management of all these wastes, along with the tens of thousands of large waste generators, 250,000 or more small generators, 16,500 transporters, and 5,000 facilities that officially treat, store, and dispose of these wastes. This, however, was the purpose of RCRA.

BOX 4.2 Hazardous Wastes Around the House

Hazardous wastes are by no means restricted to by-products of industrial production. We all share in the use of vast numbers of goods containing hazardous materials that, when discarded, become hazardous wastes. These range from the more obvious, such as gasoline and batteries, to items less conspicuously associated with hazardous waste: televisions and home computers, the ever-present household oven cleaners, paints, and dry-cleaning solvents. The National Safety Council has provided some helpful hints on how to manage some of the most prevalent hazardous wastes found around the home.

CHEMICAL HAZARDS IN THE GARAGE AND WORKSHOP

Product	Possible Hazards	Disposal Suggestions	Precautions and Substitutes
Aerosols	When sprayed, contents are broken into particles small enough to be inhaled. Cans may explode or burn.	Put only empty cans in trash. Do not burn. Do not place in trash compactor.	Store in cool place. Propellant may be flammable. Instead: use non-aerosol products.
Auto: Antifreeze	Very poisonous. Has sweet taste — attractive to small children & pets. *Toxicity 3-4**	Put in a secure container & take to a garage or service station.	No substitutes. Clean up any leaks or spills carefully.
Auto: Batteries	Contain strong acid. Very corrosive. Danger to eyes & skin.	Recycle.	No substitutes. Trade in old batteries.
Auto: Degreasers	Corrosive. Poisonous. Eye & skin irritant. *Toxicity 2-4**	Use up according to label instructions.	Choose strong detergent type over solvent type.
Auto: Motor oil & transmission fluid	Poisonous. May be contaminated with lead. Skin & eye irritant.	Recycle.	No substitutes.
Paint strippers, thinners, & other solvents	Many are flammable. Eye & skin irritant. Moderately to very poisonous. *Toxicity 3-4**	Let settle, pour off cleaner for re-use. Pour sludge into container & seal. Use up according to label instructions or save for hazardous waste collection day.	Avoid aerosols. Buy only as much as you need. Ventilate area well. Do not use near open flame. Instead of paint stripper: sand or use heat gun. Use water cleanup products as much as possible.

(continues)

BOX 4.2 *(continued)*

Product	Possible Hazards	Disposal Suggestions	Precautions and Substitutes
Paints, oil-based, & varnishes	Flammable. Eye & skin irritant. Use in small, closed area may cause unconsciousness.	Use up according to label instructions or save for hazardous waste collection day.	Ventilate area well. Do not use near open flame. May take weeks for fumes to go away. Instead: use water-based paints if possible.
Pesticides,** herbicides, fungicides, slug bait, rodent poison, wood preservatives	All are dangerous to some degree. Can cause central nervous system damage, kidney & liver damage, birth defects, internal bleeding, eye injury. Some are readily absorbed through the skin. *Toxicity 3-6**	Use up carefully, following label instructions. Save for hazardous waste collection day.	Do not buy more than you need. Instead: try hand-picking, mechanical cultivation, natural predators. Practice good sanitation. Choose hardy varieties. Use insect lures & traps. As a last resort, use least toxic suitable pesticides.

*General Toxicity Rating

Number Rating	1	2	3	4	5	6
Toxicity Rating	Almost Non-Toxic	Slightly Toxic	Moderately Toxic	Very Toxic	Extremely Toxic	Super Toxic
Lethal Dose for 150 lb. Adult	More than 1 Quart	1 Pint to 1 Quart	1 Ounce to 1 Pint	1 Teaspoon to 1 Ounce	7 Drops to 1 Teaspoon	Less than 7 Drops

For more information, contact your local public works department, hazardous waste agency, or poison control center.

**The following pesticides previously sold for use by homeowners and the general public have since been banned or are no longer recommended for use by homeowners
- Aldrin
- Arsenate
- Calcium Arsenate
- Chlordane
- Copper Arsenate
- Creosote
- DDT
- Dieldrin
- Heptachlor
- Pentachlorophenol (PCP)
- Silvex
- Sodium Arsenite
- 2-4-5T

If you have any of these pesticides, carefully store and save them for a hazardous waste collection day. Get a plastic container with a lid. (A five-gallon plastic bucket is ideal.) Fill the bucket halfway with cat litter. Keep the pesticide in its original container and put it in the bucket. Fill the bucket to the top with cat litter. Put the lid on it. Mark the container clearly, and store it on a shelf away from children and pets.

Prepared by the National Safety Council
A non-governmental non-profit organization

Source: Reprinted with permission from the Illinois Hazardous Waste Research and Information Center.

THE REGULATORY DESIGN OF RCRA

RCRA called for regulation of all three main groups involved with hazardous wastes: generators; transporters; and operators of treatment, storage, and disposal (TSD) facilities (see Box 4.3). The Act provided that hazardous wastes must be tracked "cradle to grave" through a uniform manifest system (following the approach adopted by California in 1972). Records are supposed to be maintained at each point of turnover as the wastes move from their point of origin to their final destination. For any person or firm caught violating the manifest system, the penalties can be severe, though there is no routine monitoring of the system for accuracy or as a means of spotting possible illegal dumping by haulers who sign off for a waste load but fail to deliver it to an authorized treatment facility or landfill.[16]

Regulating Generators of Hazardous Waste

The RCRA regulatory system is nowhere near as comprehensive as it sounds, however. Manifests, in fact, are required only for those wastes that leave the site of a generator to be transported elsewhere: to a treatment facility or to a landfill. Yet it is estimated that up to 90 percent of all the hazardous wastes generated in the United States have been "managed" by their industrial generators, typically by being placed as liquids into unlined pits, ponds, and lagoons or other surface impoundments on the production site. No cradle-to-grave manifests exist for these wastes, some 264 million tons annually. Hazardous wastes managed onsite escape RCRA regulation almost entirely, even though formally a RCRA hazardous waste management permit is required for self-management. (Through the 1980s, most waste generators operated with "interim status" under RCRA—not really a strict regulatory permit at all.)

These onsite facilities are monitored only to the extent states and local communities require them to be or only in the rare event of an EPA inspection. For example, in the mid-1980s, the state agency in California responsible for regulating hazardous wastes under both RCRA and state law reported it was able to inspect the 29 hazardous waste management facilities in Santa Clara County (Silicon Valley) on average only once every 24 months.[17] EPA inspections were far less frequent. And the 4,000 hazardous waste generators not needing a RCRA permit received no federal or state scrutiny at all. RCRA's regulatory grasp was, in effect, "an inch wide and a mile deep."[18]

Recognizing this problem, Pennsylvania adopted a drastically

BOX 4.3 The Reach of RCRA: Summary of RCRA Hazardous Waste Regulatory Requirements for Generators, Transporters, and TSD Facilities

RCRA Requirements	Generators	Transporters	Treatment, Storage & Disposal Facilities[a]
Determine if wastes are hazardous	X		X
Notify EPA if RCRA hazardous waste handler and obtain ID number	X	X	X
Train personnel in waste management procedures and emergency response	X	X	X
Develop preparedness and prevention measures and notify of releases	X	X	X
Prepare contingency plans and emergency procedures	X		X
Inspect facility operations periodically	X		X
Track wastes using manifest system	X	X	X
Carry out recordkeeping and reporting	X	X	X
Use proper package marking, labeling, and transport vehicle placards	X	X	X
Follow proper security measures	X		X
Use and manage containers, landfills, and other operating areas properly			X
Design and operate waste handling areas adequately[b]	X		X
Monitor groundwater			X
Provide closure and postclosure care			X
Ensure financial responsibility for closure and postclosure care			X

[a]Treatment, storage, or disposal facilities in operation on or before November 19, 1980, could continue operating under "interim status" until a hazardous waste permit was issued, at which time the facility had to be in compliance with final permit regulations.

[b]This includes the design and operation of tanks, surface impoundments, waste piles, land treatment facilities, landfills, incinerators, and injection wells.

different approach, holding its industrial and commercial facilities accountable for their hazardous waste practices. The state supplements formal RCRA-type regulation by requiring a declaration upon any transfer or sale of a facility as to whether the site had been used for hazardous waste disposal. The seller is then formally liable for any resulting contamination.

New Jersey's Environmental Compensation Responsibility Act (ECRA) goes even further, requiring actual site assessments before transfer or sale of any industrial or commercial property in that state. Again, sellers are liable for the costs of cleaning up any contamination discovered on their properties. The New Jersey law, in particular, has provided a tremendous impetus for careful site assessment, completely transforming the local real estate market.

Congress intended that generators should bear the primary responsibility for identifying and making known the composition of their hazardous wastes and for initiating appropriate recordkeeping.[19] Specifically, EPA regulations require hazardous waste generators to[20]

- register with EPA and with parallel state agencies;
- secure a RCRA permit if wastes are to be stored onsite for more than 90 days;[21]
- record through the uniform manifest system all shipments of waste sent offsite;
- deliver wastes only to transporters authorized by EPA and state agencies;
- send wastes only to authorized treatment or disposal facilities;
- comply with all packaging, labeling, and marking requirements;
- participate in EPA's biennial data-reporting system;
- develop an accident preparedness and prevention plan for their facility;
- certify they are pursuing waste minimization;
- maintain additional records if exporting to a foreign country or importing hazardous waste;
- make their hazardous waste records available to EPA and allow EPA onsite for facility inspections.

Regulating Transporters of Hazardous Waste

Although some 90 percent of industry's hazardous wastes was treated or disposed of onsite, the remainder is hauled off to landfills, injection wells, and other treatment or disposal facilities, usually by independent carriers. Before passage of RCRA, these haulers were seldom scrutinized and were the vehicles of choice for much illegal disposal (midnight dumping).

In the 1960s and early 1970s, few generators or other observers expressed concern that wastes might be disposed of illegally in the United States. Conventional landfill dumping and underground injection of liquid wastes were both quite inexpensive (and onsite ponds were even cheaper). However, more landfills began to refuse to accept hazardous wastes in the mid-1970s, and fees for disposal at the remaining landfills began to increase dramatically. As a result, the temptation to dump illegally rose precipitously. By 1976, state officials in New Jersey were some of the first to become quite concerned about midnight dumping. It was reported at the time that dumpers would cruise the New Jersey Turnpike on rainy nights, leaving open the valve at the back of their tanker truck. A nagging concern of RCRA's authors was the specter of having even a small proportion of the thousands of independent haulers exploiting these new circumstances to charge generators high prices for hauling (ostensibly because of the new regulations and landfilling fees), then turning around and dumping the wastes illegally along the nation's highways and byways. As increasingly frequent news reports of surreptitious roadside dumping began to reveal, those fears were well founded.[22]

To make sure transporters became an integral part of the nation's new hazardous waste management system, they were incorporated into the RCRA regulatory scheme. The implementation responsibilities for this subsection of RCRA—the Hazardous Materials Transportation Act (HMTA)—were placed in the hands of the U.S. Department of Transportation (see Chapter Six). Regulations were imposed on transporters' equipment, recordkeeping procedures, and overall management practices.

Under the law, all hazardous waste transporters must

- register as hazardous waste haulers with federal and state authorities;
- use the uniform manifest system to keep detailed records of all hazardous waste pickups and deliveries;
- deliver only to permitted hazardous waste treatment, storage, and disposal facilities;
- notify appropriate authorities of any hazardous accidents or spills;
- clean up any discharge of waste that occurs during transportation.

Presumably, these provisions would adequately safeguard against illegal diversion and dumping and guarantee greater awareness and safety consciousness on the part of transporters.

Regulating Treatment, Storage, and Disposal Facilities

RCRA calls for extensive EPA and state oversight for all facilities that treat, store, and/or dispose of hazardous wastes (known collectively as "TSD facilities"). All TSD facilities are required to

- secure a permit for operation—first an interim status permit, issued automatically; later a permanent "Part B" permit involving an extremely detailed, cumbersome, and costly approval process;
- follow prescribed procedures for waste analysis, security, and inspection of waste operations;
- develop a program for personnel training;
- develop a plan for spill prevention and emergency preparedness;
- participate in the manifest system, keeping precise records of points of origin of all wastes they accept and of the treatment methods used;
- institute groundwater monitoring at their facility;
- where landfilling is involved, institute a new multiple lining and leak detection system;
- clean up any onsite contamination;
- develop a closure plan and postclosure monitoring system;
- demonstrate proof of financial ability to pay for closure and postclosure care;[23]
- after the 1984 amendments to RCRA, carry out "corrective action" activities for cleanup of any hazardous contamination onsite.

Until 1984, RCRA remained silent on precisely which disposal methods were to be used by TSD facilities. Consequently, with cost considerations ever-present, land disposal and deep-well injection practices remained dominant through the 1980s—despite the fact that environmentally preferable methods of recycling, recovery, neutralization, incineration and overall waste minimization were available. We discuss this point at some length in Chapter Five.

RCRA'S EARLY YEARS: SUPERFAILURE IN NEW GARB

In 1976, Congress initially gave EPA one year to inventory all industrial and municipal hazardous waste disposal sites across the nation, and 18 months to develop regulations that generators, transporters, and TSD facilities would have to follow. By 1983, all dump sites were to be brought into full compliance with RCRA's provisions, or they would have to stop accepting any new hazardous wastes.[24] EPA was also supposed to give each of the 50 states the opportunity to assume administration of RCRA within its borders, which Congress presumed most states would want to do. Otherwise, excessive operational tasks would fall to EPA, which lacked the staff, the experience, and the will to carry them out.

When Congress later sent its watchdog General Accounting Office (GAO) into the field to see how well RCRA was being implemented, the reports sent back were most disappointing.[25] EPA's inventory of all sites had taken more than a year longer than RCRA mandated. The GAO found four of EPA's ten regional offices were still incapable of gauging the extent of hazardous waste streams within their locale.

Worse, EPA waited until 1980 to promulgate its final definition of hazardous wastes and to issue any interim permits for TSD facilities. Issuance of final "Part B" permits for all existing facilities was not expected to be completed until 1992 at the earliest. It took EPA six years (from 1976 to 1982) to issue its regulations—nearly 600 pages—covering the 2,000 existing landfills and storage ponds then handling most of industry's new toxic wastes. Regulations for incinerators and other treatment facilities were deferred for several more years.

One of GAO's most serious criticisms was that as late as 1984, EPA had failed to carry out RCRA's vital groundwater protection measures. Congress responded that year by establishing unequivocal goals for EPA on the number of effective groundwater monitoring devices that needed to be installed at RCRA sites. Even so, GAO found in 1988 that even this direct mandate had not been fully accomplished.[26]

Money is not the only or necessarily the best indicator of federal commitment to a program, but without funds a government agency will accomplish little. In this vein, it is revealing that as late as 1979, only 3 percent of EPA's financial resources were assigned to efforts related to hazardous wastes.[27] This situation worsened under the early years of the Reagan administration when all environmental programs faired poorly;[28] RCRA spending by EPA dropped sharply from $130 million in fiscal year 1980 to $94 million in fiscal year 1984.[29] To accelerate program implementation would require intense congressional action and unprecedented legislative intrusion into the administrative implementation process, as part of RCRA's 1984 renewal. These pressures did make a difference. By fiscal year 1985, RCRA had become the third largest operating program within EPA, with a budget of $175 million.[30]

A FEDERAL-STATE PARTNERSHIP

The fact that RCRA implementation depends overwhelmingly on the states is an often overlooked dimension of the nation's program. To be successful, RCRA would require effective oversight of thousands upon thousands of generators, transporters, and TSD facilities. Even more so than for Superfund, therefore, effective management of America's new wastes would be tied intimately to state-level competence, will, and initiative.

Given the importance of the hazardous waste issue, RCRA's authors assumed the states would rise to this challenge. The few that have are generally more competent than EPA. Unfortunately, this experience in federal-state partnership reveals to date that the premise of effective state management and program implementation was a largely erroneous assumption to make. EPA's failures cannot be tolerated simply by relying on the chimera of state delegation.

With a few notable and sporadic exceptions—California, Massachusetts, Minnesota, New Jersey—the states were faring no better than the federal government at developing programs for safe hazardous waste management, either on their own or under federal RCRA guidelines. And even the few exceptional states presented very spotty records when looked at in detail. Doing better than EPA was hardly the same as doing well!

As of 1978, GAO found the states had taken few steps to lay the groundwork for assuming RCRA responsibilities. They had available only rough estimates of the hazardous wastes being generated right under their noses and were still uncertain how all these wastes were being managed. None of the 26 states examined by GAO had fully inventoried its waste generators or developed an adequate enforcement program. Only 17 states had even adopted hazardous waste laws that could serve as the cornerstone of their hazardous waste management effort. The conclusion was inescapable that "few if any states have hazardous waste programs which provide the control intended by RCRA."[31]

Not until 1985, nine years after Congress passed RCRA, had even half the states conformed to EPA requirements and acquired the delegated authority to manage RCRA. This number grew to 42 states by 1988. By then, however, events had rapidly outpaced both EPA and its state counterparts. In 1984, Congress had greatly amended and expanded RCRA, passing the Hazardous and Solid Waste Amendments of 1984 (HSWA). Six years thereafter, by the end of America's first toxics decade, very few states had been delegated authority to carry out these new HSWA provisions. The cycle of delegation failure was repeating itself.

Since Congress permitted the states to impose more rigorous standards and broader coverage than EPA's, several have done so, in rather different ways. The examples of New Jersey and Pennsylvania property transfer requirements have already been noted. An Illinois innovation provides another example.

Since 1987, Illinois has required both generators and permitted disposal site operators to obtain specific authorization from the Illinois Environmental Protection Agency before placing hazardous wastes onto the land. To obtain this authorization, the generator must demonstrate reasonably that the particular hazardous waste stream cannot instead be recycled for reuse, incinerated, or chemically, physically, or biologically treated to render it nonhazardous. This approach has accelerated the transition from dumping to treatment (at least in Illinois), but it also has accelerated shipping of Illinois wastes out of state.

Several factors related to delegation criteria explain the overall unimpressive record of responses by the states as well as the wide diversity of state programs. Three basic criteria for delegating RCRA implementation to a state are (1) the state can demonstrate to the satisfaction of EPA adequate administrative capacity to run the program; (2) the state's hazardous waste program must be consistent with and at least equivalent to EPA's; and (3) the state can provide adequate legal enforcement. These are all minimum thresholds, based on formalistic assessments rather than any real analysis of a state's capacity and will.

Conceptually, the federal-state partnership called for under RCRA is a good example of "regulatory federalism," under which the federal government acquires nationwide authority in a policy area, then yields it to the states if and when they develop acceptable regulatory programs. The federal government provides grants covering 75 percent of program costs for states with approved RCRA programs; nonauthorized states get smaller grants. In effect, the federal government sets basic tenets of national policy, while ceding most program implementation—the all-important factor—to the states. In one sense, this is "a delegation of national authority, but not an abdication of national control."[32]

In truth, the federal government remains desperately dependent on state performance, coming under powerful political and budgetary pressure to relinquish control to even those states which show only slight interest in implementation. Whatever the vagaries of state performance, EPA simply does not have the resources to carry out RCRA on its own; the federal agency needs the states to assume this delegated authority, essentially on their terms. That being the case, whether any national program will work as intended—with development of needed regulations, communications, and monitoring—can be affected significantly by the working relationships between federal and state officials and the basic capacity and will of a state to act once a program is in its hands. This is especially true for RCRA, which mandates to an extraordinary degree details of regulatory action and oversight.

The factors coming into play in the RCRA intergovernmental partnership go well beyond merely good working relations, even beyond the six conditions identified by Kamieniecki, O'Brien, and Clarke in their analysis of Superfund implementation, presented in Chapter Two. As might be expected, research shows that good communication between state and federal officials is important,[33] but it is only part of the picture, as a comparative examination of the 50 states reveals. Lester and Bowman examined 14 possible hypotheses from a standard implementation taxonomy in order to isolate key elements distinguishing between those states that were and were not delegated responsibility by EPA to administer RCRA. By 1985, the date of their research, 25 states had been delegated authority.[34]

Factors considered by these authors included the magnitude of the hazardous waste problem within a state, the consistency between state and EPA estimates of the problem, a state's general support of industrial development, a state's hazardous waste management payroll, the importance of the hazardous waste management industry to the state's economy, and the availability in the state of waste management technologies besides landfilling. They also assessed the commitment to hazardous waste cleanup made by the state's political leaders, whether the state was Democratic or Republican, whether environmental problems were handled by a unified state agency, whether implementing officials were "sympathetic" to RCRA's aims, the extent of state-initiated enforcement actions, and several other factors.

Using this statistical analysis, Lester and Bowman found a good deal of overall variability in state responses to hazardous waste problems, but four factors (in order of importance) proved relevant in determining whether a state received RCRA authority. Delegation was likelier if the state had a comprehensive environmental agency, a diverse economy, a Democratic-controlled state government, and a high level of state enforcement. Delegation was less likely in states where waste generators' contributions to new capital formation were high, general state financial support for industry was high, and the payroll from hazardous waste TSD facilities was high.[35]

The failure of most states to move quickly and uniformly, combined with EPA's failure to carry out its obligations under RCRA in a timely manner, provided the backdrop to deliberations by Congress on how to advance the implementation process when the time came to renew the Act. This debate began in 1982 and culminated in passage of HSWA in 1984.

THE TRANSITION AWAY FROM LAND DISPOSAL: A REVIEW OF RCRA PROGRESS

Early RCRA implementation by EPA and the states was slow, frustrating, and incomplete, but even by the early 1980s a transformation of hazardous waste management in the United States was obviously under way. Although EPA took more time than most would have liked, its regulatory guidelines for generators, transporters, and TSD facilities eventually came into place. Consequently, many landfills decided to close rather than meet the first new technical standards promulgated from 1980 through 1982. For example, four of southern California's five hazardous waste landfills closed in 1980 and 1981; the remaining facility (BKK) soon became the largest hazardous waste landfill in the United States, accepting over 500,000 tons of wastes annually until closed too in 1984. These landfill closures, combined with the many other new national rules under RCRA, caused a rapid increase in land disposal costs at those facilities remaining open.

Although overall RCRA implementation was spotty, many changes were in progress. Following the early lead of New Jersey and California, many of the most industrialized states took selective initiatives to improve hazardous waste management within their borders, whether in conjunction with EPA or not. The uniform manifest system was instituted nationwide, covering most hazardous wastes sent offsite. Surveys of waste generators and treatment facilities initiated by EPA allowed the scope of the waste management problem to come into better focus. Eventually, the basic administrative apparatus needed to carry out RCRA was set up across all the states.

With all of this emerging regulatory underpinning came the beginnings of a profound shift in attitudes toward hazardous waste management: reliance on cheap but inadequate land disposal no longer seemed the best option. Even during RCRA's rocky early years, many forward-looking government and business leaders began to see that more was going to be needed than merely closing old landfills, lining those that remained open, and being more careful where new hazardous wastes were dumped.

It was clear America could not comply with the spirit of RCRA and respond to the high new cost of hazardous waste management unless a significant portion of its future hazardous waste stream was managed quite differently. Hazardous waste treatment garnered center stage; reliance on land disposal of untreated wastes, chiefly liquids, was no longer desirable. Some wastes would need incineration, others chemical or biological neutralization and detoxification; for some, simply dewatering and stabilizing were enough before land disposal of the treated residues.

Anticipating this policy direction, the National Conference of State Legislatures in the early 1980s polled its members and concluded that a minimum of 125 modern commercial hazardous waste management facilities would have to be sited to treat wastes being diverted from conventional landfills, which were rapidly being closed to further disposal of untreated hazardous wastes.[36]   As early as 1981, California adopted a series of rules calling for rapid phaseout of continued land disposal for many large-volume categories of hazardous wastes.[37] Later known as the "California List," these wastes would be treated instead. Strict dates were set for ending land disposal.

The attempt was designed explicitly to increase the economic attractiveness of hazardous waste treatment and thus induce investment in such facilities. Although appropriate treatment technologies were well known, the facilities to treat these wastes first had to be designed, funded, sited, constructed, and operated, either onsite or off. If new facilities were not in place, California policy leaders promised not to "ban any waste before its time"; exemptions to the deadlines would be available if treatment capacity was not.

Given the growing consternation with EPA's performance, Congress in 1982 began its major review of RCRA. By then it had become clear EPA had fallen far behind in completing its assigned tasks. The agency was then in the reluctant hands of Anne (Gorsuch) Burford, President Reagan's new probusiness EPA administrator.   In the Democratic-controlled Congress, a strong consensus began to emerge calling for sweeping changes to ensure that RCRA would be carried out as its proponents had envisioned.   These included mandatory provisions—the so called "hammers"—to enforce action by an "untrustworthy" Republican-controlled EPA. Program implementation actions desired by Congress would now take place almost automatically, it was felt, even in the face of the political resistance by the head of EPA.[38]

Congress took two years to gain agreement on the specifics of what would be one of its most detailed and prescriptive pieces of environmental legislation ever enacted. The new law reflected a sobering realization: Notwithstanding that some RCRA permits were being issued, that EPA had initiated the uniform manifest system for offsite wastes, and that states were developing some of the needed administrative capacity, America's hazardous waste problems appeared to be expanding, not shrinking. There was little evidence of any transition away from land disposal methods and deep-well injection toward neutralization, stabilization, recycling, and other methods of safer, longer-lasting methods of waste management, despite RCRA's gentle pressures in that direction and the move in that direction by a few lead states.

The Congressional Budget Office estimated that industry's generation of hazardous wastes in 1983 exceeded 293 million tons: more than a ton a year for every man, woman, and child in the United States.[39] These figures caught people's attention.   The challenging magnitude of managing all these new wastes far overshadowed the Superfund problem, despite the political intensity associated with cleanup. Even so, the sheer volume of new wastes should not have been a surprise. The RCRA law of 1976 had been aimed not at reducing waste generation or finding alternatives to landfills so much as at managing industry's vast volumes of hazardous wastes in improved, lined landfills. For all the talk in leading policy circles that source reduction was central to solving hazardous waste problems, even as late as 1985 EPA was still busily writing its rules for new double-lined landfills.

This emphasis on building a safer landfill would be changed by Congress. A growing population and an expanding economy meant that even maintaining the status quo in per-capita hazardous waste generation would otherwise result in ever-increasing volumes. Aggregate figures in the early 1980s revealed that the net impact of voluntary industry efforts to curb hazardous waste generation—of which there were already some good examples, especially by a select number of large firms[40]—was insufficient to offset the overall rate of growth in total hazardous waste generation across the nation (see Box 4.4).

As noted, the people President Reagan placed in charge of EPA in his first administration were hardly committed to aggressive implementation of RCRA, both for philosophical and political reasons. Indeed, they were quite the opposite.[41] The Reagan team realized correctly that aggressive implementation of RCRA would insert government regulators into the heart of the business community, a presence industry adamantly opposed. Even more so than for Superfund, over which there was growing debate—though in it "only" money was at stake—effective regulation of industry management of the nation's hazardous wastes would involve government intervention on an unprecedented scale.[42]

To the Reagan EPA and the Office of Management and Budget, intrusive government regulation was anathema. Therefore, the battle over RCRA quickly took on highly ideological and partisan overtones. Throughout much of the Reagan administration, Democrats capitalized on the substantial disjuncture between the president's "trust industry" posture and the growing public clamor for government to police industry's unacceptable hazardous waste habits. The downfall of Anne Gorsuch, Rita Lavelle, and their associates in 1983 over their malfeasance in Superfund execution provided Congress with the opening it needed to impose its will through a vastly revised RCRA program calling for unprecedented government intrusion into business environmental management practices.

POLICY LEARNING AND THE 1984 HSWA REVISIONS

By 1984, Congress had learned a great deal about RCRA shortcomings, lessons it incorporated into the Hazardous and Solid Waste Amendments

BOX 4.4   Alameda County: Racing to Stay in Place

Alameda County (in the San Francisco Bay Area) completed a
hazardous waste management plan in 1987. Planners looked in detail
at hazardous waste generation in the county—some 100,000 tons per
year—and developed several scenarios of its evolution to the year 2000,
based on different policy assumptions. Projected growth in economic
activity would add some 40 percent more hazardous waste, planners
felt. Introducing the most aggressive source reduction measures feasible
across the county's 7,000 total large and small waste generators would,
when combined with this growth, keep Alameda's total hazardous
waste volumes roughly at their 1986 levels: 100,000 tons per year.

(HSWA). These amendments were intended to close many of the
loopholes in the original Act that had allowed EPA to move ever so
slowly and industry to avoid shifting from land disposal to alternative
treatment technologies and waste reduction. HSWA launched a period
of upheaval in hazardous waste management far beyond that caused by
RCRA eight years earlier.

For one thing, HSWA expanded RCRA well beyond its original
boundaries, to cover more than 1 million underground storage tanks
across the nation containing hazardous materials (used primarily for
gasoline storage);[43] more than 250,000 generators of small quantities of
hazardous waste;[44] and hundreds of blenders and burners of waste
fuels. The amendments also added an additional 21 substances to EPA's
list of RCRA-regulated hazardous wastes.

The 1984 amendments moved beyond conventional civil sanctions;
RCRA violations could now be criminal offenses. Maximum penalties
were raised, and the law was amended to allow citizens to file "imminent
hazard" lawsuits against generators and storage facilities. EPA was also
authorized to conduct criminal investigations of suspected violators.

Despite these impressive new enforcement powers, EPA's enforcement
capabilities remained quite limited throughout the 1980s. Typically, EPA
relied on state environmental agencies, state attorney generals, and local
agencies to conduct most federally sanctioned inspections as well as to
initiate most actual enforcement cases. In fiscal year 1988, EPA
established RCRA inspection and enforcement as a major goal and then
only with respect to permitted land disposal facilities deemed to be
"significant non-compliers."[45] Though important, these few firms were
not even a tiny fraction of all the nation's businesses covered under
RCRA. EPA's National Enforcement Investigation Center in Colorado
had attained high proficiency by the late 1980s, but was still unable to

meet all of EPA's nationwide enforcement responsibilities for RCRA, Superfund, and the other environmental laws.[46]

Most importantly, HSWA built on the experience in several states and key industrial firms to adopt as national policy the "hazardous waste management hierarchy" (see Box 4.5). The 1984 amendments give preference, in order, first to waste reduction (generating less waste in the first place), then to recycling, then to treatment by appropriate technology, and only finally to land disposal. This was the policy statement:

> The Congress hereby declares it to be the national policy of the United States that, wherever feasible, the generation of hazardous waste is to be reduced or eliminated as expeditiously as possible. Waste that is nevertheless generated should be treated, stored or disposed of so as to minimize the present and future threat to human health and the environment.[47]

The phrase "whenever feasible" did leave wiggle room for those who would have to implement the law and were directly affected by this provision. Nevertheless, the intent seems fairly straightforward: the nation's industry was to move to source reduction.

The stark reality was that industry was generating far more new hazardous wastes than had been imagined in 1976. By 1984, it was evident that while treatment was feasible technically, far too little treatment capacity was available—and a lot more marketplace and public resistance stood in the way of developing that capacity—than had been presumed at the launching of RCRA eight years before. The situation looked even more bleak given projections of economic expansion over the next five to ten years, for with that expansion would come ever-heavier hazardous waste loads.

Congress heard from several quarters that another option was available: reduce the volume of industrial hazardous waste generation. Estimates said generation could feasibly be reduced by nearly 14 percent from 1984 to 1990—from 293 million to 252 million tons annually—if industry would rapidly adopt basic waste reduction principles and take advantage of known waste reduction technologies. Admittedly, industry would incur a substantial (estimated at 46 percent) increase in expenditures on hazardous waste management, but these expenses would fall chiefly into four key sectors: chemicals and allied products, rubber and plastic products, primary metals, and fabricated metal products.

The alternative was even less thinkable. If industry continued its past waste generation and disposal practices, the annual waste load would increase by 5.6 percent from 1984 to 1990, and the cost of managing these

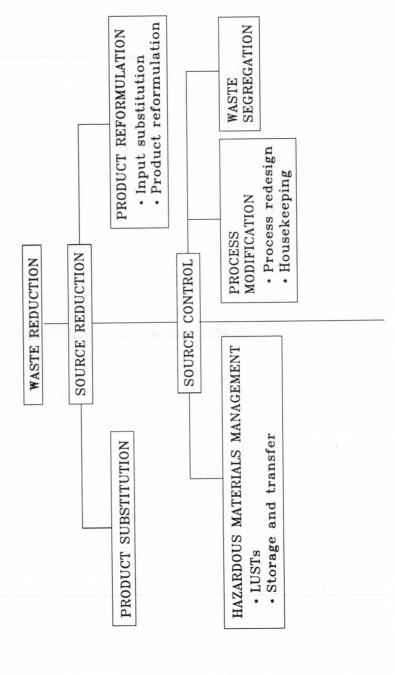

BOX 4.5 **Waste Reduction and Treatment Hierarchy**

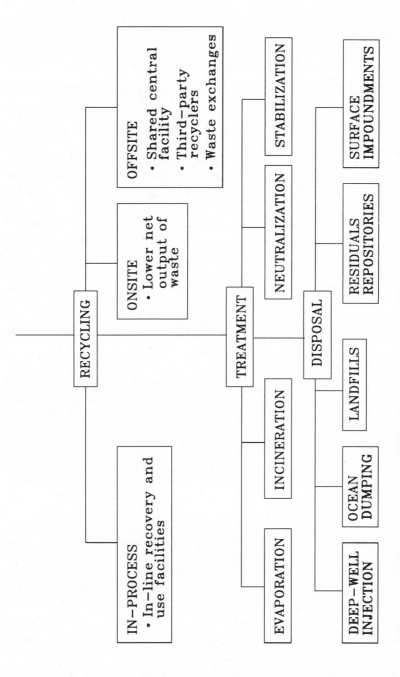

Source: Adapted from Office of Technology Assessment, U.S. Congress, "Technologies and Management Strategies for Hazardous Waste Control" (Washington, D.C.: Government Printing Office, 1983).

wastes with conventional strategies would rise by 94 percent.[48] The economic and environmental logic of waste reduction was compelling: Every gallon or ton not generated was a gallon or ton not needing costly treatment or disposal. Waste reduction could actually save industry money in the long run. Of course, this long-term view was all too rare.

The concept was clear, but in practice it would be complex and difficult for industry to make such a transition (see Box 4.6). Even so, waste reduction became the criterion against which industry and government programs would henceforth be judged.

Congress decided not to mandate waste reduction in 1984. Economic incentives alone were deemed sufficient to encourage industry to reduce rates of waste generation, combined with articulation of waste reduction as an overarching policy goal.

Congress focused RCRA's implementation on mandatory treatment of wastes rather than their continued land disposal. The inherent risks to human health and the environment that could arise from disposing of these dangerous compounds in even the safest landfills were too great to accept any longer. (As discussed in the next section, federal legislation was passed in 1990 to make unequivocal the desire of Congress to move toward source reduction as the overriding goal.)

Phasing out land disposal became the regulatory centerpiece of HSWA. The legislation drew on the lead taken by California several years earlier, with land disposal of untreated hazardous wastes to be phased out under strict deadlines. Treatment was mandated instead, with only state-of-the-art disposal units allowed to continue to manage residuals left after treatment. HSWA set specific dates for outright bans on further landfill disposal.

Starting with spent solvents and dioxins in 1986, EPA imposed restrictions on land disposal that squeezed the regulated community with a statutory series of deadlines. At each point, EPA defined acceptable treatment standards for various waste categories. These deadlines arrived one after the other. By the time generators and commercial hazardous waste management firms began to comprehend and comply with the 1986 restrictions on solvents and dioxins, the entire "California List" was being banned from land disposal nationwide.

A year later EPA set treatment standards for the first one-third of all remaining hazardous wastes. In mid-1989 the second third were restricted, and controls for all remaining waste categories were imposed in May 1990. Disposal of most wastes was banned unless EPA could prove the wastes left untreated would pose no risk of harm for as long as they remained hazardous.

Landfilling was retained as an available option only for the residues remaining after effective hazardous waste treatment and for those few

untreated wastes found safe in a land disposal setting. Exemptions of up to two years were available, but a future emphasizing waste treatment rather than disposal had clearly arrived.

New safety measures would also have to be observed at all these landfills. Landfill operators had to institute several measures to reduce possible seepage into underground aquifers, including installing double liners, leachate collection systems, and systems of groundwater monitoring to detect any seepage that might occur. Operators of all existing and new landfills had to secure bonding and to develop EPA-approved site closure and postclosure monitoring plans. (See Box 4.3 for the impact of HSWA on generators, transporters, and TSD facilities.)

Since 1984, some states have gone even further. For example, not waiting for results of EPA studies, Minnesota changed its law in 1986 to exclude further landfilling of virtually all hazardous wastes, even in double-lined landfills. Any new disposal facility sited in that state can accept only wastes rendered nonhazardous or at least treated with the best feasible and most prudent technology. The facility must also be above ground.[49] As of May 1990, no untreated hazardous wastes of any kind could be placed onto the land in California.

To preclude the possibility of further EPA foot-dragging, Congress included several dozen so-called hammer provisions in HSWA. Each of these hammers required EPA to develop a detailed regulation and meet specific implementation goals by a certain date. If EPA failed to meet these requirements, the more stringent actions spelled out in detail in HSWA would take effect automatically. It was through these uncompromising provisions that Congress intended to take charge of EPA actions directly, circumventing the Reagan White House. And although Congress had resorted before to writing detailed regulations into statutory language, the extent of HSWA was unprecedented. The hammer provisions covered a spectrum of issues, including the time EPA had to bring small-quantity generators into the RCRA program, the listing of additional hazardous substances, the phasing in of bans on placing high-priority toxic substances in landfills, the promulgation of new regulations for air emissions from TSD facilities, the final permitting of these facilities, and the development of regulations covering deep-well injection.[50] Some deadlines were only a few months away, others 60 months hence.

EPA was not the only target of the hammer provisions. They were designed to eliminate the economic incentives that previously led generators of hazardous wastes and owners and operators of TSD facilities to delay as long as possible the implementation of many of RCRA's provisions—delays they achieved through administrative appeals within EPA, court challenges, and lobbying for legislative change.

Hammer provisions were used by Congress to send as strong a message as possible that delay in effective hazardous waste management by either the regulators or the regulatees would no longer be tolerated.

LAND DISPOSAL OR TREATMENT?
THE CONUNDRUM OF CAPACITY AVAILABILITY

Unfortunately, most of the new treatment facilities needed to implement land disposal bans have not been built, even now at the end of the first toxics decade. Their absence has greatly impeded America's transition to a new era of safer waste treatment and has undermined much of the thrust of HSWA.

The reasons for this failure are again numerous. To begin, Congress made absolutely no provision in HSWA for siting of the new facilities crucial to accomplishing the transformation in hazardous waste management called for in the HSWA amendments. Decisions about land use and facility siting in America have traditionally been reserved to local communities, which respond to private-sector initiatives driven by market needs. Just as occurred with California's early land disposal bans, generalized economic incentives were presumed to be sufficient; and just as California's effort failed to bring land disposal to a halt, HSWA's mandated shift to treatment foundered for lack of new facilities.

Despite evidence that local interests and market forces were insufficient alone to site the complex facilities needed to handle modern hazardous waste treatment and thus to permit the called-for phaseout of land disposal, the federal government abdicated any responsibility for facility siting. This step significantly eroded any likelihood that RCRA and HSWA would be implemented effectively.

The transition away from land disposal was all the more confounded by the growing chemophobia, Superfund shock, and deepening public distrust of governmental decisions on environmental and health issues during the 1980s. It was hardly surprising that even where there was interest on the part of business to develop modern treatment facilities, very few would be sited voluntarily by communities (an issue discussed further in Chapter Seven). For RCRA, the result was a self-defeating downward spiral.

As long as the older landfills remained available, their very presence largely stymied the push for a more rapid transition to new treatment technologies. Waste disposal at old landfills was cheaper than treatment at a new facility. So why would a generator of waste use a new facility? And why would an investor finance a new facility (that might not be used)? Moreover, the firms owning these landfills—Chemical Waste

Management, Inc., IT Corporation, and Browning Ferris Industries (BFI), for example—were unlikely to accelerate development of the very treatment facilities that, once available, would allow EPA to implement the legislated phaseout of land disposal. Yet these were the very firms to which America still looked for leadership in hazardous waste management, primarily because they were accustomed to dealing daily with the specter of Superfund liability. Who would enter the market under these circumstances to compete with them?

In contrast, the corporations with obvious expertise in managing hazardous chemicals daily—DuPont, Monsanto, ARCO, Mobil, Chevron, and so on—were frightened by CERCLA's apparently infinite reach into their deep pockets. Despite their immense technical competence and their access to capital to build the needed new treatment facilities, the willingness of these corporations to lead America out of its hazardous waste management wilderness was diluted by the chilling effect of the liability rules crafted to deal with remediation at Superfund sites.

Moreover, although disposal costs at existing landfills were increasing rapidly, they often remained just below those of comparable treatment of waste streams. Most of these landfills had been sited and built some years earlier; their owners had time to amortize capital costs. Proposed new treatment facilities were different: Their capital-intensive costs would have to be recovered quickly. Knowing that existing landfill owners could undercut their treatment prices essentially at will, many investors considering proposed treatment facilities found the prospects of an adequate rate of return simply too uncertain.

Then, too, treatment always leaves some residue (sludge and ash) that requires land disposal. Thus, a firm operating a treatment facility but not owning its own hazardous waste landfill would find itself vulnerable to availability or price for final disposition of these residues at a competitor's landfill.

Finally, hazardous waste landfill owners were willing to lobby intensively against rapid implementation of the land disposal phaseout concept. They could spend large sums to influence legislators and senior officials of regulatory agencies (playing especially on the regulators' fear of rampant illegal dumping if available landfills were actually closed).

RCRA IMPLEMENTATION, ROUND TWO

Eight years have passed since the HSWA legislation, and it is evident that what HSWA called for and what EPA and the states and industry have delivered are not the same. Phaseout of land disposal has not proceeded smoothly, although many owners and operators of existing than meet EPA's new requirements for groundwater monitoring and financial assurance. EPA's treatment standards have been incredibly complicated, and adequate treatment capacity has failed to emerge.

The HSWA hammer provisions previously described, combined with better funding from Congress, did indeed produce some striking regulatory results. In a four-year retrospective, GAO found that small-quantity generators had been brought into the RCRA program, regulations prohibiting land disposal of highly hazardous wastes had been promulgated, and the backlog of industry petitions requesting exemption from RCRA controls had largely been processed. GAO concluded that EPA was devoting substantial resources to the extensive assessments needed to issue final RCRA permits—as opposed to its earlier interim permits. (EPA issued its final permits first to land disposal facilities and only later to incinerators—an ironic set of priorities given the HSWA land disposal phaseout program.)

November 1989 was the deadline for existing hazardous waste incinerators to obtain permits. As of then, 121 of the incinerators applying for a RCRA permit had received it; of these, 14 were commercial facilities, and 107 were onsite private units.[51]

Receiving less attention from EPA, however, were many of HSWA's nonhammer provisions and the agency's other hazardous waste responsibilities. EPA focused on the hammer issues to the exclusion of much else, including such major activities as ensuring adequate provisions were made to close many landfills that could not or did not want to comply with the strict new HSWA standards. Also not attended to were the substantial cleanup, monitoring, and remediation requirements (corrective action) to be met by the 5,000 operating land disposal, incineration, and treatment and storage facilities as a condition of their RCRA permits.

EPA's data-gathering activities remained problematic as well. For example, information collected on industrial hazardous waste generated in 1985 was not released until 1988, and the format was inconsistent with other government data bases. That was supposed to be remedied beginning with the 1989 data reports.[52]

The most serious controversy over HSWA implementation arose from what many in Congress and the environmental community saw as EPA's sidestepping, or at a minimum underplaying, of the goal of waste reduction. Rather than take on the challenge of waste reduction frontally—which would have required EPA to prod American industries into using different inputs in their production processes, responding to new economic incentives, developing new production methods or new products, all with the goal of reducing hazardous waste generation—the agency retained its more conventional regulatory function of reviewing proposed TSD facility permits (through 1988, mostly for landfills, shifting somewhat thereafter to encouraging alternative waste treatment methods).[53] Exemplifying EPA's attitude was a 1989 statement by David Cohen, director of EPA's press division: "Some argue for pollution prevention, which is a somewhat utopian ideal that may be workable in the future, but for now, the waste has to go somewhere."[54]

This is not to say there has been complete lack of progress toward waste reduction nationally. EPA redefined the concept to fit its broader definition of waste minimization. When the Office of Technology Assessment (OTA) surveyed waste generators to see if they were complying with the HSWA mandate that they develop waste reduction plans, only 40 percent could say they were.[55] Under EPA's adopted definition, that could legitimately include any proposed action falling within the hierarchy of treatment approaches, not just steps that would result literally in less waste being generated.

A number of states showed more initiative and commitment to waste reduction, introducing tax incentives, funding research and development assistance, and providing information-outreach and technology-transfer programs. North Carolina, Illinois, and Ohio were noteworthy early examples. North Carolina has been especially vigorous in reaching out to industry through educational efforts, hazardous waste auditing programs, and source reduction research. The program has prepared over 50 publications on waste reduction in several industries (textiles, fabricated metals, food processing, and furniture) as well as technical guides that industry can follow. The program also operates a clearinghouse and offers matching grants for developing source reduction technologies. North Carolina's program is comparatively small in scale but quite effective and is clearly a model of aggressive leadership in a cooperative public-private drive for better toxics management.[56]

Funding for government source reduction activities has been minimal, however, even for the most ambitious state programs.[57] Many large firms have had the economic incentive and the capital and technical resources to complete waste reduction audits, to implement new techniques, and to install new waste reduction technology, but the nation's hundreds of thousands of small generators face a vastly different situation. Federal, state, and local government programs are still struggling to fill that gap.

In 1990, Congress passed a significant new piece of legislation: the Pollution Prevention Act (PPA). PPA mandates that all facilities required to report releases of toxic substances under SARA Title III (known as the *toxics release inventory*, or TRI; see Chapter Six) must also report on their in-house waste minimization efforts. All information, including the TRI, is made available to the public.

Under the new federal law, all facilities generating over a certain quantity of toxic chemical emissions must file annual "toxic chemical source reduction and recycling reports" as of July 1, 1992. These reports must include the following information:

- amount of wastes entering the waste stream and percentage change from the previous year;
- amount of wastes expected to enter the waste stream and to be reported for the next two calendar years;
- amount recycled, percentage change in amount recycled from the previous year, and process used;
- source reduction practices used;
- ratio of reporting year's production to previous year's production;
- techniques used to identify source reduction opportunities;
- amount of toxic chemical(s) released as a result of one-time events (e.g., remediation or accident).

Finally, the closure of conventional landfills combined with the many new requirements on remaining TSD facilities to produce an unanticipated consequence in the late 1980s: a growing shortfall in hazardous waste management capacity in the United States. Congress's response was to instruct each state to assess its waste management needs and capacity, the aim being to reconcile the two. As a matter of expediency, Congress placed this requirement in its amendments to the 1986 Superfund renewal (SARA), though the topic clearly falls within the framework of RCRA. By 1990, each state had assured EPA it had adequate hazardous waste management capacity for 20 years. (Failure to provide such assurance could result in loss of federal Superfund cleanup money.)

In part, most states met their capacity assurance requirements by proposing to accelerate waste reduction, by promising to build new hazardous waste treatment and incineration facilities to meet their needs, and by citing landfill capacity available in other states. Given the recalcitrant local opposition to siting new facilities throughout the entire toxics era, it is difficult to believe that mere promises by states to bring many new facilities on line will turn out to be anything better than "paper compliance" (see Chapter Seven).

As with Superfund implementation, arrival of the Bush administration injected a breath of fresh air into RCRA, especially for its long-neglected source reduction directive. EPA established a new Pollution Prevention Office and in 1989 launched a $12 million pollution-prevention initiative involving all EPA program offices. A year later, this group began aggressive implementation of the Pollution Prevention Act.

EPA Administrator William Reilly then set a new tone for the source reduction campaign in early 1991 by calling on America's 600 largest corporations to reduce significantly their generation of 17 major toxics emissions; he asked for reductions of 33 percent by the end of 1992 and at least 50 percent by the end of 1995.[58] This was not to be achieved through EPA prescriptive or top-down regulation, however, but through asking industry for "voluntary" compliance. Reilly's goal was to move expeditiously but also to avoid "an adversarial relationship"[59] with the nation's industrial leaders (the traditional friends and backers of the Republican administration he serves). Noted too by the *Wall Street Journal* was that mounting statutory pressure and rising costs of hazardous waste disposal gave industry good economic reasons for taking Reilly up on his suggestion; at long last, the message was beginning to hit home among America's business community that pollution prevention just might pay.[60] This evolving perspective is obviously a very positive step. Only time will tell if it will help stem the tide of the hazardous wastes problem.

Further RCRA amendments were on the congressional agenda as the second toxics decade got under way. The continuing problems of administering the wide-ranging toxics program were ever-present, particularly the need to shift smoothly from the land disposal reliance of the past (and the present) to a new focus on both treatment of hazardous wastes and successful waste reduction.

To the extent an aggressive EPA can make a difference in resolving these issues, there is renewed hope. However, to the extent these issues are deeply embedded in the independent decisions of firms and communities across America, the challenges of the 1990s to change patterns of waste management and waste production remain daunting.

NOTES

1. The first alarm sounded to the broad public about the dire consequences of chemicals being poured on the land—not primarily from hazardous waste practices but from the application of pesticides and herbicides—came from books by Rachel Carson, *Silent Spring* (Greenwich, Conn.: Fawcett, 1962); James S. Turner, *The Chemical Feast* (New York: Grossman, 1970); and Barry Commoner, *The Closing Circle* (New York: Alfred A. Knopf, 1971).

2. Walter A. Rosenbaum, *Environmental Politics and Policy*, 2d ed. (Washington, D.C.: Congressional Quarterly Press, 1991), 228.

3. Roger C. Dower, "Hazardous Wastes," in Paul Portney, ed., *Public Policies for Environmental Protection* (Washington, D.C.: Resources for the Future, 1990), 151–194, esp. 177–178.

4. Marcia E. Williams, "Strategies for Managing Present and Future Wastes," *Risk Analysis* 11 (March 1991), 77.

5. Richard C. Fortuna, "Comments on 'Strategies for Managing Present and Future Wastes,'" *Risk Analysis* 11 (March 1991), 87.

6. Lawrence G. Brewster, *The Public Agenda: Issues in American Politics* (New York: St. Martin's, 1984), 135.

7. RCRA, Pub. L. No. 94-580, section 1004 (5); 42 U.S.C. section 6903 (October 21, 1976).

8. Congressional Budget Office (CBO), U.S. Congress, "Hazardous Waste Management: Recent Changes and Policy Alternatives" (May 1985), 18.

9. Seymour I. Schwartz, Wendy Pratt Cuckovich, Nancy Steffenson-Ostrom, and Cecilia F. Cox, "Managing Hazardous Wastes Produced by Small Quantity Generators," Senate Office of Research, California Legislature (April 1987).

10. Environmental Protection Agency, "National Survey of Hazardous Waste Generators and Treatment, Storage, and Disposal Facilities Regulated Under RCRA in 1981" (1984) 135.

11. CBO, "Hazardous Waste Management," 22.

12. Steve Lohr, "Siting for Toxic-Waste Cave Stirs Texas Political Fight," *New York Times* (May 6, 1991).

13. For example, California's number one Superfund site, the Stringfellow Acid Pits in Riverside County, received a total of some 20,000 tons of hazardous liquid wastes during its 20 years of operation in the 1960s and 1970s. In contrast, the BKK landfill in nearby Los Angeles County, regulated under RCRA, received nearly 500,000 tons of regulated hazardous wastes during 1984 alone, its last full year of operation.

14. Keith Schneider, "The Data Gap: What We Don't Know About Chemicals," *The Amicus Journal* 7 (Winter 1985), 15–24.

15. Rosenbaum, *Environmental Politics*, 215.

16. Christopher H. Schmitt, Pete Carey, and Scott Thurm, "State Fails to Track Toxic Waste Cheaters," *San Jose Mercury News* (March 31, 1991); Dower, "Hazardous Wastes," 163.

17. Letter from DHS/TSCD Regional Office Director to David Morell (personal correspondence, 1987).

18. Williams, "Strategies for Managing," 77.

19. Andrea M. Fike, "A *Mens Rea* Analysis for the Criminal Provisions of the Resource Conservation and Recovery Act," *Stanford Environmental Law Journal* 6 (1986–87), 191.

20. Requirements covering generators, transporters, and TSD facilities are drawn from various EPA documents and from Bradford S. Gentry, "Regulation of Hazardous Waste in the United States and Great Britain," *Environmental Reporter* (February 24, 1989), 2321–2328.

21. The 90-day provision created a massive regulatory loophole because hazardous wastes may be "stored" up to 89 days without any RCRA permit. To avoid cumbersome EPA permitting procedures, many generators simply operate full-blown storage facilities, but ship their wastes offsite every 89 days. The

absence of a permit ensures the lack of effective regulatory control, monitoring, or inspection of these storage facilities.

22. Steven Ferrey, "Hard Times: Criminal Prosecution for Polluters," *The Amicus Journal* 10 (Fall 1988), 11–17; Marx Wexler, "Strike Force," *National Wildlife* (June-July 1985), 38–41; Jonathan Weber, "Corporate Crime of the '90s," *Los Angeles Times* (November 11, 1989).

23. In 1980, Congress established a national trust fund from fees on hazardous waste disposal to cover postclosure financial liability and postclosure monitoring costs. See Richard Riley, "Toxic Substances, Hazardous Wastes, and Public Policy: Problems in Implementation," in James Lester and Ann O'M. Bowman, eds., *The Politics of Hazardous Waste Management* (Durham, N.C.: Duke University Press, 1983), 35.

24. By 1988, two-thirds (956) of the offsite land disposal facilities nationwide had not received RCRA certification and therefore finally had to close. See U.S. General Accounting Office (GAO), "Hazardous Waste: New Approach Needed to Manage Resource Conservation and Recovery Act" (July 1988), 39.

25. The General Accounting Office became deeply involved over the years in monitoring EPA progress in implementing RCRA's hazardous waste provisions, issuing 30 major reports on the subject between 1983 and 1988. We have drawn on several of these reports.

26. GAO, "Hazardous Waste: New Approach Needed," 33–35.

27. Brewster, *The Public Agenda*, 119.

28. Norman J. Vig, "Presidential Leadership: From the Reagan to the Bush Administration," in Norman J. Vig and Michael E. Kraft, eds., *Environmental Policy in the 1990s* (Washington, D.C.: Congressional Quarterly Press, 1990), 33–58.

29. GAO, "Hazardous Waste: New Approach Needed," 7, 14.

30. CBO, "Hazardous Waste Management," 6.

31. Quoted in Riley, "Toxic Substances," 36.

32. James P. Lester and Ann O'M. Bowman, "Implementing Intergovernmental Policy: A Test of the Sabatier-Mazmanian Model," *Polity* 21 (Summer 1989), 734.

33. Karen B. Wiley, "State-EPA Relations in the RCRA Program: A Report on an Interview Study," monograph (October 1986).

34. Lester and Bowman, "Implementing Intergovernmental Policy."

35. Lester and Bowman divide those states not delegated RCRA administration (as of 1985) into "strategic delayers" (e.g., California, Connecticut, Hawaii, and New York) and "recalcitrants" (e.g., Alabama, Nevada, and Pennsylvania). They underscore that the former group often tried to develop programs different from—sometimes more expansive than—EPA goals and were denied delegation not just because they refused to develop a state-level program along EPA's preferred lines.

36. National Conference of State Legislatures, "Hazardous Waste Management: A Survey of State Legislation" (Denver, Colo.: NCSL, 1982).

37. Liquids containing certain metals, cyanides, PCBs, strong acids, and chlorinated compounds at high concentrations.

38. Dower, "Hazardous Wastes," 165–168.

39. CBO, "Hazardous Waste Management," 9.

40. David Sarokin, Warren Muir, Catherine Miller, and Sebastian Sperber, *Cutting Chemical Wastes: What 29 Organic Chemical Plants Are Doing To Reduce Hazardous Waste* (New York: Inform, Inc., 1985).

41. Christopher Harris, William Want, and Morris Ward, *Hazardous Waste: Confronting the Challenge* (New York: Quorum Books, 1987), ch. 7; Jonathan Lash, Katherine Gillman, and David Sheridan, *A Season of Spoils: The Reagan Administration's Attack on the Environment* (New York: Pantheon Books, 1984).

42. Imposition of federal Occupational Safety and Health Administration (OSHA) rules for worker safety beginning in 1970 represented a similar threat to industry and suffered a similar fate.

43. It was obvious that with the number of underground tanks involved, the administrative task of overseeing their upgrading and replacement would be beyond EPA's capacity and would require new approaches. See Sheldon Kamieniecki and Steven A. Cohen, "Strategic Regulatory Planning in the Management of Hazardous Materials," *Policy and Politics* 18, 3 (1990), 207–216.

44. Congress lowered to 220 pounds (100 kilograms) of hazardous waste per month the threshold for inclusion in the federal program, set originally by EPA under (Gorsuch) Burford at 2,200 pounds (1,000 kilograms).

45. "Office of Solid Waste and Emergency Response: Annual Report, Fiscal Year 1988," U.S. Environmental Protection Agency (November 1988), 31–33.

46. By contrast, in the late 1980s EPA had about 14,000 employees devoted to all aspects of environmental protection; the Internal Revenue Service, devoted largely to monitoring and enforcement, had some 74,000 employees; the Bureau of Land Management in the Interior Department had about 17,000.

47. CBO, "Hazardous Waste Management."

48. CBO, "Hazardous Waste Management," tables 13 and 15, 48–51.

49. Peter M. Sandman and Emilie Schmeidler, "Getting to Maybe: Decisions on the Road to Negotiation in Hazardous Waste Facility Siting," Environmental Communications Research Program, Rutgers University (January 1988), 299.

50. CBO, "Hazardous Waste Management," table 9, 36–37.

51. Permit requests were denied 37 facilities, which ceased operating; another 17 facilities missed the deadline, though they were later reviewed by EPA. Forty more incinerators decided to close before late 1989 because they were unable to meet EPA's new performance standards.

52. GAO, "Hazardous Waste: New Approach Needed," 25–30.

53. Office of Technology Assessment (OTA), U.S. Congress, "Serious Reduction of Hazardous Waste: For Pollution Prevention and Industrial Efficiency" (September 1986).

54. Quoted in "News and Analysis," *Hazmat World* (September 1989), 13.

55. OTA, "Serious Reduction of Hazardous Waste," 45.

56. "North Carolina's Roger Schecter," *EPA: Pollution Prevention News* (April 1989), 3–4.

57. OTA, "Serious Reduction of Hazardous Waste," table 1.3, 35.

58. "EPA Unveils Pollution Prevention Strategy: 17 Chemicals Targeted for Reduction in Strategy's Industrial Toxics Project," *EPA: Pollution Prevention News* (January/February 1991), 1, 8. The chemicals involved include benzene, cadmium and its compounds, carbon tetrachloride, chloroform, chromium and its compounds, cyanides, dichloromethane, lead and its compounds, mercury and its compounds, methyl ethyl ketone, methyl isobutyl ketone, nickel and its compounds, tetrachloroethylene, toluene, trichloromethane, trichloroethylene, and xylenes.

59. Robert L. Jackson, "EPA Appeals to 600 Firms to Curtail Toxic Pollution," *Los Angeles Times* (February 8, 1991).

60. Scott McMurray, "Chemical Firms Find That It Pays to Reduce Pollution at Source," *Wall Street Journal* (June 11, 1991).

CHAPTER FIVE

Engineering, Economics, and Politics: Technologies for Safe Hazardous Waste Management

It was one thing for Congress to pass RCRA and especially its HSWA amendments, thereby calling on America's industry to convert to the treatment and safe management of its hazardous wastes and to minimize generation of those wastes. It may be quite another to carry out this transformation, as we have seen. The challenge is not fundamentally technical—technologies are generally available to accomplish the desired changes in hazardous waste treatment practices. Yet the question remains: Why have these technologies not been brought into widespread use in the United States?

Nearly all hazardous wastes regulated under RCRA (perhaps up to 90 percent) can be treated effectively with methods known for decades.[1] Indeed, many U.S. firms are already using off-the-shelf technologies to accomplish cost-effective onsite treatment, including distillation, burning wastes as fuel in industrial boilers, chemical oxidation/reduction, neutralization/precipitation, biodegradation, incineration, reverse osmosis, and ion exchange. As mentioned in Chapter Four, however, these operations remain the exception; at the close of the first toxics decade, most of America's hazardous wastes were still being placed on the land.

That being true, the pressing question is why treatment methods have not been introduced on a scale sufficient to bring about the overall changes needed in America's hazardous waste management practices (and to reduce the total hazardous waste load). The answer involves a complex set of constraints on technology, including competitive costs, regulatory processes, marketplace uncertainties, financial risks, concern over liability, and, unexpectedly, public perceptions and local opposition to needed new facilities. America's failure to adopt available technologies is in stark contrast to the success many other advanced industrial nations have had introducing new techniques of waste management and source reduction. These countries are well ahead of the

United States in realizing the necessary transformation in many (though certainly not all) of their hazardous waste practices.

SAFE HAZARDOUS WASTE
MANAGEMENT ALTERNATIVES

The aim of hazardous waste treatment is to transform these wastes into something less (or not at all) hazardous or to reduce greatly their volume. As discussed in Chapter Four, a broad spectrum of American industry generates a comparable range of hazardous wastes: Solvents, dyes, and resins come from the chemical industry; metal-containing sludges, liquids, and dusts come from the metal-finishing and electroplating industry; waste motor oils come from many industries as well as consumers. Appropriate treatment techniques differ for various wastes.

The metallic sludges generated as a by-product of the metal-finishing, electroplating, and printed circuit board industries often come from these industries' pretreatment of liquid wastes, with the treated liquids then discharged to the sewer (under standards set by the federal Clean Water Act). A typical sludge might consist of hydroxides, salts, metals, and water. Treatment involves dewatering and metals recovery. Traditionally, such sludges have been sent to landfills without any attempt made to reclaim the metals. Disposal costs were low, and costs of reclamation were relatively high. Treatment technologies are readily available, however.

Organic solvents are used in a wide array of firms to prepare and separate compounds; they serve as degreasing and cleaning agents in industries as diverse as electronics and latex or vinyl polymer production; and they are used in the production of pesticides and fertilizers. Many organic solvents in mixed solutions can be distilled and recovered for reuse by their generators or for use in other industries that can accept solvents with slightly lower purity.

Many wastes can be chemically neutralized (bases can neutralize strong acids) or stabilized to render them no longer chemically reactive. In these cases, the volume may not change significantly, but the degree of hazard is altered substantially.

Evaporation applies the principle that "the solution to pollution is dilution," the premise being that hazardous volatile gases become so dilute in the atmosphere as to make them inoffensive. This option has limited merit and is certainly not acceptable when industry releases dangerous gases in concentrations harmful to human and animal life.

By-product gases from organic solvents can be precursors to smog and are thus strictly regulated in many locales under the Clean Air Act.

Because incineration can destroy completely certain organic wastes which are highly toxic and difficult to break down, this technique is a preferred treatment option for such wastes. Certain wastes may be incinerated as fuels (added to a cement kiln, for example) to take advantage of their high BTU value. Although incineration can produce dangerous air emissions, these can be controlled strictly with modern scrubbers and other smokestack equipment. (By contrast, emissions from evaporation are much tougher to control.) Incineration often produces ash that is a hazardous waste residual requiring land disposal.

As indicated in Chapter Four, disposal of nearly all raw hazardous wastes ceases to be a legal option in the United States as of May 1992, provided the RCRA/HSWA provisions remain on schedule. Currently, variances may extend these deadlines to 1993 or 1994 at the latest. How wastes actually will be treated and how their treatment residues will be disposed of remain unclear. The preferred order of hazardous waste management from an environmental and health perspective moves down the hierarchy described in Box 4.5: source reduction, source control, recycling, effective treatment, and finally disposal.

Disposing even of treatment residues in a lined landfill is less preferable than placing them in a liquid-free residuals repository because the latter can be constructed to store wastes securely (without leachate) and the wastes can remain available for future mining of their contents after that technique becomes economically attractive.

No matter how much we prefer otherwise, even with aggressive source reduction, America's hundreds of thousands of hazardous waste generators will continue to produce large quantities of hazardous wastes well into the next century. Either onsite or offsite, these wastes require effective management in a range of appropriate facilities, several of which are described in the next section.

THE TECHNOLOGICAL OPTIONS

Typical characteristics apply to different components of the full range of hazardous waste management technologies or facilities. Each technology group may be described in terms of the following:

- purpose of the technology (e.g., solvent recovery reclaims solvents from a liquid organic waste stream);
- types of wastes to which the technology applies;

- specific technologies included in that category;
- scale and operating capacity of a typical facility (in tons of hazardous waste per year, truckloads of waste per week, and number of employees), information that can be provided for both large and small facilities;
- controls employed at a typical facility to prevent release of hazardous substances into the environment.

Frequently, the various technology groups are combined into single larger offsite facilities. For instance, tank and drum storage is often combined with recycling and treatment capabilities and maybe with a residuals repository landfill. Recycling facilities may have treatment units such as incinerators and tank treatment to manage materials that cannot be recovered. A typical residuals repository might have solidification capabilities. Bulking and transfer facilities may carry out limited kinds of treatment. The size of a facility (its area) may not increase proportionally when different types of waste management units are added to it, because support services and loading and unloading facilities would probably continue to serve the entire facility.

Drum Storage and Transfer Facilities

Drum storage and transfer facilities accumulate small volumes of wastes from various generators. Once volumes accumulate, these facilities contract with haulers periodically to take these wastes elsewhere for recycling, treatment, incineration, or disposal. Usually, transfer stations are a central location for collecting wastes from generators in a particular area. They combine similar wastes (acids, solvents, metals) until they have enough to ship economically to another waste management facility. Many of these facilities also handle "lab pack" wastes: bottles of used chemicals in small amounts, packed with absorbent filler into 55-gallon drums.

Typical drum storage and transfer facilities have a truck loading and unloading area and a series of concrete pads on which 55-gallon drums (or smaller canisters) can be kept. These facilities often have steel tanks in which they collect larger volumes of compatible liquid wastes. The concrete pads and the areas around the tanks are each surrounded by lined concrete walls (berms) designed to prevent liquid wastes from migrating from that storage area. Incompatible wastes (those that can react with each other) are stored in separate areas. Typically, these facilities are equipped with air monitoring and control systems to limit volatile and particulate emissions; many have a groundwater monitoring system too. Commonly, they have a laboratory onsite for analyzing chemical samples and maintain a complex recordkeeping system.

As the cost of hazardous waste management increased sharply in the second half of the 1980s, many existing transfer and storage facilities began to offer a new, very important service: waste blending. Blenders use their knowledge of available treatment and incineration facilities—their costs and their physical constraints (not more than a specific percent of chlorine, no more than a certain minimum fuel value, and so on)—to combine materials appropriately for maximum economic advantage. In a way, these transfer and storage facilities have become modern "waste stream arbitrageurs," helping to "make the market" for cement kilns, solvent recovery plants, deep-injection wells, rotary-kiln and fluidized-bed incinerators, and stabilization plants.

Typical transfer stations occupy from one to ten acres and have between two and ten employees. The amount of waste moving through these facilities may range from 10,000 to 40,000 tons a year. Weekly incoming traffic can range from 6 to 75 (or more) trucks.

Treatment Facilities for Liquid Hazardous Wastes

Although many different processes can be applied to treat liquid hazardous wastes, they usually fall into three categories: physical, chemical, and biological.

Physical treatment processes separate water from the rest of the waste stream or prepare liquid wastes for further treatment. Organic waste streams (wastewater contaminated with solvents or other organic materials) are treated by distillation, evaporation, steam stripping, gravity settling, flotation centrifuging, reverse osmosis, carbon/resin adsorption, or solvent extraction. Physical processes to treat inorganic wastes (metals and caustics) include gravity settling, flotation and centrifuging, filtration, and flocculation.

Chemical treatment processes reduce concentrations of contaminants in a waste stream by separating hazardous constituents or by rendering them less harmful. These techniques employ chemical dechlorination, wet air oxidation, chemical oxidation, ion exchange, and reduction.

Biological treatment processes increase degradation of hazardous constituents by injecting microbes into the liquid waste stream. Biological treatment processes are usually used to treat organic wastes and include activated sludge, trickling filters, aerated lagoons, waste stabilization ponds, and anaerobic digestion. Under current RCRA guidelines, processes using lagoons and ponds for hazardous waste treatment are prohibited after 1992.

Neutralization is common for treating acids (or bases). An aqueous stream (containing few or no metallic contaminants) with either a high or a low pH is neutralized by adding an acid or a caustic, producing as a by-product an inert salt that can usually be disposed of as nonhazardous. Neutralization can also stabilize inorganic compounds and reduce reactivity or corrosivity of a waste. A reduction in hazardous waste volume of 85 to 100 percent can often be achieved by neutralization.

Commonly, precipitation is used to treat liquid waste streams containing heavy metals. This process is easy to operate and relatively inexpensive. Once the waste stream is neutralized, oxidizing or reducing the waste stream causes the metals to form insoluble salts (precipitates) that are subsequently removed from the solution as sludges.

Carbon adsorption can also be used to treat liquid waste streams containing relatively low levels of organic compounds, such as pesticides. Organics are attracted to and captured on the surface of highly porous powdered, activated carbon and are thus removed from the waste stream. When the carbon reaches its capacity to hold additional organic wastes, it is removed and replaced. The spent carbon may then be regenerated to its original condition and reused, although this is a costly process feasible only for large carbon adsorption systems. Otherwise, spent carbon is either incinerated or disposed of in a hazardous waste landfill. Carbon adsorption can achieve an 80 to 100 percent reduction of contaminants, depending on the organic contaminant.

Most hazardous waste liquids treatment facilities consist of storage tanks, pipelines, and several groups of tanks in which the various treatment processes take place. Wastes received by the facility are analyzed and stored in an appropriate tank until they are transferred to another for treatment. Usually, tanks have roofs to minimize air emissions and are surrounded by berms placed on concrete pads to prevent surface and groundwater releases. Groundwater monitoring is usually required. Treated wastewater effluent is discharged either to a sanitary sewer or (if no longer hazardous) into an evaporation pond. The sludges formed are sent to an incinerator or a biological waste converter or are stabilized for subsequent land disposal.

The annual operating capacity of typical aqueous treatment facilities ranges from 70,000 to 350,000 tons. A smaller unit may cover from five to seven acres, with larger facilities occupying between ten and thirty acres. Such facilities might employ from 15 to 40 people. A facility with an annual capacity of 70,000 tons might have approximately 84 truck deliveries (4,000 gallons each) each week.

Solvent and Oil Recycling

Several technologies are available for solvent and oil recycling. These include distillation, solvent extraction, carbon/resin adsorption, filtration, and reverse osmosis. Each technology separates waste solvent or oil from the liquid solution so that the product can be recovered for reuse.

To an observer, a solvent or oil recovery facility resembles a miniature modern petroleum products refinery, with some storage tanks, pipelines, distillation towers, a few industrial buildings, and a warehouse that trucks enter to load and unload. Storage tanks are surrounded by berms to contain spills.

Small facilities can process between 10,000 and 15,000 tons of materials a year and usually occupy from one to three acres of land. Larger facilities can handle up to 40,000 tons of hazardous wastes a year and would require as much as ten acres. A large facility may employ up to 60 people.

Processing units are fitted with seals to prevent emissions; leaks are contained by dikes, drains, and basins. Most storage tanks and transfer lines are equipped with vapor recovery systems. Detectors, alarms, and process controls prevent and monitor air emissions and liquid effluents. All these facilities are required to have emergency response plans and trained personnel to respond to accidents (fires, explosions, spills).

During the distillation process, organic wastes such as oils or solvents are heated in a sealed vessel at temperatures that cause the materials to vaporize. These vapors are condensed and the oil or solvent recovered, leaving behind a by-product known as "still bottom," consisting primarily of organic degradation, other waste by-products, and inorganic contaminants. Large commercial processing plants are designed for high process rates, are very energy-efficient, and are usually expensive to set up and run. Smaller solvent stills are relatively inexpensive and easy to operate, but are not very efficient. Most distillation processes achieve a 70 to 80 percent recovery depending upon the waste material to be recovered. Typically, still bottoms are later incinerated.

Incinerators

Incinerators destroy organic liquid, gaseous, and solid hazardous wastes that cannot be recovered. Burning wastes produces ash, which can be moved to a residuals repository, often after being stabilized. All modern incinerators use sophisticated air pollution control systems.

Several different types of incinerators can be used for thermal destruction of hazardous wastes. A rotary-kiln incinerator is the least waste-specific and most flexible, capable of handling various wastes. Other incinerators, each with particular advantages, include fixed-hearth, liquid-injection, and fluidized-bed types. A fixed-hearth incinerator with liquid injection can consume liquid waste, but a rotary-kiln or fluidized-bed unit can burn solid hazardous wastes and sludges as well. Waste handling is a crucial design aspect in selecting an incinerator process.

In a rotary kiln, solid, gas, or liquid waste organics are injected into a rotating cylinder where thermal destruction occurs by radiant heat transfer from the walls of the kiln to the waste material. The ash is composed typically of silica salts and trace metals; the exhaust gases are typically scrubbed (treated) to remove gaseous contaminants. Rotary kilns can be used with any combustible waste and have high waste-destruction efficiency. For hazardous wastes with mixed organic content, these kilns are often the preferred treatment method. However, any form of incineration entails substantial capital costs, significant maintenance, and potential problems controlling gaseous emissions. Most cement kilns are large rotary kilns. They can destroy certain kinds of liquid hazardous wastes, especially organic solvents too complex to recycle.

As for many other treatment technologies, destruction efficiencies for a rotary-kiln combustor can be contaminant-specific. The best data available show that thermal destruction of most hazardous organic wastes is from 99.98 to 99.999-plus percent complete. Federal regulations require that incinerators be capable of destroying at least 99.99 percent of the hazardous constituents.

A typical incinerator facility has a tall smokestack, bermed storage tanks, a truck unloading area, and some support buildings. As with all hazardous waste management facilities, containment systems must be adequate to keep any liquid spills from migrating.

Small rotary kilns can handle about 30,000 tons of waste a year, large ones 100,000 tons. Typically, eight to twelve acres would be needed respectively for small and large incinerators. A large one could accept 100 trucks a week. Federal regulations require operators to monitor waste feed streams, stack emissions, and ash residuals to make sure operating specifications are met continuously.

Incinerators must also meet the discharge requirements set forth in their air quality permits. In many cases, incinerators are fitted with scrubbers or operate with additives to keep emissions at acceptable levels. Ash residuals exhibiting very low concentration levels and sludge from the air pollution control system are collected and taken periodically to a landfill for disposal, either as is or after stabilization.

Solidification and Stabilization Facilities

Solid hazardous wastes and sludges are often solidified further or stabilized before disposal in a residuals repository. These wastes would typically be residues from liquid waste treatment processes, ash from an incinerator, or bottoms from recycling or distillation processes. Contaminated soils may also be stabilized before land disposal.

Wastes are solidified by applying additives to the material that prevent leaching and chemical reactions. Inorganic sludges can be fixed by adding lime and fly ash. Other wastes can be bound in asphalt or plastic (polymer) coatings.

Compared with most other treatment processes, stabilization adds bulk to the waste stream—as much as 20 to 40 percent in weight and a commensurate increase in volume. Consequently, such facilities are often (but not always) located right at landfill sites. This minimizes transportation costs.

Solidification facilities look like large industrial buildings with several tall silos for storing of dry additives. The facilities can be as small as one acre and as large as ten, employing five to thirty people. Stabilization units can be designed to handle a wide range of treatment capacities. Typical offsite facilities might handle from 50,000 to 250,000 tons a year. Like other facilities, solidification units use modern monitoring and containment systems to detect and control releases to the environment.

Hunter Environmental Services, a Texas company, has proposed building a stabilization facility in a large salt dome in Dayton, Texas, ten miles from Lake Houston. If the plan is approved, the company would drill ten 1,800-foot caverns into the salt dome, and waste would be mixed with ash and cement, solidified, then crushed into gravel before being dropped into the cavern. Salt domes are routinely used to store oil and gas, but their use as hazardous waste repositories has not been allowed in the United States. The decision to let the permitting process go forward rests with the Texas Water Commission, but local opposition remains high, and Hunter Environmental's case is not helped by Ann Richards, the Democratic governor elected in 1990.[2]

Transportable Treatment Units

Increasingly, many waste generators are using transportable units to treat hazardous wastes. Such treatment is often cost-effective for smaller or periodic generators of hazardous wastes who can afford neither to buy permanent onsite treatment units nor to ship their wastes to expensive offsite commercial facilities. Transportable units may offer an economically attractive alternative.

Primarily, generators use transportable treatment units (TTUs) to treat their lower-risk liquid waste streams. Physical processes separating water from hazardous constituents, such as filtration and flocculation, are most often used. Acid neutralization units are increasingly common.

Transportable air stripping units can treat contaminated groundwater as it is drawn from withdrawal wells, incinerate vapors, or pass liquids over carbon to collect organics. Transportable rotary-kiln and fluidized-bed incinerators have helped clean up several Superfund and RCRA corrective-action sites.

TTUs must meet applicable federal and state regulatory requirements. They may operate at many different sites, yet qualify for a single regulatory permit. Generators, however, are responsible for properly handling the effluent from these units (meeting local sewer discharge and air pollution control requirements).

In several states, use of effective TTUs is being encouraged by new permit-by-rule approval procedures that assess technical characteristics and capabilities of specific treatment units and define the waste streams for which they are appropriate. Once a transportable unit is approved, any generator can move that unit onsite to treat the kinds of wastes designated without having to apply for a site-specific permit.   In California, such accelerated and simplified permitting procedures now apply only to non-RCRA California-regulated hazardous wastes. Any single generator may use a transportable unit no more than 180 days in any calendar year. So far, EPA has not developed similar rules under RCRA.

New modular incinerators are also becoming available, including rotary-kiln and fluidized-bed. Transportable incinerators can be moved onto specific locations, used to complete their assigned tasks—remediation of a contaminated site, for instance—then moved to their next assignment. In some cases, national EPA permits have been issued allowing a designated unit to incinerate selected waste streams (in at least one case, PCBs) at any particular type of location. However, additional site-specific environmental approvals are also required. Transportable incinerators have been used successfully in cleanup activities in Alaska, Illinois, Mississippi, Missouri, and New Jersey.

Residuals Repositories

A residuals repository landfill can dispose safely of waste residues from many different waste treatment plants. Of the noted treatment sequences, only neutralization of high or low pH solutions typically generates no hazardous residual for a repository. All other waste types and treatment techniques leave some amount of hazardous waste not amenable to further treatment and ultimately requiring land disposal.

A residuals repository looks like a modern landfill with several areas in which wastes can be placed. Operation of these facilities is subject to several new limitations, however, compared with traditional hazardous waste landfills. First, they receive only solid wastes that have first been sufficiently treated. (As of 1990, RCRA rules required all hazardous wastes to be treated to acceptable concentration levels before being placed in a residuals repository facility.) Second, treated wastes must not contain any free-standing liquids. Third, hazardous organic wastes cannot be placed in these units without being solidified first. Such facilities already operate at several locations in Europe, but are still lacking in the United States.

Repository facilities are designed to be covered (with a plastic liner sheet) at all times to avoid any penetration of rainfall (and thus avoid any buildup of leachate). The cover or movable roof is moved aside during good weather to allow access to the landfill cells; in inclement weather, only specially covered wet-weather disposal cells can be used. This intense effort to prevent liquids from entering the facility distinguishes it from traditional landfills.

Repository facilities must meet all federal and state land disposal regulations, including double liners underneath, leachate control and monitoring systems, run-on and run-off controls, and groundwater monitoring. These facilities cannot be sited in areas with permeable soils. A small residuals repository might accept 75,000 tons a year and occupy 100 acres. A larger one could handle as much as 360,000 tons a year, cover 250 acres, and employ as many as 50 people.

Costs of Some Treatment Technologies

According to the California Governor's 1986 Task Force on Toxics, perhaps 80 percent of the hazardous wastes sent to land disposal in that state in 1984 could have been treated using technologies that were then commercially and technically available. Land disposal costs have risen several hundred percent since 1984, making treatment costs look even more competitive with the direct costs of most land disposal. Treatment is even more economically advantageous if the indirect costs of land disposal (liability and the scarcity of landfill sites) are considered. And in any event, land disposal is no longer legal for many kinds of untreated hazardous wastes. Box 5.1 provides examples of the approximate costs of treatment technologies for a selection of hazardous wastes.

As mentioned, metal sludges are generally sent to landfills but at a high cost: about $485 a ton. Ultimate generator liability under CERCLA is an ever-present concern. Modern hydrometallurgical recycling methods permit these sludges to be digested with acids, distilled, and further purified to produce salable metals and salts at an estimated cost (including credit from sale of the metals and salts) of only $195 a ton, notably lower than the cost of land disposal.[3]

BOX 5.1 Waste Treatment Technologies and Estimated Costs

Technology Type	Costs
Incineration[a]	
Offsite, low BTU content	$250–725/ton[b]
Onsite, low BTU content	$300–425/ton[b]
Offsite, high BTU content	$50–250/ton[b]
Onsite, high BTU content	$100–175/ton[b]
PCBs, less than 500 ppm	$350–450/ton[b]
PCBs, more than 25,000 ppm	$850–1,350/ton[b]
Landfill[a]	
Bulk solids, regulated in California, no EPA number	$113/ton, $65/drum[c]
Bulk solids, EPA-regulated, assigned EPA number	$230/ton, $198/drum[c]
Drums, local facility	$25–250/drum[b]
Bulk, local facility	$30–100/ton[b]
High hazard, local facility	$100–300/ton[b]
Low hazard, out-of-state	$100–300/ton[b]
Liquids requiring extensive pretreatment to meet land disposal restriction	$2.75/gallon, $220/drum[c]
Liquids needing only stabilization treatment before land disposal	$1.95/gallon, $160/drum[c]
Specific Wastes and Treatment Types	
Cyanide, by chemical oxidation	$2.30–2.80/gallon or $210/drum, including disposal. Range reflects cyanide concentration.[c]
Cyanide, by sodium hypochlorite	$0.65–4.00/gallon[d]
Cyanide, by calcium polysulfide	$0.05–1.00/gallon[d]
Metal sludges, by hydrometallurgical recycling	$195/ton[e]
Industrial waste acids, by electrodialysis	$0.57/gallon[f]
Halogenated and nonhalogenated organic solvents, by distillation	approximately $0.26/gallon[g] to $1.42/gallon[h] small system: $0.47/gallon[i] large system: $0.20/gallon[i]
Wastewater, by solar evaporation	$0.65/gallon, $84/drum[a]
Waste oils, by re-refining[j]	$0.10–0.40/gallon for a 10-million-gallon plant[d]

(continues)

BOX 5.1 *(continued)*

"Traditional" treatment and disposal costs vary widely. Evaporating volatile solvents, where permitted, may cost only a fixed permit fee, e.g., $50–1,000 per source. Sewer discharge fees range from about $20/ton to $400/ton and will be more expensive as they become subject to tighter controls. Susan Sherry, "Reducing Industrial Toxic Wastes and Discharges" (Sacramento, Calif.: Local Government Commission, 1988), 6–9. Landfilling hazardous wastes typically costs about $350/ton, but this figure will also rise as disposal capacity shrinks; furthermore, liability costs would inflate this figure if they were factored in. High-temperature incineration can be very expensive (as much as $1,500/ton) for difficult-to-destroy wastes that require long residence times in the kilns as well as very high temperatures. David J. Sarokin, Warren R. Muir, Catherine G. Miller, and Sebastian R. Sperber, *Cutting Chemical Wastes: What 29 Organic Chemical Plants Are Doing to Reduce Hazardous Wastes* (New York: INFORM, Inc., 1985), 145.

[a]Gordon M. Evans, "Cost Perspectives for Hazardous Waste Management," in Harry Freeman, ed., *Standard Handbook of Hazardous Waste Treatment and Disposal* (New York: McGraw-Hill, 1988), 14, 15.

[b]1985. Cost information was not available for the range from 500 to 25,000 ppm.

[c]Price quote as of July 31, 1991, for services at Chemical Waste Management's Kettleman Hills facility in California.

[d]California Department of Health Services, Toxic Substances Control Division, Alternative Technology and Policy Development Section, "Alternative Technology for Recycling and Treatment of Hazardous Wastes: The Third Biennial Report" (July 1986), 72–73, 75–78.

[e]S. Wayne Rosenbaum, "Hydrometallurgical Recycling of Metal Sludge," in California Department of Health Services, symposium proceedings, *Metal Waste Management Alternatives: Minimizing, Recycling, and Treating Hazardous Metal Wastes* (September 12–13, 1989, Pasadena, Calif., and 18–19, San Jose, Calif.), 147.

[f]Carolyn H. Byszewski and K. N. Mani, "Aquatech™ Systems: A Technology for Metal Waste," in California Department of Health Services, symposium proceedings, *Metal Waste Management Alternatives*, 126.

[g]Virginia Polytechnic Institute and State University, "Hazardous Waste Management in Virginia: Alternatives to Land Disposal of Untreated Wastes," final report (December 1, 1984), 61–63.

[h]California State Governor's Task Force on Toxics, Waste, and Technology, final report, vol. 1 (May 1986), 125.

[i]Seymour I. Schwartz, Wendy Pratt Cuckovich, Nancy Steffenson-Ostrom, and Cecilia F. Cox, "Managing Hazardous Wastes Produced by Small Quantity Generators," Senate Office of Research, California Legislature (April 1987), 88.

[j]Waste oils, especially automotive oil, can be re-refined or recycled using various techniques such as filtration, distillation, chemical treatment, and solvent treatment. Unfortunately, waste oils tend to be burned as fuel without any such treatment and are still considered "recycled" by most administrative standards.

It may be difficult to generalize about cost savings from solvent distillation because solvents vary so widely in base price, and because the costs of process changes have not always favored recovery. But as with the example of metal sludges, solvent distillation can produce valuable products, in some cases worth as much as $600 a ton.[4]

Source Reduction and Waste Minimization

Rather than relying on traditional land disposal or available treatment technologies, both industry and government by the end of the 1980s had begun to pay increasing attention to methods for producing less waste, thereby achieving what is generally termed "source reduction." These activities go to the heart of modern manufacturing and production processes and as such cannot easily be illustrated fully.

There are probably as many ways to accomplish source reduction as there are separate manufacturing technologies and methods. The basic principle remains clear: Adopt a strategy that moves hazardous waste management as high up as possible on the source reduction hierarchy (shown in Box 4.5). The concept is to maximize the efficiency of our industrial processes in terms of their generation of hazardous waste by-products.

In general, the hierarchy favors reducing the use of hazardous materials, then lowering the extent to which industrial processes generate wastes, then controlling management of those wastes that have been generated. It is not feasible for all industries to follow the exact order of this hierarchy all the time; some options simply do not exist for all firms, and many firms will find themselves operating simultaneously at several different points on the hierarchy.

Source reduction can be achieved by producing a different product (product substitution), by reformulating industrial processes to produce the same end product by using fewer hazardous raw materials, or by generating fewer hazardous wastes. Product substitution can be attractive if a firm can market the new product successfully, but it may require larger investments.

Consumer reluctance can be a problem, too, as Monsanto Company's experience demonstrates. Monsanto reformulated an adhesive to avoid a filtration step that had produced waste particulate matter and contaminated filters. Two years of marketing and persuasion were needed, however, before Monsanto could convince its major customer that the reformulated product retained all its former attractive adhesive properties.[5]

Source reduction combines economic and environmental advantages by saving money while helping lessen burdens on the environment. Ventura County, California, decided in 1986 to provide county assistance and incentives for local firms to ease dependence on land disposal of hazardous wastes, mainly through implementing onsite programs for source reduction. The county health department identified the region's 75 largest waste generators and visited all of them personally to help them conduct waste audits and to identify attractive opportunities for source reduction. In less than two years, these generators as a group were able to achieve almost a 90 percent reduction in land disposal (mostly through source reduction and, to a lesser extent, with onsite treatment).

In San Diego County in 1987, General Dynamics decided to implement a comprehensive source reduction program targeted at chromium wastes. After an intensive waste stream audit, the company carried out the steps identified, at a cost of some $4 million. The company achieved a 98 percent reduction in chromium waste generation, recovering its costs in less than four years because the firm had been paying about $1 million a year to dispose of these wastes.

Hazardous materials management is an important part of source control, because it can make the difference between contaminating groundwater (if hazardous materials are stored in leaky underground storage tanks), releasing life-threatening emissions (as in the case of Bhopal, India), or simply posing a fire hazard where hazardous materials are stored (these issues are covered in depth in Chapter Six). In some cases, hazardous materials management involves high costs. Requiring all underground storage tanks to be double-lined imposes large retrofit costs on many companies. Sound materials management also calls for expensive monitoring and careful employee training.

Modifying a process generally involves some kind of equipment or procedural change. Often, these steps save money while reducing waste streams. When Exxon installed 16 floating roofs in chemical storage tanks (at a cost of $5,000 to $13,000 each), it saved annually nearly 700,000 pounds of organic chemicals valued at over $200,000.[6] The investment in source reduction paid for itself in the first year. Apel, Szabo, and Ludwig describe a plant using a bead-blast paint stripper to remove paint mechanically—rather like a sand-blaster—instead of stripping surfaces chemically with methylene chloride.[7] This process modification did not change the endproduct in any way, but saved the company from having to dispose of 10,000 tons of methylene chloride wastes a year, though paint chips produced still had to be sent offsite for incineration. Process modifications can return savings in production costs, and they demand some research and development expense and capital investment that may be localized by certain firms, diminishing the broader impact.[8] Better "housekeeping" can be a relatively easy way to cut back on excessive use of hazardous materials, thereby reducing the possibility of spills or accidents.

The step below source reduction in the hierarchy is to manage better those hazardous wastes still being generated. Separating wastes from each other usually involves fairly simple changes that can be attractive economically. Once segregated, valuable wastes can be recycled and others treated at relatively low cost, leaving a smaller volume of waste for expensive treatment and disposal.

At times, recycling can even be done in-line, within the production process, with recycled materials returned to the process. This method can avoid the need to obtain a complicated and costly RCRA permit. Other systems recycle after production. Recycling can also take place offsite at commercial facilities. Onsite recycling saves substantial material input costs and may also lower a company's liability because it can control the fate of most of its wastes at first hand. In contrast, offsite operators do not necessarily assume all liability for the wastes they accept and recycle. Private recyclers have other difficulties. They must obtain an EPA or state RCRA Part B permit; often require relatively uniform waste streams; must establish long-term business relationships to guarantee reliable sources of waste streams; and must set their prices to make a profit and a return on investment.

In-process recycling has great regulatory advantages because it is exempt from formal RCRA permitting. Well-designed systems can be very attractive economically too. A zero-discharge reverse osmosis recycling system developed by a firm in Minneapolis can completely recycle the waste stream from many metal-plating baths. The system separates the waste stream into clean water suitable for return to the rinse tanks in the process line, and plating-strength liquids ready for reuse. Liquids between these extremes are reprocessed through the reverse osmosis membrane until finally ready for reuse either in the plating or the rinse tanks.

CONSTRAINTS ON THE DEVELOPMENT
OF NEEDED CAPACITY

Not enough onsite and commercial offsite treatment facilities of the types described in this chapter are appearing in the United States, despite land disposal bans, mounting costs (and cost-effective alternatives), and hefty policy pressures favoring treatment over land disposal. Why? A number of complicated factors have come together to constrain successful development. The factors are outlined briefly in the following discussion;

some of the issues, such as facility siting and local opposition, are treated more fully later.

Permitting Requirements

It is extremely difficult to obtain the RCRA Part B permit normally required to operate a hazardous waste treatment facility. The permit process is complex, cumbersome, costly, time-consuming, and frustrating in the extreme. Neither EPA nor the states have yet devised effective mechanisms for reviewing permit applications, responding to both technical concerns and public comments, and issuing RCRA permits in a timely fashion. Often two or three years elapse and perhaps $500,000 to $1 million of costs are incurred before a company reaches the end of the federal permitting process; even then, further state permits and local land-use approvals may be needed before the treatment facility can be built.

After 1984, the new corrective-action requirements in HSWA made Part B permitting even more undesirable for most applicants. Now any application for a RCRA permit triggers full scrutiny for any past hazardous waste spills, leaks, or other mismanagement. Although identification of these problems at thousands of industrial sites not previously covered under RCRA—except as generators exempt from the permitting process provided they get rid of their hazardous wastes every 90 days—may be excellent environmental policy overall, the requirements to complete a RCRA facility assessment and perhaps even a more detailed RCRA facility investigation under HSWA's corrective-action rules have a definite chilling effect on any firm's willingness to pursue onsite treatment options that would require a RCRA permit.

Most hazardous waste treatment systems also call for a slew of additional permits from an alphabet of federal, state, and local regulatory agencies. These permits cover emissions under federal and state clean air rules; discharges of liquids under the federal Clean Water Act and similar state laws; hazardous materials storage and use of underground storage tanks; and local land-use permissions. Any or all of these requirements may prove troublesome and engender further public scrutiny of the firm's activities as a whole.

Facility Siting

Economic and political constraints to development of new hazardous waste treatment facilities are discussed in great detail in Chapter Seven, but we should note here that public opposition has been a constraint on siting not only traditional land disposal facilities but also the newer, safer treatment facilities. Local opposition to any facility remotely connected with hazardous materials and wastes has remained high. Many people feel a facility of this kind, no matter how small or safe, could set a precedent for more such operations in the area. Furthermore, citizen groups often feel betrayed after their experiences with former dump sites and with dangerous, older leaky hazardous waste facilities. Residents near any prospective site find it difficult to grasp the advantages to society of developing safer new treatment facilities over the disadvantages of maintaining the status quo. Thus, even though it seems rational to push for more and safer treatment facilities so that less-safe landfills can be closed, local opposition in the immediate areas selected is still heavily influenced by the nagging memories of past hazardous waste mismanagement practices.

Liability

Firms, especially large corporations, are desperately afraid of Superfund's overarching liability provisions—and for good cause,[9] as noted in Chapter Two. Most do not see any way the potential profits from owning and operating a new hazardous waste treatment facility can possibly compensate for the potential risks of being held accountable for the cleanup of a spill, leak, or other accident involving hazardous materials at that facility. Investors are convinced that they can make more money on condos or junk bonds—with a lot less risk—than on a new hazardous waste treatment facility. Even when the facts dictate otherwise, fear of Superfund liability makes many firms unwilling to proceed into the hazardous waste treatment business.

Moreover, the great difficulty in obtaining pollution liability insurance further constrains corporations' willingness to proceed with financing, siting, and developing new hazardous waste treatment facilities.

Marketplace Uncertainty and Competition from Cheaper Facilities

Overall, the market for hazardous waste management services is fraught with uncertainty. Data are unavailable, inaccurate, obsolete. Regulations change constantly. Volumes projected to arrive at a new offsite facility may never emerge. Wastes flow across state and even national boundaries; local generators may send their wastes to out-of-state facilities. Some firms will generate more wastes in the future, but others will practice source reduction, thereby significantly cutting back their waste streams. Many firms may choose to treat their wastes onsite, using new fixed or transportable treatment units of various kinds. All these factors make highly uncertain the projections of future demand for treatment capacity at a particular treatment unit.

Even if these fundamental market uncertainties could be eased, developers of new facilities would face potentially severe competition from both existing and new ones. Existing landfills, as long as they are allowed to remain in operation, can undercut the prices a new treatment facility will charge to cover its capital and operating costs. These existing landfills were built some years ago and capitalized (except for cleanup costs) at that time. Consequently, as long as federal and state land disposal restrictions are not fully enforced, price competition makes investments in many treatment facilities a very risky proposition. (Of course, in the absence of any newly funded and built treatment facilities, full enforcement of the land disposal bans remains highly unlikely. Where are these wastes supposed to go?) This aspect of the facility-siting conundrum represents an important constraint on development of needed new treatment capacity.

In a similar vein, developers of proposed new treatment facilities are concerned about potential competition for critical waste streams from existing or new treatment facilities. Potential owners of new incinerators, for example, might be concerned that high-BTU waste streams that compose an important and profitable portion of their projected market might be sent instead to existing (or new) solvent recovery plants, or to cement kilns.

Part of this complicated puzzle of competitive advantage or disadvantage relates to the truth that all hazardous waste treatment systems leave some residue (ash, sludge, and so on) requiring ultimate land disposal. Firms that do not own licensed, permitted hazardous waste landfills often express concern that they will be unable to dispose of their treatment residues, at least at prices that will be acceptable, because their competitors own the landfills and thus would be able to dictate both price and availability.

Furthermore, any developer of a new treatment facility is concerned about competition from an opposite direction: the next facility to be built, perhaps one incorporating newer, more efficient technology and thus able to undercut the first developer's prices. This is a typical problem in any technology-related market segment, but it seems particularly vital in hazardous waste management because many of the acceptable treatment technologies are being defined by the EPA treatment standards associated with land disposal bans. Onsite and transportable technologies that might enter the market in the near future represent further threats to the potential market share of any new offsite treatment plant.

Source Reduction as a Constraint on Siting

The many attractive advantages of source reduction and waste minimization are a central component of any successful modern toxics management strategy. At the same time, ironically enough, the growing focus on source reduction further constrains the ability of the hazardous waste management industry to develop new offsite treatment capacity. Much of the reason behind this counterintuitive situation lies in the increased marketplace uncertainty already noted. More source reduction means fewer wastes to be treated; but how much reduction will really occur? Besides, the very focus on source reduction makes siting harder, because every facility-siting proposal now encounters the same refrain from environmental groups and local communities: "We prefer source reduction instead." Developers are hard-pressed to respond effectively when that specific citizen challenge combines with the inherent strengths of the "not-in-my-back-yard" (NIMBY) movement to make siting approval even less likely.

LESSONS FROM ABROAD

We have reviewed some of the options already available for hazardous waste treatment and reduction as well as some cases of industry success with waste minimization. The United States can learn powerful lessons from the success of other industrial societies in managing their hazardous wastes. Indeed, many such countries today are applying treatment technologies to a much larger proportion of their waste stream than is the United States. This further suggests that constraints on successful hazardous waste management in the United States are not primarily technical but organizational, institutional, political, and economic.

Many of the data-collection problems existing in the United States also plague other countries. As here, only very rough aggregate figures of hazardous waste generation over time are generally available abroad. Questionnaires or surveys of particular industries suffer from shaky reliability, and it is often difficult to find waste data classified consistently. As a result, it is hard to establish baseline figures that can serve reliably to evaluate the effectiveness of hazardous waste treatment or waste minimization programs.[10] These uncertainties point to the utility of comparing waste minimization based on relative program inputs and efforts.[11]

Most industrial countries that have hazardous waste management programs that can be compared with those in the United States are much smaller, with substantially different political economies. Is it realistic to compare, say, Denmark—a country with a population and per-capita hazardous waste stream only 3 percent that of the U.S. counterpart—with the American experience? Yes, if only because Denmark and several other countries appear to have dealt more successfully with similar wastes and similar political and economic obstacles.

Denmark is often cited as the country with the world's most progressive overall hazardous waste management program.[12] This country consciously offers substantial economic incentives and subsidies to those industries willing to adopt process modifications or new, low-waste technologies, both of which are subsidized at 25 percent of their cost to that industry.[13]

For the remaining wastes, Denmark insists on comprehensive treatment, either onsite (by those larger firms that choose to do so) or at a central treatment facility that accepts almost all the hazardous wastes treated offsite in the country. This central facility offers incineration for organic chemical wastes and solvents, oil re-refining, and waste neutralization, followed by land disposal of the hazardous sludges and filter cakes obtained from these treatment processes.[14] These dewatered sludges and solids are placed in a specially designed repository (landfill) continuously covered on top (as well as on its bottom and sides) with a plastic liner. This cover prevents entry of precipitation, thus reducing to near zero the chances of leachate that would threaten the area's groundwater. An extensive network of collection sites (at least one in each municipality) reduces the distances hazardous wastes must travel (primarily by rail) to reach the central treatment facility, which makes it easy and economical for Danish industries to use the facility. In addition, Denmark is in the vanguard for new approaches to collecting household hazardous wastes (see Box 5.2).

The entire Danish system is owned and operated by Kommunekemi, Inc. (Community Chemical Company). An interesting hybrid entity neither fully private nor fully governmental, Kommunekemi is a private corporation, exempt from civil service, all the stock of which is owned by the Danish government and the country's several municipalities. Kommunekemi received extensive subsidies and low-interest loans from the Danish government to construct its initial facilities in the early 1980s; modernized, expanded facilities were then built in the late 1980s without further subsidy.

Japan, too, has successfully sited numerous hazardous waste treatment facilities tailored to specific industries. Akin to the Danish system, a public-private partnership—the Environmental Pollution Control Service Corporation—provides subsidized loans to firms for purchasing and installing pollution control equipment and onsite treatment systems. This

138

 BOX 5.2

Which Way Is Best to Collect Hazardous Wastes?
by Michael Johansson

A regulation effective January 1, 1991 mandates the 275 Danish municipalities to collect household hazardous waste such as oil, chemicals, paint, solvents, etc. Although the government mandates collection, municipalities may design their own collection schemes.

Some cities have arranged with paint shops, for example, to accept household paints and solvents. The shops receive a token payment from the city for this service. The municipalities are responsible for further handling of the waste. Major advantages of these schemes are that most people live or work near a shop, and that the shop staff can assist with advice on how to handle the waste. Major disadvantages are that the shops—unlike the municipal installations—accept only fractions of the waste, and that they are not given a sufficient economic incentive to run the schemes.

Manned mobile containers have been widely used. The manned containers are placed in neighborhoods or near shops once or twice a year. . . .

Last year, some municipalities tried to improve the mobile container scheme by introducing a special collection van. The van, manned with skilled staff, takes a fixed route six to twelve times a year, stops every 100 to 200 yards, and rings a bell. Each stop lasts approximately five to seven minutes, and all kinds of hazardous waste are accepted. The van has the great advantage of minimizing the distance the consumers have to carry their waste. A serious drawback is the short duration of the stop. Even if you're just a few minutes late, you have to take your waste back home. Again, some people solve this problem by putting out their waste in advance.

At present, the highest level of service is offered by a few municipalities who supply the households with a special hazardous waste plastic box (approx. 2 cubic feet) and a sorting instruction (what is hazardous waste and what is not). Normally, all types of hazardous waste are accepted. The boxes are collected from the households on fixed dates at least twice a year, and, in some cases, every month. The households must normally put their own box out in advance. . . .

(continues)

BOX 5.2 *(continued)*

Recently, the Danish Association of Local Municipalities and the Danish Consumer Council have compared a number of the collection schemes with regard to price, efficiency and participation. . . .

. . . [T]he "proximity" of the scheme influences the quantities separated. Thus, the permanent installations are the least efficient, while the box and perhaps the van are the most efficient. It is also evident that a price must be paid for high efficiency. The more efficient schemes are also the more expensive ones. This simple conclusion does not pay respect to the fact that cheaper schemes will sometimes be sufficient to ensure that a significant part of the hazardous waste is separated from the rest of the waste. A choice between collection schemes must depend on the actual urban and socio-economic situation in the area where the scheme is to be used.

Source: Reprinted with permission from *BioCycle* (J.G. Press, Inc.), June 1991, p. 39. Permission granted to reprint as adapted.

corporation also constructs new offsite treatment facilities where needed. Japan is even more constrained geographically than are most heavily industrialized Western European nations. Consequently, land disposal has long been out of favor there as a hazardous waste management option. Another quasi-governmental organization, Clean Japan Center, offers awards for waste minimization, conducts research, and introduces new low-waste technologies through demonstration pilot plants.[15]

Similar programs and facilities exist in other industrial countries like Sweden, the Netherlands, and West Germany. Some important conditions exist in all these countries that might make their experiences difficult to apply to U.S. policymaking. First, size matters. For example, New Jersey or California might never be forced to "contain" all their hazardous waste management options within their own borders, because there is the perception that there will always be states like Nevada or New York or Arkansas available to receive some of their wastes. However, opposition to out-of-state waste is growing, as indicated by the formation in 1990 of States for Responsible and Equitable Waste Management, a group of 13 states that are "tired of being the country's hazardous waste dumping grounds."[16] Such thinking is more difficult for a nation-state like Denmark or Japan, where many conflicting demands are placed on land and where transboundary pollution effects are quickly felt and widely understood.

Size also plays a role if a small country generates a relatively small per-capita waste stream, as in the case of Sweden or Denmark. A small industrial base, coupled with good recycling programs, may be served well by just a few treatment facilities; fewer facilities may mean fewer battles with local communities for siting acceptance.

The European picture has not been entirely rosy, however. Wastes that do not enter the modern treatment system (the amount may be as high as 50 percent in many countries) are often sent to unlined landfills or dumped untreated into the Atlantic Ocean, Baltic, North Sea, or Mediterranean. Many West German hazardous wastes were sent to a large landfill in East Germany, reportedly one from which leachate enters groundwater at a rapid rate. In Denmark, the Kommunekemi incinerator destroys large volumes of waste oils from the nearby ferry system for their high BTU value (perhaps because of Europe's high energy costs compared with U.S. costs); such wastes are typically recycled in the United States today. The United Kingdom remains highly dependent on the kinds of land disposal facilities no longer favored in the United States. The situation in Eastern Europe is even worse.

Italy received its share of bad publicity in 1987 and 1988 when it was discovered that several shipments of Italian hazardous wastes were being refused entry all around the world. Indeed, whether it is an East Germany accepting West Germany's "worst wastes," or Guinea-Bissau or Nigeria refusing U.S. and other European wastes, the picture is the same: Governments pressed for hard currency are becoming more and more reluctant to address economic concerns by forfeiting environmental safety.[17] These practices raise serious questions about the efficacy of European hazardous waste management efforts as a whole, despite the good track records several countries have in treatment and facility siting.

The second factor affecting easy transference of other countries' experience to the U.S. situation is that the environmental agencies of most European countries that sited treatment facilities in the 1970s and early 1980s enjoy more political legitimacy than do U.S. agencies that handle environmental policies. European counterpart agencies are considered to be reasonably competent on issues of waste management and policymaking in general. In Denmark and West Germany, the facility-siting process traditionally has been open to citizen involvement. Siting negotiations have lacked the NIMBY characteristics so prevalent in the United States, where confrontation is accepted as the norm. Moreover, traditional tolerance for central authority decisions is much stronger in Europe than in the United States, though Europeans do admit that since the late 1980s, they have encountered far more NIMBY-style resistance to siting proposals than was true earlier.

Third, these countries have relied on interactive corporate

arrangements to a greater extent than has been possible in the United States. Instead of merely pushing regulations on industry, West Germany, the Netherlands, and Denmark have brought industry directly into the policymaking process. These countries have also consciously blurred the distinction between public and private roles, especially regarding the financing, siting, building, and management of hazardous waste treatment facilities.[18] The assignment of responsibility for hazardous waste management programs to sympathetic agencies or concerned political leaders means that guidelines and standards are often set by the same people who will later be responsible for their implementation. Once again, the contrast with the United States is striking.

Finally, liability and insurance issues have not paralyzed waste management actors in Europe or Japan as they have in the United States. In Scandinavia or Japan, for example, social norms dictate less reliance on litigation than in the United States. Furthermore, Japan has embedded within that country's environmental agency a compensatory fund: the Pollution-Related Health Damage Compensation Association.

In general, these four crucial aspects have led to more and better treatment abroad of hazardous wastes through use of available technologies. Again, the issue for the United States is not the availability of technology but its political and economic underpinnings. Not surprisingly, the relationship between treatment and source reduction in Europe and Japan has been similar to the U.S. situation. In light of other countries' experiences, U.S. advocates of source reduction may be right to fear that the availability of treatment facilities may relieve the perceived need to reduce the use of hazardous materials at the source. As far as we know, source reduction has been almost as difficult to implement abroad as it has in the United States. Moreover, U.S. policymakers in the late 1980s were supporting source reduction more overtly than were their counterparts abroad, although implementation of these policy goals has been slow and difficult to evaluate.

Western European and Japanese approaches to hazardous waste management appear to have relied more on end-of-the-pipe treatment rather than on reduction of the waste stream in the first place, an emphasis that may reflect different starting points in these two regions regarding industrial efficiency (and energy use) in general. U.S. consumption patterns tend to make source reduction more difficult than in Europe or Japan.

However, that attitude may be a result of the nature of source reduction and state intervention in industrial societies. It is difficult to (1) impose or induce source reduction practices in industry or (2) confirm the effects of municipal and industrial policy or program changes on hazardous materials use and generation. In the face of such uncertainty, it is naturally attractive to do what can be done—build treatment plants and collection facilities, close landfills, set up waste exchanges, and so on. Once facilities are operating, U.S. policymakers depend on treatment and disposal costs to encourage source reduction, although that linkage is very difficult to establish.

Geiser, Fischer, and Beecher have summarized the lessons to be learned from Europe in the following points. First, government can play a significant and effective role in aiding, guiding, and encouraging hazardous waste minimization efforts among industries. Second, this role does not replace the need for strong and well-enforced environmental regulations; rather, guidance and support reinforce the impact of regulations. Third, such programs place some sections of government in a cooperative and collaborative relationship with the innovative and planning-oriented elements of private industrial management. Fourth, such programs comprehensively link the prevention of environmental pollution with the need to improve and develop overall industrial productivity.[19]

Given America's enormous hazardous waste load and the current growth in federal and state waste minimization policies, source reduction is assuming a growing priority in the new technology improvements being adopted by industry. New policy options will greatly accelerate this process by favoring incentives for process or product modifications requiring fewer hazardous materials inputs.

Modular treatment technologies can also be emphasized and easily adapted to a number of different situations. For example, a modular hazardous waste incinerator may encounter less local opposition if it can be shown it will be installed only for, say, five years or for the duration of a specific cleanup task. Similarly, that same incinerator could be transferred from one municipal or corporate entity to another in a regional association or compact. We pursue these issues in Chapter Eight, but first we consider hazardous materials management and facility siting.

NOTES

1. By *effective* waste treatment, we do not mean the kinds of waste disposal practices so prevalent in the past and often still in use today. Such disposal methods include deep-well injection, discharge into sewers and waterways, impoundment of wastes in surface ponds or lagoons, disposal of untreated wastes in clay-lined hazardous waste landfills, inadequate ("phony" or "sham") recycling, and incomplete incineration.

2. Steve Lohr, "Site for Toxic-Waste Cave Stirs Texas Political Fight," *New York Times* (May 6, 1991).

3. S. Wayne Rosenbaum, "Hydrometallurgical Recycling of Metal Sludge," in California Department of Health Services, symposium proceedings, *Metal Waste Management Alternatives: Minimizing, Recycling, and Treating Hazardous Metal Wastes* (September 12–13, 1989, Pasadena, Calif., and 18–19, 1989, San Jose, Calif.), 147.

4. David Sarokin, Warren Muir, Catherine Miller, and Sebastian Sperber, *Cutting Chemical Wastes: What 29 Organic Chemical Plants Are Doing to Reduce Hazardous Waste* (New York: INFORM, Inc., 1985), 382.

5. Sarokin et al., *Cutting Chemical Wastes*, 89.

6. Sarokin et al., *Cutting Chemical Wastes*, 310–325.

7. M. Lynn Apel, Michael F. Szabo, and Robert Ludwig, "Pollution Prevention Through Innovative Source Reduction Technologies," paper presented at the Air and Waste Management Association, 82d Annual Meeting and Exhibition, (Anaheim, Calif., June 25–30, 1989), 8.

8. Virginia Polytechnic Institute and State University, "Hazardous Waste Management in Virginia: Alternatives to Land Disposal of Untreated Wastes," final report (December 1, 1984), 58.

9. David Stipp, "Toxic Turpitude: Environmental Crime Can Land Executives in Prison These Days," *Wall Street Journal* (September 10, 1990).

10. Katy Wolf, "Source Reduction: What Is It and How Can We Accomplish It?" unpublished manuscript (June 1989), 1–3; Kenneth Geiser, Kurt Fischer, and Norman Beecher, "Foreign Practices in Hazardous Waste Minimization," report to the U.S. Environmental Protection Agency (Medford, Mass: Center for Environmental Management, Tufts University, August 1986), 9.

11. Office of Technology Assessment, U.S. Congress, "From Pollution to Prevention: A Progress Report on Waste Reduction" (June 1987), 23–25.

12. William R. Mangun, "A Comparative Analysis of Hazardous Waste Management Policy in Western Europe," in Charles E. Davis and James P. Lester, eds., *Dimensions of Hazardous Waste Politics and Policy* (New York: Greenwood Press, 1988), 213.

13. Geiser, Fischer, and Beecher, "Foreign Practices," 185.

14. Operators of the Danish treatment system keep the cost of incineration for recoverable solvents high, thereby ensuring the survival of small recyclers of solvents. A similar situation exists in the case of copper and precious metals.

15. Geiser, Fischer, and Beecher, "Foreign Practices," 54–55.

16. Marie Frohnauer, "States Cry for CAP Enforcement," *Hazmat World* (November 1990), 12.

17. Tyler Marshall, "West Europe Has Its Fill of Toxic Waste," *Los Angeles Times* (February 28, 1989); Carol Cirulli, "Toxic Boomerang," *The Amicus Journal* 11 (Winter 1989), 9–11; Harry Anderson, Ruth Marshall, Christopher Dickey, Michael Meyer, Theodore Stranger, and Taiwo Obe, "The Global Poison Trade," *Newsweek* (November 7, 1988), 66–68; H. Jeffrey Leonard, ed., *Divesting Nature's Capital: The Political Economy of Environmental Abuse in the Third World* (New York: Holmes and Meier, 1985). For a global analysis of the hazardous wastes trade

and policy options, see Christopher Hilz and John R. Ehrenfeld, "Transboundary Movements of Hazardous Wastes—A Comparative Analysis of Policy Options to Control the International Waste Trade, *International Environmental Affairs* 3 (Winter 1991), 3–25.

18. Mangun, "A Comparative Analysis," 212.

19. Geiser, Fischer, and Beecher, "Foreign Practices," 24.

C H A P T E R   S I X

Beyond Hazardous Waste: Safe Management of Hazardous and Toxic Materials

America's first toxics decade began with deep concern for how poorly America had managed its hazardous wastes. By middecade that issue had mushroomed into an all-out drive for better and safe management not only of wastes but of all hazardous materials in the workplace, the home, and throughout the environment.

The Bhopal accident in late 1984 and similar industrial accidents elsewhere revealed that inadequate waste management alone played only a minor part in the overall toxics problem. Everyday industry as well as agriculture and consumers were exposed to and using hazardous *materials* thousands of times greater in volume, accessibility, and potential harm than all the *wastes* from industrial and commercial activities.

In the mid-1980s it became obvious that the underground aquifers so vital to the nation's drinking-water supply were threatened far more by leaks from the "normal" storage of gasoline and chemical feedstocks in underground tanks than from any leaks from Superfund hazardous waste sites. Cleanups of waste sites numbered 10,000 to 30,000; cleanup of underground tanks numbered perhaps 3 million.

Similarly, fire fighters and emergency response workers were far likelier to be exposed in the course of their daily activities to risks from all kinds of hazardous materials used and stored by business and industry than from the onsite ponds and lagoons where those firms' wastes may have been dumped. Hazardous waste management was not of much concern to fire departments; hazardous materials management was.

Once it was public, detailed information on hazardous materials usage at existing industrial facilities engendered enormous and intense public interest, particularly from the communities surrounding those facilities. Risks of toxic accidents suddenly seemed plausible even from plants believed previously to be perfectly safe. Consequently, in some areas facilities once considered desirable economically were being questioned.

The NIMBY phrase that represented resistance to siting new facilities gained a new sibling: GOOMBY (get out of my backyard).

It had become painfully clear that hazardous wastes were merely the tip of the toxics iceberg. In a few short years, public concern over industry's management of hazardous materials had begun to rival in intensity the focus on cleaning up the toxics legacy of the past. The overall problem of what to do about toxics was far more difficult for the nation to cope with than had ever been imagined. No longer could toxics management be restricted to hazardous wastes; by the mid-1980s, and with increasing attention thereafter, effective management of hazardous materials became the focus.

Abandoned hazardous waste sites and even the management of on-going generation of hazardous wastes had been primarily in the federal domain, with federal legislation providing much of the impetus for activity. In contrast, the hazardous materials management effort began at state or even local levels of government; these jurisdictions still handle most of these activities today. For example, underground tank regulations emerged initially in Suffolk County (Long Island), New York, and in Santa Clara County (Silicon Valley), California, in response to local uproars over contamination of underground aquifers serving as primary drinking-water sources. Reporting on hazardous materials usage began with state laws in New Jersey and California; their local and state regulatory innovations quickly spread nationwide, especially after toxics disasters in Bhopal and elsewhere became major media stories.

In 1986, Congress took its first step toward dealing with effective hazardous materials management nationwide. Title III of the Superfund amendments (SARA) had nothing to do with Superfund site cleanup. It required industry to begin to report on its overall use of hazardous materials. In 1990, federal law upped the ante substantially, this time in requirements embedded in amendments to the Clean Air Act. Firms using particularly dangerous chemicals must now devise and implement comprehensive risk management plans.

As with other aspects of America's first toxics decade, our incremental approach to dealing effectively with the vast volumes of dangerous chemicals in use, storage, and transport through the industrial complex brought numerous small successes—and generalized failure. The scope of the problem and one example of success in dealing with it were evidenced in the ability of 15 different fire agencies in Silicon Valley to issue permits to over 4,000 facilities that store and use hazardous chemicals. Each facility was inspected at least once by a fire department hazardous materials team; some were revisited several times. (To expand this local program nationwide would involve issuing hazardous materials storage permits to some 500,000 facilities.)

The complexity of managing hazardous materials is illustrated by the failure, also in California, to implement the new state laws requiring strict management of extremely hazardous substances. Once again, as in other aspects of toxics management, rhetoric far outpaced reality. Passing new laws in response to public outcry was far easier than implementing those laws successfully. Dealing with this kind of superfailure would be the primary challenge of the second toxics decade.

STATE INITIATIVES: STRONGER ENFORCEMENT AND REGULATION

During the second half of the 1980s, a number of states adopted strict enforceable rules designed to control purchase, transportation, storage, use, and ultimate disposition of a wide range of hazardous materials. These stringent state regulatory efforts seem likely to spread rapidly during the 1990s throughout the nationwide system of environmental federalism.

Within this aspect of toxics management, federalism has been particularly pronounced; several states have passed strict laws regulating use of especially dangerous materials, far beyond what has so far been required nationally. Again, actions in New Jersey and California are noteworthy.

New Jersey's Toxic Catastrophe Prevention Act

The Toxic Catastrophe Prevention Act (TCPA) was enacted by New Jersey's legislature in 1985 as an explicit response both to Bhopal and to a score of accidental chemical releases in New Jersey involving storage and use of extremely hazardous substances. The state's Department of Environmental Protection (DEP) has primary responsibility for implementing TCPA, but local agencies are also involved.

TCPA defined a set of 11 extremely hazardous substances (EHSs), accidental release of which could produce acute health effects. This law set threshold quantities for each substance, above which TCPA's reporting and planning requirements took effect. DEP later expanded the list to well over 100 chemicals, with thresholds varying from 10 to 34,000 pounds.

Any facility in New Jersey handling any of these substances in excess of defined volumes must register with DEP. Information to be provided includes

- an inventory of each EHS generated, stored, or handled at the facility, with quantities for each;

- general description of processes and principal equipment involved;
- overall extent of risks and hazards involved;
- profile of the area where the facility is located;
- names of all insurance carriers underwriting a facility's environmental liability and workers' compensation risks.

TCPA goes far beyond the subsequent federal SARA Title III requirements (detailed later) by ensuring that every facility handling EHSs in New Jersey develops a full-fledged risk management program designed to minimize the effect of any accidents involving the chemicals. The plans must include review of the facility design from a safety viewpoint; standard operating procedures; preventive maintenance programs; operator training; accident investigation procedures; risk assessments for specific pieces of equipment; and detailed emergency response planning. These plans are akin to those now required nationally under the 1990 Clean Air Act.

By mid-1989, existing facilities in New Jersey had to develop such programs. All proposed new facilities handling EHSs must submit a safety review, hazard analysis, and risk assessment at least 90 days before construction can begin. The rules also apply to proposed modifications to existing plants. After reviewing the risk assessment, DEP can order selected facilities to undertake risk reduction plans. The state agency has other strong enforcement powers, and the law contains provisions for substantial penalties for violations. Local ordinances inconsistent with TCPA—including any that attempt to impose stricter requirements—must be approved by DEP.

California's Approach

California began in the mid-1980s to introduce a number of innovations in managing highly toxic materials and is adding new requirements at an accelerating pace. Some innovations extend to many more California facilities several planning and reporting requirements similar to those of federal SARA Title III. Others impose stringent risk management requirements on selected facilities (as in New Jersey). And one California voter initiative places unique restrictions on discharging and using chemicals that cause cancer or birth defects and requires public notification of exposures to a broader list of toxics.

Overall hazardous materials planning. Under one set of new rules, all local governments in California must develop programs to regulate hazardous materials storage by business as well as plans for emergency response to hazardous materials releases. Similar in many ways to subsequent SARA Title III planning requirements, these actions are being implemented in California by all 58 counties and an additional 62 cities in the state. Adopted in 1985, this statewide legislation was based on a model hazardous materials storage ordinance devised in 1983 by Santa Clara County. The state Office of Emergency Services (OES) has developed a model business plan reporting form and reviews the area plans developed by each of the 120 local "administering agencies." To help explain the welter of conflicting requirements, OES has also written a manual: "Hazardous Materials Emergency Planning and Community Right-to-Know: A Comparison of California and Federal Requirements."

Any California business handling hazardous materials or hazardous wastes above state threshold quantities must submit a business plan to its local administering agency and update it once a year. The business must also notify the local agency within 30 days of any substantial changes, including the introduction onto its premises of any new hazardous material. Reporting thresholds under this state law are consistent for all hazardous materials, but differ from federal standards.

Originally, the targets were simply 55 gallons of liquid, 500 pounds of solid, and 200 cubic feet of compressed gas. However, in an attempt to mesh state and subsequent federal (Title III) requirements facing the same businesses, the California legislature in 1988 amended the law to extend state requirements to those businesses previously covered only by federal rules (which have different reporting thresholds).

California business plans must contain detailed inventory information, including all chemicals and hazardous wastes handled by the firm, the amount of each material onsite, and where in the facility the chemicals are located (typically shown on a detailed site map).

Each business must report immediately the actual or threatened release of any hazardous material to its administering agency and OES. Any regulated business renting or leasing its location must notify the property owner if state reporting requirements apply and must provide the owner upon request with a copy of its plan. Business plans are open to public inspection at the administering agency's offices.

Besides reports from each business covered under the state law, each local administering agency must develop and maintain a plan for its area describing emergency response to actual or threatened releases of hazardous substances. These plans define procedures for public notification and evacuation, mutual aid among various local jurisdictions, containment of the accident, and subsequent follow-up. The plans must be updated every three years. Although they differ from the plans prepared under the federal hazardous materials planning program and indeed cover different geographic jurisdictions, these area plans are incorporated into SARA Title III plans on an ongoing basis.

Moreover, all these activities are integrated into the usual building and occupancy permit requirements enforced locally by every city and county in the state. Now local governments in California must include in all building permit applications (except for residential units) a space for applicants to identify whether they are subject to the state's hazardous materials planning requirements, to the state's risk management and prevention program rules, or to permitting requirements of the local air quality district. No city or county may issue a final occupancy permit for any facility unless the applicant provides proof from the appropriate government agencies that all such requirements have been or are being met.

Controlling risks from acutely hazardous materials. In 1986, the California legislature—partially in response to Bhopal—adopted legislation to expand regulatory control over materials that can produce toxic fumes after a fire, explosion, or other accident. The legislature drew on and expanded New Jersey's TCPA by designing a stringent planning and enforcement mechanism for all businesses handling acutely hazardous materials. The chemicals covered were those on EPA's list for chemical emergency preparedness. Adding unneeded complexity, California called these chemicals "acutely hazardous materials" (AHMs); EPA calls them "extremely hazardous substances" (EHSs).

In theory, every firm covered under California's program must register with the local administering agency. All new or modified facilities, and others if the local agency so chooses, must then develop and implement a detailed risk management and prevention program (RMPP) designed to prevent accidents involving acutely hazardous materials. They must also plan to respond effectively both to onsite and offsite consequences of any such accidents.

The RMPP covers specific equipment and procedures for handling AHMs; maintenance, control, and safety systems; and auditing and recordkeeping systems. Each RMPP also includes a study of the potential risks of such releases as well as an analysis of the consequences from a complete release of chemicals under adverse air quality conditions. Results of such studies will obviously engender intense interest from residents in the areas surrounding a particular facility.

This program is implemented by the same 120 local government agencies administering the state's basic hazardous materials program, again with limited state guidance from OES. Local agencies have the option of requiring an RMPP at any existing facility handling acutely hazardous materials. All new or modified facilities must submit a complete RMPP before they can begin handling these chemicals, and all RMPPs must be updated every three years.

In 1989, California introduced a further innovation, mandating that all firms required to have an RMPP consider explicitly in their risk assessments the proximity of any schools, hospitals, or long-term healthcare facilities. No new facility handling acutely hazardous materials can be located within 1,000 feet of a school unless an RMPP has first been approved by the local administering agency and certified by the local air quality district. Moreover, now an RMPP can be required even from facilities located that close to a school which do not handle acutely hazardous materials but pose "a reasonably foreseeable threat of a release of an air contaminant" if that release would cause "injury, detriment, nuisance or annoyance . . . or endanger the comfort, repose, health or safety" of any significant number of people at the school. Traditional air pollutants, even odors, are covered by this definition.

Local administering agencies are supposed to inspect each registered AHM facility at least once every three years to ensure it is fully implementing its RMPP (if one has been prepared) and is otherwise complying with the law. Finally, these overarching regulatory requirements for toxics are linked to local building and occupancy permit ordinances.

The California statute goes well beyond its New Jersey model and much beyond federal SARA Title III requirements, both of which focus almost entirely on reporting. RMPPs are comprehensive and complex documents. The analysis they contain of offsite risks can potentially produce a sharp emotional response from the surrounding public, especially from anyone living near existing facilities who has never before been given a reason (or any data) to be concerned about a particular industrial facility. The very real possibility is emerging that the now-widespread NIMBY opposition to proposed new hazardous waste management facilities (see Chapter Seven) may be joined by an emerging GOOMBY response to existing industrial plants.

Unfortunately, California has been very slow to implement these strict requirements. Administering agencies, swamped with their responsibilities for carrying out the basic hazardous materials law, have left the RMPP requirement and related rules for subsequent implementation. Only in 1991 was administrative momentum apparent from a significant number of administering agencies.

FEDERAL REPORTING AND MONITORING
OF HAZARDOUS MATERIALS

Frightened by the specter of a Bhopal-style toxics disaster striking the United States, Congress in 1986 expanded on state and local efforts like those in New Jersey and California. Added to the Superfund law was a new SARA Title III, the Emergency Planning and Community

Right-to-Know Act of 1986.[1] This law created four distinct sets of complex reporting and planning requirements covering these aspects of hazardous materials:

- planning for emergency response regarding extremely hazardous chemicals (SARA sections 301 to 303);
- reporting chemical inventory materials in the workplace (sections 311 and 312);
- reporting continuous emissions of selected toxic chemicals to air, water, or land (section 313);
- reporting leaks or spills of extremely hazardous substances (section 304).

Unfortunately, each of these four federal regulatory initiatives is built around a distinct—and different—list of toxic chemicals (see Box 6.1). The information being made public certainly comes in a highly complicated format.

Although reports of continuous emissions have captured the greatest public attention, the overall set of SARA Title III rules is rapidly bringing businesses throughout the country into a whole new era of toxics management. Rules on reporting and planning regarding industry's use of hazardous materials have been adopted nationwide. They require thousands of firms using specified hazardous chemicals to report details on the volumes being purchased, stored, and emitted. All these rules are having an enormous impact on businesses in terms of costs and compliance capabilities and an equally great effect on public attitudes toward businesses using hazardous materials.

Even so, enforcement has not paralleled data reporting, and some programs have foundered in confusion over agency roles and public/private responsibilities. As in other aspects of toxics policy in the 1980s, there is evidence of policy learning and some specific successes, but this progress is taking place against a backdrop of rapidly escalating public expectations and legal demands about the need to manage toxic materials wherever they exist—and of the near impossibility of doing so effectively. This overall policy failure further intensifies public fear and leads to demands for passage of still more toxics laws.

Emergency Planning

SARA requires each state governor to designate a state emergency response commission, which in turn designates local emergency planning districts, each with its own local emergency planning committee. Each committee must prepare a plan for responses within that district to any

BOX 6.1 Sections of SARA Title III

	Applicability	Requirements
Extremely Hazardous Substances (EHSs)	Based on threshold planning quantities (TPQs)	Submit inventory data
Section 311: Reporting Chemical Inventory	Facilities handling hazardous chemicals that require an MSDS, or any EHS in excess of either 500 pounds or the federal TPQ	Inventories must include CAS number, chemical and common names, and hazard category
Section 312: Annual Hazardous Materials Inventory Statements	Facilities that handle threshold quantities of hazardous material or any EHS	Report names, quantities, and location of all hazardous chemicals that are onsite for less than 24 hours if (1) the amounts are in excess of the established reporting thresholds and (2) the chemicals are not exempt from reporting under SARA Title III
Section 313: Toxic Chemical Release Inventory	Businesses that employ 10 or more people; and businesses classified in SIC codes 20-39; and businesses that use, manufacture, or process toxic chemicals above levels listed on EPA's toxic chemical list for SARA Section 313 reporting (Reporting thresholds may also apply to other businesses)	Requires firms to submit EPA Form R: Information on released substances and on response
Section 304: Spill Reporting	Releases that are a CERCLA-defined hazardous substance above EPA reportable quantity (RQ) or are an EHS and exceed RQ.	Report chemical identity, release media, health risks, time and duration or release, response measures

Source: Derived by the authors from SARA Title III.

releases of "extremely hazardous substances" (EHSs). These are the chemicals included by EPA on its list for chemical emergency preparedness. EPA has revised the list several times; it now contains more than 350 chemicals.

These local district plans include

- identification of all facilities in the district subject to SARA Title III reporting;
- routes suitable for transporting extremely hazardous substances;
- emergency response procedures applicable to local facilities and local government agencies;
- notification procedures in the event of any emergency;
- methods to identify releases;
- inventories of emergency response equipment and personnel;
- evacuation plans;
- training programs for emergency response and medical personnel;
- methods to revise and update the local plan.

Each state commission reviews all these plans from its local districts.

To provide the information needed to complete these local plans, SARA requires facilities handling more than a stated amount of any chemical on EPA's list to submit detailed inventory data to local and state planning agencies. (See Box 6.2 for thresholds and exemptions.) EPA structured this process in a complex manner, using six different levels for

BOX 6.2 Facilities Required to Submit Annual Hazardous Materials Inventory Statements Under SARA Title III (Section 312)

Thresholds	Exemptions
Facilities that handle (1) more than 10,000 pounds of any hazardous material, or (2) any EHS in excess of either 500 pounds or the federal TPQ	• Any food, food additive, color additive, drug, or cosmetic regulated by FDA • Any toxic chemical in solid form in a manufactured product that under normal conditions of use would not cause the user to be exposed • Any toxic chemical used for personal, family, or household purposes • Any toxic chemical used in a research lab or medical facility • Any toxic chemical used in normal agricultural operations or any fertilizer sold to the ultimate consumer

the hundreds of different EHS chemicals. These thresholds range from 1 pound to 5 tons.

But even this sixfold division is misleadingly simple. For some reason, all the EPA thresholds are expressed in pounds, even for gases (normally defined in terms of cubic feet at standard temperature and pressure) and liquids (normally measured in gallons). Furthermore, EPA's regulations require thresholds to be met individually for each EHS chemical, even when it is in a mixture with other chemicals. The complicated formula to calculate the threshold is based on the percentage of the chemical in the mixture, with reporting thresholds set at 1.0 percent for most of the extremely hazardous substances and .01 percent for any substances identified as carcinogens.

Reports of Hazardous Substances in the Workplace

The second set of SARA Title III reporting requirements covers the thousands of hazardous materials for which the federal Occupational Safety and Health Act of 1970 has required preparation of material safety data sheets (MSDSs). In this instance, no precise list yet exists to define the chemicals covered. Each firm's inventory must include all chemicals that were present at the facility during the preceding calendar year. These reports thus go far beyond the EHS reporting previously described.

The Occupational Safety and Health Administration has given general guidance on the sorts of hazards that should trigger preparation of an MSDS.[2] Chemical users must then determine the specifics of their compliance. To err on the safe side, some manufacturers even prepare MSDSs for common materials such as sand, table salt, and deionized water. For this aspect of SARA reporting, facilities are allowed to group their many different chemicals into five "hazard categories": immediate or acute, delayed or chronic, fire, risk from sudden release of pressure, and potentially reactive.

Initially, each business must provide local fire departments and the district and state Title III planning agencies with lists of all the chemicals onsite for which MSDSs were being maintained (alternatively, they can submit copies of the MSDSs).

As firms acquire additional chemicals or determine that chemicals they are already using are now subject to federal MSDS requirements, they have three months to prepare and submit updated information. At first, these voluminous reporting requirements applied only to manufacturing establishments, but by early 1989 EPA greatly expanded the coverage. Only research laboratories, transportation firms, and most household and agricultural products retain their exemptions from MSDS requirements and thus from this aspect of SARA Title III reporting.

Most facilities must also file annual inventory statements covering all chemicals for which an MSDS is being maintained if these chemicals are onsite in amounts over EPA's thresholds. (To add to the potential confusion, the chemicals and categories of activity covered by these annual inventory statements differ from those required in the annual continuous emissions reports described in the next section.) These reports can include either summary MSDS information or more detailed information, depending on the specific requirements of the district and state emergency planning agencies. SARA allows any member of the public to request this information from the appropriate planning agency, but these agencies are not required to do anything with the MSDS information and the annual inventories except to ensure public access.

Estimates of Continuous Emissions

The third set of toxic chemicals addressed by SARA Title III involves yet another different list of 300-plus chemicals, commonly referred to as the "Maryland/New Jersey list" because those two states were already requiring reports on such chemicals when Congress passed SARA. All manufacturing businesses with "continuous" (that is, nonaccidental) releases of these chemicals in any form must provide annual estimates of the volumes of all such emissions. Such a report is called a *toxics release inventory*, or TRI. Once again, EPA has defined reporting thresholds differing from other aspects of the SARA Title III reporting scheme. Here reports must be submitted if either (1) 10,000 pounds of the chemical were used at the facility during the year, (2) 25,000 pounds of the chemical were manufactured at the facility during the year from nonlisted chemical constituents, or (3) for any EHS, 500 pounds or the threshold planning quantity (TPQ) was exceeded (see Box 6.1). Most firms report using EPA's Form R (Toxics Chemical Release Inventory Reporting Form).

Form R asks for a great deal of information. The facility first lists its name and location and then for each listed toxic chemical (unless its identity is claimed to be a trade secret) the following information:

- whether the chemical is manufactured, processed, or otherwise used;
- the general category of each chemical (from among five hazard classifications: fire hazard, sudden release of pressure hazard,

reactive hazard, immediate health hazard, and delayed health hazard);
- an estimate of the maximum amount of the chemical onsite at any time during the preceding calendar year;
- an estimate of the total amount of each toxic chemical released to water, air, and land during the year;
- for each waste stream, the method of treatment or disposal and an estimate of the "treatment efficiency";
- the offsite locations to which the firm shipped wastes containing the toxic chemical, and the quantities of the toxic chemical sent to those locations;
- the onsite treatment or disposal methods used for wastes containing the toxic chemical and estimates, for each toxic chemical, of their treatment efficiency;
- certification by the owner, operator, or "senior management official" of the truth and completeness of information and the reasonableness of assumptions.

For purposes of reporting, firms may use already available data or, when necessary, make reasonable estimates.

Firms reporting continuous emissions of selected toxic chemicals under section 313 have additional reporting and recordkeeping obligations as of July 1, 1992. They are required to submit information about in-house hazardous waste minimization efforts for the previous calendar year. As noted in Chapter Four, this includes information on the size of the waste stream, how it is being reduced, and the methods used.

The law requires facilities covered by these various requirements to send toxic chemical release reports both to EPA and to the state in which their facility is located. At EPA, the Office of Toxic Substances is responsible for receiving and processing the data.

EPA is required by law to make the data in these reports available to the public through a computer data base. Community right-to-know laws grant citizens the right to obtain such information from all administering agencies and from businesses that handle hazardous materials.[3] The EPA data base is intended to help answer citizens' questions about a firm's hazardous materials inventory, accidents, reporting system, emergency response plan, and plans for and methods of source reduction.[4]

As reports on the 1987 TRI survey of emissions from the nation's industry became known, they created a considerable furor in many states and local communities that, for the first time, had quantitative statistics on the large volumes of chemicals regularly being released to the air, water, and land by industries in their area. Analysis of the 1989 TRI reports showed that 22,560 firms released 5.7 billion pounds of toxic chemicals into the nation's environment in the year reported, a statistic that made national headlines. People had little prior information and little frame of reference with which to comprehend the meaning of these new data, and existing fear and outrage redoubled in many areas over toxics in the local environment. Lost sight of was the fact that the figures appeared to represent a decline in releases of up to 18 percent over the 1987 reports (differences in reporting procedures make it difficult to be certain about the change from 1987 to 1989).[5]

This confusion in communication was one example of how SARA Title III has overwhelmed America with data about toxics but not with usable information on which to base informed policy decisions. In a few cases in Southern California (one case involved a large refinery), release of the raw data led to local pressure to close certain manufacturing facilities operating there for many years.

At the same time, the TRI reports caused many firms to reassess their use of toxic chemicals. Source reduction incentives intensified in the face of direct citizen pressures to stop putting so many toxics into the local air, water, and land. For example, 25 Silicon Valley companies decreased their collective releases of toxics from their facilities in Santa Clara County, California, by 74 percent between 1987 and 1990: a reduction of 2,150 tons in total. Releases in 1990 alone were 40 percent less than in 1989. These reductions were due primarily to seven kinds of actions: chemical substitution, improved inventory techniques, improved pollution controls, improved process controls, recycling, use reduction, and waste minimization. Reductions of toxic emissions to different media were as follows:

- releases to the air: 1,250 tons
- chemicals sent to offsite TSD facilities: 650 tons
- releases to sewage treatment plants: 222 tons.

Of total reductions in toxic air emissions since 1987, 59 percent involved releases of chlorofluorocarbon (Freon 113); 15 percent were trichloroethane, 10 percent hydrochloric acid, and 6 percent dichloromethane emissions. The two largest reductions for offsite chemical shipments were acetone (37 percent) and trichloroethane (13 percent). Large reductions in sewage releases were seen for sulfuric acid (49 percent) and hydrochloric acid (29 percent).[6]

Reporting Spills and Leaks

The fourth set of SARA Title III reporting requirements covers leaks or spills of any extremely hazardous substance and of any other substance already subject to emergency notification requirements under the cleanup portions of Superfund. Unfortunately, the reportable quantities here not only differ from the planning thresholds; many have not yet been established by EPA.

Facilities leaking or spilling listed chemicals in reportable amounts (many are as low as one pound) must immediately report any such discharge to local emergency response agencies and to the district and state Title III planning agencies. Subsequently, they must provide written follow-up reports that detail the chemicals involved, time and duration of the release, known or associated health risks, and precautions taken in response to the leak or spill. Thirty days later a formal report on the incident is due, including a full status report of the cleanup effort.

Funding to Implement Title III Requirements

As with so many aspects of modern environmental federalism, SARA Title III provided only minimal financial assistance to states and localities to implement these vast new reporting and planning requirements—and no assistance at all to the thousands of firms, large and small, caught up in the expanding net of toxics data reporting. The Federal Emergency Management Agency (FEMA) received $5 million annually from 1987 to 1990 to train state and local governments; these funds were spent primarily on information seminars (by satellite link) and on printed materials.

In large part, therefore, states and localities were left on their own to receive and store all these new data on use of toxic chemicals; to make the data generally available to the concerned public; to protect industry trade secrets adequately; and to prepare emergency response plans. Individual firms were left entirely on their own to comply with these complicated and clearly inconsistent reporting requirements. Finally, the public was left to make some sense of all this information or, at times, to respond emotionally.

To be sure, the record of performance across the country has been checkered. Overall, governments are awash as never before in industry-provided toxics-use data. The public is trying to determine the salient differences between raw data and useful information, and a number of states have moved aggressively on their own to shift from data collection and planning to enforcement of the increasingly strict requirements on industry's use of toxic materials. All this activity involves an unprecedented degree of intervention by government regulators into industrial decisions and manufacturing processes.

Federal Requirements to Prevent Accidental Releases

Under the 1990 Clean Air Act (CAA) amendments, Congress required EPA to promulgate rules to prevent accidental releases of extremely hazardous substances. These requirements go far beyond the reporting mandated by SARA Title III; now many facilities across the country must for the first time prepare detailed risk management plans patterned after those required by state laws in New Jersey and California.

Owners and operators of stationary sources producing, processing, handling, or storing regulated hazardous substances must identify the hazards that may result from accidental release of such substances. They must then design and maintain their facilities to prevent such releases and to minimize the consequences if such releases do occur.

EPA's proposed list of at least 100 substances that pose the greatest risk from possible accidental releases was slated to be available in fall 1991. Substances on this list are to be drawn from the 360 or so substances already included on EPA's list of extremely hazardous substances published under SARA Title III. EPA will also set threshold quantities for each substance listed.

Congress mandated that the list begin with 14 known hazardous air emissions: ammonia, anhydrous hydrogen chloride, anhydrous sulfur dioxide, bromine, chlorine, ethylene oxide, hydrogen cyanide, hydrogen fluoride, hydrogen sulfide, methyl isocyanate, phosgene, sulfur trioxide, toluene diisocyanate, and vinyl chloride. EPA is to develop procedures to add and delete substances from the list and to review and revise the list at least every five years.

By November 1993, EPA must promulgate regulations and guidance for facilities to prevent, detect, and respond to accidental releases of the substances it has listed. These regulations will require the preparation and implementation of a formal risk management plan. This plan must include a hazard assessment, a prevention program, and an emergency response program. The plan must be registered with EPA; submitted to an independent new national Chemical Safety and Hazard Investigation Board established by the CAA amendments, the state emergency agency, and local emergency response agencies; and made available to the public. EPA is required to develop an auditing system to review and require revisions to risk management plans. The financial, bookkeeping, and technological challenges the new CAA amendments pose to business have not gone unnoticed.[7]

CONTROLLING LEAKS FROM
UNDERGROUND STORAGE TANKS

Today, management of underground storage tanks (USTs) containing solvents, chemical feedstocks, and even gasoline has become another national priority. Effective management of materials stored in underground tanks of various types, sizes, and ages poses a challenge of enormous importance and equal complexity. With tens of thousands of owners involved, millions of tanks in place, and hundreds of millions of dollars at stake, tensions have run high. Groundwater aquifers serving as basic sources of drinking water for millions of Americans are at risk of contamination from leaking underground storage tanks that contain gasoline or numerous chemicals. How can government possibly regulate a universe of potential toxics problems of this dimension?

State Regulation of Underground Tanks

This regulatory process was once again built from the local level up. State regulation of hazardous materials storage in underground tanks began in California in 1983 when a model hazardous materials storage ordinance, first developed in Santa Clara County, was adopted by a number of other localities around the state. (Santa Clara's program was modeled in part on an ordinance in effect in Suffolk County, New York.) Soon thereafter, a new law dealt with underground tanks across the state.

California's legislation required state environmental agencies to devise statewide standards that would be implemented by counties and cities, a concept that in turn formed the model for subsequent federal legislation on UST regulation.

In California, all owners of existing tanks had to register them with the State Water Resources Control Board (the state agency responsible for water quality, including groundwater). All new USTs had to be registered before installation and use. Registrations included the location of the tank and its characteristics, the hazardous substances stored in it, and the methods in use to detect any leakage.

The California program began in 1984; by 1987, the state had registered 161,000 underground storage tanks. Every month thereafter local programs have continued to identify more than 100 previously unregistered tanks.

With this statewide information base and a program of such magnitude, California moved to local implementation of its UST regulations. Program design shifted from mere reporting to action designed to protect groundwater from contamination.

As in the subsequent federal program, California's rules prescribe specific technical standards for both tanks and monitoring systems. All new tanks had to have both primary and secondary containment (typically, double walls), plus monitoring systems. Tanks installed before 1984 had to be equipped with an approved monitoring system by mid-1985. When leaks were detected at existing tanks, those tanks had to be removed and replaced with new ones meeting the latest technical standards.

These massive monitoring efforts detected huge numbers of leaks. Contamination was found at more than 30 percent of all existing tanks. However, when the presumably guilty tank was then removed as required by the law, its structural integrity was often found to be intact. Leaks apparently had occurred in the pipes, through spills during filling, or through other spills in handling liquid materials in the vicinity of the tank. Even small spills were found to cause large problems: A spill of one gallon of pure solvent can contaminate millions of gallons of water at a few parts per million (or even per billion). For example, a one-gallon spill was responsible for creating one Superfund site in the Silicon Valley.

Although state agencies commonly provide technical and policy guidance, California's effort is being implemented by local agencies. Every one of the state's 58 counties is required to designate an agency (typically the county health department) to implement its program. Some 43 cities also chose to carry out the program on their own, independent of county efforts. Those local programs (as in Santa Clara County) already in effect before 1984 continued in force provided their requirements were amended to be at least as strict as the newer state mandates; stricter local regulations were explicitly allowed.

Local regulatory programs issue five-year permits for all tanks and require annual information updates and amendments when new hazardous substances are to be stored. Implementing agencies inspect facilities at least once every three years. Local inspectors must be present whenever an underground tank is to be removed, closed, or abandoned. Because tank replacement has become so common, this has placed an extraordinary demand on inspector time. California's UST laws require local agencies to recover their program costs through permit fees. The law includes both civil and criminal penalties for tank owners who fail to comply.

New federal UST regulations were modeled after California's law. However, two major differences presented the state with significant coordination requirements. First, under the federal rules, all existing tanks are required to comply with new double-liner standards within 10 years. By that time, all single-containment tanks would have to be closed, even if no leaks had been detected under California's strict monitoring efforts. The state law had allowed these older tanks (with no leaks found) to remain in operation. Second, federal financial responsibility requirements added a new dimension on top of the California program.

During the second half of the 1980s, as this massive statewide regulatory effort emerged, local regulatory officials began to assume some roles in onsite supervision of the cleanup of contamination detected around underground tanks. This effort vastly expanded their program responsibilities into areas of action previously reserved to state water quality agencies or to EPA. State and federal Superfund programs made limited funds available on a pilot basis to selected local programs willing to undertake this new function. The federal program has focused particularly on cleanups of leaking fuel (gasoline) tanks. However, cleanup supervision has proved to be as difficult for these local agencies as for the others; progress has been frustratingly slow and enormously costly both in time and resources.

In the San Francisco Bay Area alone, leaks have been identified at more than 4,000 of the area's 16,000 underground fuel tanks. These leaks pose a serious threat to the area's drinking-water supplies and frustrate regulators and environmentalists, who find totally inadequate the system that is supposed to facilitate cleanup of this contamination. Each week brings five to fifteen new tank-leak reports, yet only about ten contamination episodes are being cleaned up every year. Despite state requirements, most tank owners fail to carry out the appropriate cleanups; enforcement of the laws is hampered by bureaucratic confusion over federal, state, and local responsibilities and by state unwillingness to provide sufficient staff and financing.[8]

Federal Regulation of Underground Storage Tanks

In 1984, Congress amended RCRA to begin to deal nationally with the UST problem. This part of the HSWA amendments covered all underground tanks that store petroleum and other hazardous substances with only a few exceptions (e.g., farm and residential fuel tanks under 1,100 gallons, tanks storing heating oil for onsite use, and septic tanks). Federal regulation of USTs includes all underground piping as well as the tanks themselves.

Given the enormity of regulating several million underground tanks and their many thousands of owners, Congress and EPA left implementation of this massive new regulatory program almost entirely in the hands of the states. All tank owners had to register with their state, providing information on characteristics and uses for all existing tanks and for all tanks removed from service since 1973. Each state had to prepare separate inventories of those underground tanks storing petroleum as well as all other USTs.

Akin to the California program, HSWA also required EPA to issue regulations establishing a variety of new technical requirements: construction standards for new underground tanks; leak detection; reporting of releases and corrective actions; onsite practices and recordkeeping; tank-closure standards; and financial responsibility. Not surprisingly, EPA proved unable to meet the strict deadlines imposed in the 1984 law.[9]

Underground tanks installed after passage of HSWA had to meet interim standards for corrosion prevention; cathodic protection; and use of construction and lining materials compatible with the hazardous substance to be stored in the tank. New tanks for petroleum could continue to be single-walled under the federal program, but new tanks designed to hold hazardous substances had to have double containment. All new tanks installed after December 1988 had to have spill and overflow protection devices and to provide leak detection capability. Existing tanks and associated piping either had to be upgraded to meet the new federal standards or be removed. These actions follow a 10-year schedule extending to 1998. Specific deadlines depend on the age of the tank, with older ones requiring attention first.

During the period before a tank is upgraded (or closed), its owners can choose between monitoring and leak detection options that narrow and become more onerous as the tank ages; thus, a cost incentive favors earlier tank upgrading. Those tanks meeting EPA's new-tank standards can be monitored by using inventory reconciliation and by testing the tightness of the tank and its piping (typically every five years). Other tanks must use more expensive monitoring devices.

EPA has also established detailed requirements for reporting any releases from an underground tank and for subsequent cleanup. These requirements apply to releases of petroleum products of 25 gallons or more; for other hazardous substances, the threshold is the reportable quantity established under Superfund. Once a release has been confirmed, the tank's owner/operator must follow a specific schedule of documenting and reporting the release, follow a predetermined cleanup procedure, and file all appropriate forms with local and state agencies and EPA.

EPA's regulations also impose recordkeeping requirements on tank owners and operators, with emphasis on registration and monitoring.

Finally, owners of tanks containing petroleum products must demonstrate sufficient financial responsibility to pay for leak cleanups. In a complicated legislative maneuver typical of so much U.S. toxics legislation, Congress added these requirements to the RCRA framework in 1986 as part of the bill enacting amendments to Superfund. The basic statutory requirement is $1 million for each tank containing petroleum, although EPA is authorized to set lower or delayed requirements for different types of tanks or classes of owners.

EPA's final regulations became effective in January 1989. Tank owners may use a variety of mechanisms to demonstrate financial responsibility: insurance; surety bond; guarantee; letter of credit; self-insurance; trust fund; or state fund. Both the federal legislation and the regulations recognize that currently, some of these financial options are difficult or even impossible to exercise, especially by smaller independent companies. Therefore, EPA has provided two sorts of flexibility. The first scales down the per-tank monetary amounts applicable to owners of more than one tank; the second varies compliance dates by which owners must be able to demonstrate their financial responsibility.

EPA is authorized to order cleanup at any UST site. To further assist UST cleanups, the 1986 SARA amendments provided for a $550 million fund to finance remedial action.

Texas was the first state to introduce the impressive innovation of providing state funds for all cleanups of contamination from gasoline tanks, paying up to $1 million for each tank. This program is funded by a tax on petroleum at bulk terminals in the state and covers any tank owner, from the smallest "mom and pop" store to the largest oil company. Each owner pays the first $10,000 of cleanup costs (as a deductible), the state pays the rest. The owner can perform the cleanup and request reimbursement from the state fund. This program appears to be operating efficiently, encouraging rapid cleanups at hundreds of contamination sites. In that respect, it stands in sharp contrast to the failures evident in federal Superfund and in many other state UST cleanup programs. Other states, including California later adopted programs like that of Texas.

RCRA gives each state the opportunity to assume EPA's regulatory responsibilities under the federal UST program as well as under RCRA as a whole. Given its many other program responsibilities and its limited financial and personnel resources, EPA has been eager to have states take over these tasks.

The tank program has been at the forefront of federal efforts to encourage delegation to states. Indeed, EPA's Underground Storage Tank Office adopted an explicit "franchising program" to encourage rapid delegation of these responsibilities. In general, states must demonstrate that their programs are at least as stringent as federal requirements. For the first three years of the program, Congress in HSWA budgeted $25 million each year to provide grants to the states to develop and implement UST programs, which can be more stringent than federal requirements if the states choose.

With these extensive federal requirements covering millions of underground tanks and with the increasing federal involvement in issues of hazardous materials use by millions of businesses across the country, the scope of toxics policy has expanded dramatically. Effective hazardous *waste* management has become only a small fraction of the total policy problem.

REGULATING TRANSPORTATION OF HAZARDOUS MATERIALS

Transportation of hazardous materials and hazardous wastes is regulated under both federal and state laws. The U.S. Department of Transportation (DOT) administers the Hazardous Materials Transportation Act (HMTA), enacted in 1976 as part of RCRA. Under the Act, states oversee vehicles and driver safety requirements and restrict, to some degree, the routes and timing for hazardous materials transport. California, for example, spreads these responsibilities among a number of different agencies, including the Highway Patrol, Department of Motor Vehicles, Department of Transportation, Department of Health Services, and various local policing agencies.

HMTA provides a minimum standard of regulation for all hazardous materials transport, by rail, motor vehicles, aircraft, and vessels. It also prohibits overly strict state and local regulations. However, the law makes no special distinction between hazardous wastes and materials, though DOT regulations incorporate the list of hazardous wastes devised under RCRA and the hazardous substances and reportable quantities designated by EPA under Superfund.

DOT hazardous materials regulations cover packing and repacking; labeling, marking, or placarding; handling; vehicle routing; and manufacturing of packaging and transport containers. Vehicles must prominently display a placard identifying the hazard class of the contents. DOT is currently bringing its regulations in line with United Nations recommendations for international shipping requirements.[10]

DOT regulations address qualifications for drivers based on physical examinations, driving record, and written and practical driving tests. States may impose additional requirements on drivers and vehicles, and state agencies inspect hazardous materials transport vehicles to determine compliance with state requirements. HMTA imposes civil and criminal penalties for violations of its provisions.

Since 1990, all shippers of hazardous materials have had to provide additional emergency response information. The new regulations require that this information must accompany each shipment and be immediately accessible to the transporter and regulatory or fire agencies for use in responding to an accidental release. In addition, each firm that offers hazardous materials transport must provide a 24-hour emergency response telephone number, monitored by personnel able to provide callers with additional information about the hazardous materials being transported. All major accidents or incidents affecting transport of hazardous materials must be reported under DOT regulations; the reporting and safety requirements pertaining to transport under RCRA also are applicable.

Finally, each hazardous waste transporter must apply for an EPA identification number, which must then be used on all documents to allow federal and state agencies to track each transporter's activities. Each shipment must be accompanied, of course, by its RCRA hazardous waste manifest (see Chapter Four).

Despite all these requirements, serious transportation accidents involving hazardous materials continue to occur (see Box 6.3).

REGULATING HAZARDOUS AIR POLLUTANTS

The 1970 Clean Air Act (CAA) required EPA to establish and maintain a list of hazardous air pollutants and to set emission standards for several specific sources. The regulatory process was cumbersome, however, essentially requiring EPA to amass conclusive evidence that a particular air toxic was indeed "hazardous" before regulation could take hold. As a result, only eight national emission standards for hazardous air pollutants (NESHAPS) were promulgated in 20 years; they covered asbestos, benzene, beryllium, coke oven emissions, inorganic arsenic, mercury, radionuclides, and vinyl chloride. The overall scale of the program paled in comparison with the scope of the air toxics problem. This was one more example of macrofailure.[11]

In 1990, Congress decided to act decisively. In amending CAA, it extended the law to cover tens of thousands of sources of air toxics nationwide and required them to apply specific technologies to control their ongoing emissions of hazardous air pollutants (HAPs). All stationary sources—businesses, firms, facilities—that emit HAPs will have to comply with emission standards to be promulgated by EPA over the course of a decade.

All major sources of HAPs will now have to apply the "maximum

BOX 6.3 A Hazmat Disaster by Any Other Name

Make Roads, Rails Safer from Toxic Cargo Spills

Latest string of toxic chemical spills
uncovers dangerous gaps in regulation.

Recent road and rail accidents reveal glaring and dangerous weaknesses in the nation's rules for transporting hazardous substances.

The accidents had two elements in common: Each did enormous damage. And each was acceptable under law.

That shouldn't be possible.

In the first accident, a railroad car tumbled off a bridge and was punctured on rocks below, spilling 19,000 gallons of pesticide into the Sacramento River. The spill killed fish and other life in 45 miles of the river before washing into a reservoir, where workers still are battling to reduce the threat to humans.

The chemical, metam sodium, can be fatal, yet like the vast majority of agricultural chemicals, the government does not list it as a hazardous substance. Therefore, no one pays much attention to where it moves or how it is moved.

The railroad car carrying it in this instance is vulnerable to puncture. The route taken was known to be dangerous.

The second derailment, near Los Angeles July 18, tied up traffic on the California coast's major interstate for days.

This time, the chemicals were regulated, but inadequately. Even though emergency workers gained quick access to the cargo manifest, and even though it complied with federal rules, it was too vague for the workers to know how to respond.

A week later, near Washington, D.C., a truck carrying hazardous chemicals caught fire, tying up another interstate after similar uncertainty.

Changes obviously are needed:

- The list of hazardous substances must be expanded.
- Detailed cargo lists must be carried on trains and trucks and always filed with state agencies, so they can be accessed rapidly by emergency crews.
- Vehicles carrying dangerous substances must be built to survive common accidents. Inspections must assure that they live up to standards.
- Emergency crews must be trained and equipped for spills. Toxic shipments now exceed 1,000 a day.

The recent accidents sounded an alarm. Safety and common sense demand a fast response.

Source: *USA Today* (August 5, 1991), 10A. Copyright 1991, *USA TODAY.* Reprinted with permission.

achievable control technology" (MACT), to be defined by EPA; smaller "area sources" will also be regulated. These technology-based standards are applicable to all facilities in the specified source category, regardless of their location, age, or size. In addition, all major sources of air toxics will fall under a new air permit program. In November 1991, EPA published its list of all the different categories of sources that emit HAPs.

As with the 1984 HSWA amendments to RCRA (see Chapter Four), the new air toxics program includes a "hammer" provision. If EPA fails to promulgate a MACT emission standard for a given category of toxic pollutants, each major generator of that pollutant must apply for a new emissions permit, which will require meeting specific limitations on HAP emissions.

In addition to mandating MACTs, Congress instructed EPA by 1995 to devise a strategy to control HAPs from all sources in urban areas. EPA is to identify the 30 or more HAPs that present the greatest threat to public health and identify those sources generating 90 percent or more of each of these HAPs, including both major sources and smaller area sources. The strategy must show how EPA intends to reduce by at least 75 percent the public health cancer risk posed by the release of HAPs from all stationary sources. A nine-year implementation plan for the reduction strategy is also required.

If the experience with Superfund and RCRA (and previous congressional mandates to EPA about toxic air emissions) is any guide, it is unlikely that the new CAA amendments will be met within the time frame and with the detail and precision called for. Nonetheless, Congress's mandate is an extraordinary statement of the nation's intent to address the problem of toxic substances in our environment. In the face of superfailure in Superfund cleanups and RCRA implementation and past toxic air emissions policy, the challenge is extraordinary. But read as a moral imperative of modern American society, it underscores the importance of finding effective implementation strategies for better management of toxics.

TOXICS POPULISM: CALIFORNIA'S PROPOSITION 65

The anger, fear, and frustration among Californians concerning toxics may be no stronger than elsewhere across the United States, but the openness of the California political system, especially when it enables voters to lash out at entrenched powers and governing elites through the initiative process, means those instincts can be more easily vented. Toxics policymaking in California provides a vivid example of how the battle against toxics can take a direction quite different than the rule-bound, command-and-control approach inherent in existing RCRA and Superfund programs and the new Clean Air Act as well.

In the mid-1980s, after years of intense controversy within that state over the siting of new hazardous waste facilities and over revelations about Superfund sites and contaminated aquifers, local activists began in earnest to organize. Eventually, they joined together first as a loose coalition, then later formed the Toxics Coordinating Committee (TCC). Most TCC members shared the belief that the root of the toxics problem was America's growing reliance on synthetic organic chemicals, production of which had expanded from a billion pounds annually in the 1940s to 400 billion pounds a year by the 1980s.

If government and industry had failed the people of California and could no longer be trusted to curb industry's appetite for toxic substances, the more aggressive factions in the environmental movement and those who were simply most scared were quite prepared to help the public take matters into its own hands.

The instrument for doing that was the ballot initiative Proposition 65, the Safe Drinking Water and Toxics Enforcement Act of 1986. This proposition was approved by voters statewide by a two-to-one margin, passing in every one of California's 58 counties even though its proponents were outspent six to one.

Proposition 65 was vintage populism in its underlying assumptions: corporate domination of the political process, government collusion with business, bureaucratic ineptitude, and the need of the people to alter the course of policy through that most direct form of democracy—the ballot box. In the words of one of its authors, the purpose of Proposition 65 was "to give citizens more direct power to protect themselves against the risks of hazardous chemicals, and to compensate for failures of state government."[12] More than 70 labor, environmental, and neighborhood groups organized behind the initiative, announcing they were "tired of hearing about piecemeal solutions to toxic problems" and therefore "developed a unified position."[13]

The Proposition 65 campaign was waged around three basic themes:

First, prevent toxics pollution before it occurs. Under conventional rules, government is obliged to show a substance is harmful before it can be controlled or banned under state or federal law. Establishing with scientific certainty the harmful effect of toxic materials is extremely difficult and time-consuming, as evidenced by the years of frustrating experience with the federal Toxic Substances Control Act, the Safe Drinking Water Act, and the Clean Air Act.

Moreover, EPA and responsible state agencies were typically

underfunded and seemingly susceptible to enormous pressures from industry and agriculture to act only in the most blatant instances of "proven" harm. This meant that thousands of new substances were being introduced into the environment with little known about their ultimate impact and with those introducing them largely free of moral responsibility or legal liability.

Proposition 65, its proponents claimed, would cut through all of that bureaucratic inertia by prohibiting the knowing release or discharge onto the land or into any source of drinking water in the state of any chemicals known to the state to cause cancer or reproductive problems. Covered are discharges into either surface waters or underground aquifers through disposal in holding ponds, lagoons, and landfills, through deep-well injection, or through surface runoff. The only exception to these prohibitions is when dischargers can prove a discharge will cause "no significant risk" to public health. These prohibitions apply to all chemicals once they are included on a list prepared by the governor upon recommendation from a scientific advisory panel.

Twelve months after a chemical first appears on this list, businesses may not expose any individual (worker or consumer) to the chemical without "clear and reasonable warning." Twenty months after a chemical is listed, businesses are prohibited from releasing it "into waters or onto the land where such chemical passes or probably will pass into any source of drinking water."

In effect, Proposition 65 shifts the burden of proof to demonstrate real or potential harm from government to the users of toxic materials. Under these circumstances, industry has a strong incentive to demand that the state provide clear, enforceable standards for scores of toxic substances and to reduce its reliance on those chemicals covered under Proposition 65. Until health thresholds were established and substances listed, no dischargers of anything remotely toxic could assume they would not be the targets of litigation.

Second, let the public decide what is in its best health and safety interests. As a matter of good populism (and common sense), if government and industry cannot be trusted, who better to turn to than citizens themselves? Under Proposition 65, this became the cornerstone of toxics policy with the requirement of full toxics disclosure in all walks of life: "No person in the course of doing business shall knowingly and intentionally expose any individual to a chemical known to the state to cause cancer or reproductive toxicity without first giving clear and reasonable warning."[14] With this knowledge, shoppers could decide for themselves the extent to which they wanted to be exposed to known toxics in their food, in their households, and in the places they visited.

Likewise, workers would also have full knowledge of workplace exposure and could respond accordingly.

In keeping with the public's right to know, the new law required public employees, when they became aware of an illegal hazardous waste discharge, to notify within 72 hours the affected county board of supervisors and local health officials. In turn, those officials must immediately notify the public. Clearly, citizens would no longer be kept in the dark by those elected and appointed to serve them. Businesses with fewer than 10 employees were exempted from coverage. Public water supply systems and local, state, and federal governmental entities were also exempted.

Third, remove enforcement from the hands of government officials alone. An important populist precept is that neither big business nor big government pays much attention to common citizens. Proposition 65 therefore entrusted enforcement not solely to the state attorney general and local district attorneys but also to individual citizens, as described in this excerpt from a piece of campaign literature: "Once you tell your local district attorney someone is violating your rights under this act, the d.a. has sixty days to take that violator to court. If the d.a. doesn't, *you can.* You will no longer need to depend upon chemical companies or government bureaucrats for protection."[15]

To encourage citizen enforcement, a "bounty" provision was included promising 25 percent of the penalties imposed to "any person" who brought suit under the Act. These penalties could run as much as $250,000 a day and up to three years in jail for violators of the Act. To encourage local enforcement, a similar provision was provided for local health and police departments if their actions lead to suits.

The Success of Toxics Populism

Whatever else its results, Proposition 65 has matched neither the dire predictions of its opponents nor the dramatic changes in the practices of California business promised by its authors. For several reasons, the scientific advisory panel established under the Act, charged with developing the list of known cancer-causing and reproductive toxicants, has moved slowly under pressure from the governor. After much delay and several suits brought by proponents of the Act, some 300 substances have been listed. The most controversial decisions by the panel—and those least anticipated at the time of the initiative campaign—have been to identify alcohol and tobacco products for inclusion.[16] Moreover, most of the attention on implementing the Act has not been on the toxics disposal and water contamination issues at all but on labeling and on public notification of toxics spills and accidents.

To date, the most comprehensive assessment has identified only seven suits brought under the new law; these have dealt mainly with substance listing and exemptions to coverage sought by business.[17]   In vain, business has argued that federal law should preempt Proposition 65's coverage of pesticides, foods, drugs, and cosmetics as well as issues of occupational health and safety. In an appellate ruling on the governor's attempt to circumscribe narrowly the listing of toxic substances, the court made it clear public sentiment could not be ignored. Affirming the rights of the people in the best tradition of popular democracy, the appellate judge stated:

> Proposition 65 clearly reflects the result of public dissatisfaction with the state's effort at protecting the people and their water supply from exposure to hazardous chemicals. It is not our function to pass judgment on the propriety or soundness of [the Act]. In our democratic society in the absence of some compelling, overriding constitutional imperative, we should not prohibit the sovereign people from either expressing or implementing their own will on matters of such direct and immediate importance to them as their own perceived safety.[18]

Other issues have been settled out of court. For instance, the state attorney general brought suit against tobacco manufacturers for their refusal to provide Proposition 65 warnings on their products. That issue was settled out of court when several supermarket chains notified manufacturers that without the warnings they would no longer carry their products.

Gillette settled out of court on a suit initiated by the Sierra Club, the Environmental Defense Fund (EDF), and others for its failure to provide a Proposition 65 warning on its Liquid Paper correction fluid. It agreed to pay $300,000 in penalties and to begin making a safe version of the product.   Gillette has also launched a public relations campaign announcing the change in its product.

Business failed to get the Reagan White House to back its drive for federal preemption over Proposition 65. In 1988 the President's Domestic Policy Council could find little adverse effect on business and concluded the economic burdens alleged by industry were vastly overstated.

Business may or may not be correct in contending Proposition 65 will profoundly affect them. If EDF attorney David Roe is correct in his assessment, it would be difficult ever to know for sure. For him, the essence is not only to shift the burden of proof to industry but for industry to assess the potential harm from its use of toxic substances and to change accordingly.   In Roe's view, this "quiet compliance" far outweighs more vocal grumbling about the law.[19] If that is true, and it may well be, then the impact of Proposition 65 will be revealed only over the long term as toxic substances are gradually removed from products or are no longer in need of disposal as waste.

TOXICS POLICY: FROM REVOLUTION TO EVOLUTION

Toxics policy has evolved dramatically in the United States from an initial concern with the safer management of hazardous wastes at the beginning of the first toxics decade to a heightened scrutiny of the pervasive use of toxic materials and their possible release into the environment today. The precise extent of health and environmental risk, acute or chronic, posed by the use and release of these hazardous substances is only now beginning to be understood for all but the most obviously harmful of such substances now listed by the EPA. Furthermore, it is exceedingly difficult for the scientists, lawmakers, and community at large to know how best to arrive at the optimal level of use and most viable strategy for managing these substances, either as the feedstocks of industry or when they become society's wastes—or when, after all the pros and cons are considered, to conclude that the potential harm so outweighs any imaginable use benefit that industry must simply stop using a hazardous substance altogether.

Despite these uncertainties, toxics policy has acquired an ever-widening scope: the substances covered; the range of activities affected (from everyday business practices to the ultimate disposal of these substances, initially on the land and discharge into underground aquifers); and the regulatory efforts made (CERCLA, RCRA, all the corollary state and local regulations, and the new CAA).

The burden of proof has also shifted radically. It was once the case that aggrieved parties needed to document conclusively an alleged harm from toxics releases before they could bring suit against the responsible business or industry or before a governmental agency would act on behalf of public health and safety. Today, the liability provisions introduced for the first time in Superfund and those embedded in Proposition 65 have gone far toward shifting the burden of proof onto those parties who choose to use materials known or presumed to be hazardous. Although Superfund's strict joint and several liability provisions are extraordinary in this regard, they are limited in application to hazardous substances found only at Superfund sites. Proposition 65, which pertains to the disposal by industry of any potentially hazardous wastes identified by the state and disposed of anywhere in California in a way that might adversely affect the water supply, is a more sweeping doctrine.

In addition, the source reduction mandate explicit under RCRA and PPA and implicit in CAA's insistence that industry adopt maximum achievable control technologies makes clear that policymakers do not believe that better management of hazardous wastes and hazardous materials alone is sufficient. Their use in industry must be curtailed as a major step toward reducing their impact on the environment.

Yet source reduction is not sufficient as a solution to the hazardous waste management problem confronting the United States. Industrial and commercial production remains the essence of our economic system and material well-being, and this is not going to change in the foreseeable future. Thus, hazardous wastes will continue to be generated in substantially large volumes, though one hopes not at the rapidly rising per-capita and possibly even overall levels experienced until quite recently.

The toxics policy story thus circles back to the beginning: What must be done to better manage our hazardous wastes? The answer demanded by America's toxics policy is to implement to the fullest the waste management hierarchy outlined in Chapter Four. This requires, of course, that waste management moves rapidly away from landfilling and deep-well injecting to sorting, recycling, treatment, and ultimate placement of what remains in dry and well-managed residuals repositories. But as we have noted throughout, citizens have adamantly resisted the siting of any new hazardous waste facilities in their midst. This has become a major stumbling block to the successful implementation of the entire toxics policy strategy adopted for the nation by Congress. How and why this has occurred and what steps might be taken to overcome it are the subjects of Chapters Seven and Eight.

NOTES

1. For a detailed section-by-section outline of Title III, see Deborah Lukesh and Anthony Neville, "The Community Right-to-Know Law—Sara Title III," in Shyamal K. Majumdar, E. Willard Miller, and Robert F. Schmalz, eds. *Management of Hazardous Materials and Wastes: Treatment, Minimization, and Environmental Impacts* (Easton: Pennsylvania Academy of Science, 1989), 126–146.

2. Thaddeus E. Tomczak, "Occupational Safety and Health Guidance: Rules, Regulations, and Protective Equipment," in Majumdar, Miller, and Schmalz, *Management of Hazardous Materials,* 264–275.

3. For a full discussion, see Susan Hadden, *A Citizen's Right to Know: Risk Communication and Public Policy* (Boulder, Colo.: Westview, 1989).

4. Maura Dolan, "Industries Begin Revealing Toxics They Have Released," *Los Angeles Times* (July 2, 1988).

5. "1989 TRI Data Released," *EPA: Pollution Prevention News* (June 1991), 1, 7.

6. Thomas D. English, *Environmental Releases for 1987, 1988, 1989 and 1990—Based on Data Submitted under SARA Title III, Community-Right-to-Know* (Santa Clara, Calif: Santa Clara County Manaufacturing Group, 1991), 2–7.

7. The case has been put starkly by Jim Bishop, "Opposing Forces," *Hazmat World* (July 1991) 4, in his review of the new CAA requirements and the already extensive RCRA and other environmental regulations of the past several years: "The fact that this near frenzy of legislative, regulatory and enforcement activity is fundamentally at odds with current and historical industrial practice—as well as available technology, in some cases—has been deemed virtually irrelevant. The premise that total environmental protection and industrial survival may be contradictory seldom is faced. EPA is forcing the issue, intentionally or not. Industry, as well as the public—which shows little sign of disavowing its keen appetite for the pollution-producing fruits of industrial labors—must face the contradictions and make critical choices."

8. *San Francisco Chronicle* (February 12, 1990).

9. See Kathy J. Huber and Sheldon Kamieniecki, "The Implementation of Federal Underground Storage Tank Regulations: Some Preliminary Findings," paper presented at the Annual Meeting of the American Political Science Association (August 30–September 2, 1990). For a full discussion of the effort to implement the underground storage tank provisions, see Steven Cohen and Sheldon Kamieniecki, *Environmental Regulation Through Strategic Planning* (Boulder, Colo.: Westview, 1991).

10. The international conventions and several international organizations involved in the discussions are reviewed by Deborah L. Boothe, "Hazardous Materials Transportation," in Majumdar, Miller, and Schmalz, *Management of Hazardous Materials*, esp. 212–215.

11. Walter A. Rosenbaum, *Environmental Politics and Policy*, 2d. ed. (Washington, D.C.: Congressional Quarterly Press, 1991), 193.

12. Letter from David Roe to the Deputy Attorney General, Department of Justice, Sacramento, California, December 31, 1986.

13. Larry Stammer, "70 Groups Unite in Battle Against Pollution," *Los Angeles Times* (February 19, 1986), part I, 19.

14. Section 25249.6, Safe Drinking Water and Toxics Enforcement Act of 1986.

15. Campaign letter signed by the American Cancer Society, California League of Conservation Voters, Consumers' Union, and Assemblyman Tom Hayden.

16. Christine Russell, "Forewarned Is Fairly Warned," *Sierra* 74 (November/December 1989), 36–44.

17. Bruce H. Jennings, "California's Experience with Proposition 65: Implementing the Safe Drinking Water and Toxics Enforcement Act," California Senate Office of Research (draft, August 1989).

18. Jennings, "California's Experience," 30.

19. Roe's views are presented by Robert Pool, "A Corrosive Fight over California's Toxic's Law," *Science* 243 (January 1989), 306–309.

CHAPTER SEVEN

Just Say "No" — Facility Siting and the Failure of Democratic Discourse

So far we have established that the driving influence on America's toxics policy in the late 1970s and first half of the 1980s was the effort to cope with the environmental and political disasters created by past hazardous waste mismanagement. First came the clarion call to clean up contaminated, leaking hazardous waste sites by using federal and state Superfund programs. That approach was matched by the common expectation—naive as it may seem now, but reasonable considering available technologies—that safer methods for hazardous waste disposal would rapidly be introduced under the pressure of local, state, and federal RCRA programs and because of all the publicity about hazardous wastes, especially after Love Canal. Ended or phased out would be all those older, less-safe disposal methods of landfilling, deep-well injection, and dumping of wastes into sewers, lagoons, and settling ponds. Instead, safer treatment methods would be adopted to neutralize, stabilize, and recycle wastes. Only after the wastes were treated would the much smaller volumes of waste residues be stored indefinitely in residuals repositories.

These early conceptions of how to manage wastes better were followed in the second half of the 1980s by a call to change production methods and product designs to reduce in the first place the amounts of hazardous waste being generated. Most observers realized, however, that even if the push for source reduction and waste minimization were realized, a substantial amount of hazardous waste being generated by America's industry would still remain to be treated and disposed of.

The policy logic was compelling: Clean up the old dump sites and close the old commercial landfills, while simultaneously introducing source reduction throughout industry and a move to waste treatment. But in practice, only closing out the old landfills has been realized to any degree of satisfaction. The combined failure to move forward more rapidly on cleanup, treatment, and source reduction and on siting of new hazardous waste treatment facilities has become a significant stumbling block to realizing the overall goal of managing America's hazardous wastes more safely.

A national survey of the states conducted by the New York legislature in 1987 underscores vividly this point. Between 1980 and 1986, when the move to close older facilities was at its peak, only eleven new hazardous waste facilities were permitted in the entire country, and only seven were actually built.[1] The efforts of federal or state officials, business leaders, technical experts, and mediators, supported by promises of all sorts of services and payments to communities, failed to alter appreciably the stiffening resistance of local communities to any proposed new facilities.

The failure to locate modern treatment, storage, and disposal facilities is as important a dimension of the toxics policy experience of the first decade as the failure to clean up Superfund sites. It has enormous implications for the safer management of hazardous wastes not only for today but well into the future. The question before us is whether this failure to site new facilities can be explained and changed.

WHY NEW FACILITIES ARE NOT BEING SITED

When it became obvious that siting was not going forward, a good deal of attention was given to determining why. There is no simple explanation, though several major factors have been identified: the resistance from the people in the affected communities and from environmental and healthcare groups; the sheer complexity of governmental regulations; the absence of market tests for the proposed new treatment technologies; the fundamentally different perceptions of the risks involved in the new facilities; and an underlying distrust of business and government leaders who have been advocates of siting new facilities.

The assessment of the siting experience has also helped clarify the conditions likely to lead to success. Although no two experiences are ever fully alike, one of the more important findings in this regard is the need for facility siting to be resolved within a broader community consensus on long-range and broad strategies for regional economic growth and environmental protection, arrived at through a legitimate and open community decisionmaking process.

We examine first, however, the reasons given most often for siting failures.

The Not-in-My-Backyard (NIMBY) Syndrome

The simple answer to why new hazardous wastes facilities (and today almost any facility dealing with large quantities of hazardous materials) have not been developed throughout the first toxics decade in the United States is local opposition. Local citizens have resisted the siting of such facilities in their midst because they believe they are being asked unfairly to shoulder the hazardous waste burden of others. They see the costs to themselves in terms of community aesthetics, property values, and potential health and environmental harms. And they do not see vividly the benefits to either their community or to society as a whole. Wherever a local opposition group has emerged, it has been aided and abetted by environmental and health groups of every stripe and persuasion.

The battles over siting played out across the nation's landscape eventually brought together thousands of local citizens, loosely organized initially through existing environmental and health groups, into an active national movement. The Citizens Clearinghouse for Hazardous Wastes (CCHW) and the National Toxics Campaign (NTC) have grown to include thousands of members who share information and tactics on how to defeat new hazardous waste treatment facility proposals.[2] Using the myriad of local, state, and federal rules and regulations at their disposal, these citizen groups have been extremely effective at blocking the facilities, as the record of the first decade attests. Citizen power as the ability to say "no" is undeniably alive and well in America today.

The initial contention by facility proponents and sympathetic federal and state officials was that the locals were simply acting selfishly (protecting their own backyard), indifferent to the broader communitywide need for better and safer hazardous waste facilities. They were acting out of fear and misinformation about the potential harms from these facilities. This was obvious, it seemed to proponents, because the opposition was mounted in the face of "expert" opinion that modern hazardous waste treatment facilities were essential for society and that the risks involved were small and "acceptable."[3]

Self-interest and misunderstandings certainly have been a part of local opposition, but the explanation for both the opposition and the support it has garnered in the broader political arena goes much further. Opposition to facilities may seem selfish and irrational to outsiders and policy experts, but from the perspective of the communities directly affected—and the principle is a basic tenet of the democratic process—just saying "no" is quite the opposite. To date, opposition has often been the only avenue open to communities, environmentalists, and health advocates, who have fought not only particular facilities but also the hazardous waste policies behind them and how those policies were being made.[4]

Parenthetically, one of the claims of local citizens has been that a hazardous wastes treatment facility in the neighborhood would lower their property values. It appears the fear is not unfounded. The limited evidence available shows that locally unwanted projects (hazardous waste landfills or treatment facilities) have an adverse effect on adjacent residential property values.[5] Even more disturbing, property values are undermined most not merely by the existence of a facility but by the negative publicity about it as well as by perceptions of risk citizens have about being close to the facility. The implication is perverse: People living near a troublesome landfill or treatment facility better not blow the whistle or their property values will suffer. The corollary: When in doubt, err on the side of keeping potentially harmful new facilities out of the neighborhood. Thus, NIMBY-ism becomes part of the story.

Government Regulations

Every new proposed hazardous waste facility is confronted with the "too many checkpoints" problem of permits, multiple jurisdictions, delays, and ever-changing government regulations. These extend from local zoning ordinances, to federal statutory requirements pertaining to air and water, to RCRA, to occupational health and safety provisions, and many more. Almost any project proponent would find maddening the frustrations of gaining numerous clearances, responding to different and changing rules and expectations, and wading through endless bureaucracies. Combined with shrill citizen opposition and often mandatory public hearings, this regulatory maze has added to the already substantial delays and costs of doing business, frequently to the point of discouraging completely any potential new hazardous waste facility operators. Point two.

Uncertainty About Technical Capabilities and Market Conditions

Although a strong case can be made for the availability of the technologies for sound and safe hazardous waste treatment (see Chapter Five), there are always unknowns associated with any proposed commercial hazardous waste facility, if only because few of the modern variety were built in the United States before the 1980s. The technical risks associated with installing and operating the newer technologies were knowable, however, and builders and operators could incorporate them into their business plans.

From the potential financial investor's viewpoint, significant marketing and liability risks were associated with becoming involved with the new treatment facilities. To begin with, it was difficult to estimate accurately the probable financial return from such an investment. The federal government and several states had declared the old landfills must be closed and a shift to treatment emphasized, but that transition would be costly for business. Consequently, firms would rely for as long as possible on the older landfill methods or even on upgraded landfills before incurring the costs of modern treatment, and they could be counted on to resist implementation of the policies banning land disposal.[6]

Resistance to the new treatment regime and delays in implementation surfaced first in California, which in the early 1980s had mandated land disposal phaseout and a switch to treatment. The state's land disposal bans had been delayed for years because sufficient treatment capacity had not become available by the time of the deadlines set by the state. Therefore, landfills remained open and continue to this day to compete with the proposed treatment facilities. Those who had invested in more expensive treatment facilities found that as long as the old landfills stayed open, their treatment plants could not attract enough business. In some important cases, new facilities were not built even when they did manage to receive siting approval. As a result, lacking new treatment capacity, the state had to retreat from enforcing its restrictive policies. That scenario will likely be repeated nationwide as the land disposal bans in the 1984 RCRA amendments are implemented.

Of course, under Superfund and RCRA (see Chapters Two and Four), there were enormous liabilities associated with anything to do with hazardous waste as long as strict joint and several liability prevailed. How to assess the financial risk associated was not at all clear, which also dampened the enthusiasm of many potential investors.

It is not difficult to see why these uncertainties, added to NIMBY movements, meant few facilities would be built, even if they could be sited and permitted successfully by local officials. Just as local citizens in the 1980s found reasons to say no to new facilities, so too, for their own reasons, did financial investors and commercial developers.

Differing Perceptions of Risk

Much of the controversy over siting has centered around assessing the relevant risks of a hazardous waste facility. What is now clear, though it was not at all clear throughout much of the first toxics decade, is that project proponents and opponents in using the same words—"risk," "risk assessment," "acceptable risk," and the like—were usually talking past one another. That they could never come to agreement should not be surprising.

Developers of hazardous waste treatment facilities thought of risk in terms of calculating the potential returns on their investment—the classic sense of risk assessment that every entrepreneur and investor makes about his or her chances of succeeding in the marketplace. The developers' technical advisers thought of risk in terms of the mechanical and other internal operations of proposed facilities. Government scientists considered risk in terms of the likelihood (in large-number statistical probabilities) of the potential adverse health effects that could result from the operations of facilities. And government regulators and elected officials typically considered the risk to the broader community if the new treatment facilities were not brought on line: where would the wastes go instead? Elected officials may think of risk in a more parochial fashion, as the political threat that approval of a proposed facility may pose to their reelection.[7]

The basic premise of thinking about risk in these terms is what has come to be known as *technical rationality*: "a mindset that trusts evidence and the scientific method, appeals to expertise for justification, values universality and consistency, and considers unspecifiable impacts to be irrelevant to present decision-making."[8]

In stark contrast, local citizens, environmentalists, and health advocates saw risk in terms of health and safety effects on the people who would be living adjacent to the proposed facility or elsewhere, not of how such effects were revealed in statistical averages. Or they thought about risk as a matter of fairness and social equity: Why them and why their community over others? Or, especially among a small group of environmentalists and politically more radical activists who were drawn to the siting controversies, hazardous waste facilities came to symbolize the profound risk they saw to humanity embodied in capitalism and the modern industrialized world.

These are not issues of technical but of *cultural rationality*, which instead "appeals to traditional and peer groups rather than to experts, focuses on personal and family risks rather than the depersonalized, statistical approach, holds unanticipated risks to be fully relevant to near-term decision-making, and trusts process rather than evidence."[9] When presented with the arguments for the facilities by the proponents, their complex cost-benefits analyses, and their assurances of minimal "risk," citizens were confused and often incensed by the reeling off of so many facts and figures. After all, they were not scientists or technical experts. They wanted it in plain and unequivocal language. No wonder their retort was a resounding "no."

Acceptable risk, for them, is not a matter of science and numbers but of morality and decency and the health of their family and friends. Toxics policy had moved from being a matter of finding the best technical solutions to the problems of industrial waste to being an issue of more basic social and cultural concerns, and it would need to be addressed accordingly.

There are other dimensions to risk as well. It appears to be part of human nature to consider certain risks, such as exposure to toxic substances, as more serious than the "facts" seem to warrant. Moreover, people more actively resist involuntary, rather than voluntary, risk exposure. And they fear far less naturally occurring risks such as floods than they do the manmade risks such as exposure to industrial toxics or harmful drugs.[10]

Risks that cannot readily be detected by the human senses, such as radiation or chemicals in drinking water, are more mysterious and emotionally charged, thus to be avoided at all cost. In the political context, these effects have often been translated into demands by potentially affected communities for zero exposure to any toxins that might escape from hazardous waste facilities. Their reasoning is understandable: When faced with a frightening unknown, always err on the side of caution.

Willingness to accept risks is also associated with the relationship between beneficiaries and bearers of cost, an issue that may be more a matter of perceptions of "justice" than of risk. The greater the symmetry between those communities seen to be bearing the costs and those benefiting from the proposed facility, the more politically and socially acceptable those risks become. Most commercial landfills and hazardous waste treatment facilities were designed to serve fairly large geographical areas, whereas their potential harm is always seen as concentrated primarily in the host community.

Finally, everyone is more likely to accept risks when new technologies are clearly linked to new jobs, economic growth, and increased standards of living.[11] It has been difficult to show any local community it will benefit appreciably by accepting a new hazardous waste facility. (Changes in existing facilities and approvals of proposed onsite treatment processes may gain local clearance more readily, precisely because they are associated with economic advancement.) This lack of economic advantage from proposed new commercial hazardous waste management facilities has been true despite the side payments held out to host communities by several states in their siting statutes: provisions for new roads, special taxes on wastes delivered to a facility, and so forth.

Public Distrust of Business and Government

Exacerbating all of the problems just described was the near-pervasive public distrust of business and political leaders that undermined their credibility when they supported proposed new hazardous waste facilities.[12] That feeling of distrust, which has grown inexorably in the

United States since the mid-1960s, stems from many and complex roots: the Vietnam War and the Watergate scandal of the 1970s, a popular president who throughout the 1980s constantly reminded the voters of public-sector failures, and a seemingly endless string of technological and environmental calamities government and business were clearly ill-prepared to handle—from Love Canal to Three Mile Island to *Challenger* to the *Exxon Valdez*.

The failure of business and government to anticipate what would become of many Superfund sites across America and to act decisively when they were discovered appear to have reinforced this skepticism. Why, the public wondered, would proposed new facilities be any cleaner or safer over the long haul? Distrust reigned. Regardless of what was promised, the public saw every campaign to win siting approvals for proposed new facilities only in terms of their "danger."

Indicative of how low public confidence in business and government leadership had fallen was an extensive survey in California in the mid-1980s showing that on issues of hazardous waste and toxics management, the public had much more confidence in environmental organizations than in the governor, state and local elected officials, business and labor leaders, or any of the state's other organized interests.[13] No wonder Proposition 65, the toxics ballot initiative, passed so readily (see Chapter Six). No wonder it became nearly impossible to site a new hazardous waste facility.

RESPONSES TO THE FAILURE TO SITE

For all these reasons, it became evident by the early 1980s that new facilities were not going to be sited anytime soon and that the situation was nearing crisis proportions. Stemming the tide of local rejections demanded overturning one of the deepest-held American political values: local control over land use. At least that was the view of project proponents and their allies in government.

Undeniably, local government and community residents are closest to the issue and will experience most directly the harm or benefit of any siting decision. In principle, local officials are indeed the most responsive to the will of their communities. The case for local "self-determination" is compelling, as underscored by the observations of Richard Andrews in his examination of hazardous waste siting controversies around the states:

> If such facilities *are* especially hazardous, the local jurisdiction has a responsibility to ensure that its citizens' health and welfare are not

sacrificed by more remote state or federal officials who are not at risk; and if they are *not* any more hazardous than other businesses that use the same materials, they should negotiate with local governments just like any other business, and not receive special help by invoking the power of state government.[14]

Yet in the late 1970s and early 1980s, when local self-determination meant almost no new hazardous waste facilities would be sited, pressures built for state intervention. It was obvious Congress was not about to get the federal government involved in this hot topic, not with the political vulnerability present at every step.

Repeatedly over this period, Congress sidestepped the issue of siting. Neither the original or revised RCRA nor either Superfund statute directly addresses siting. Under the Hazardous and Solid Waste Amendments of 1984, Congress did instruct EPA to develop technical guidelines for hazardous waste facility siting, which EPA proceeded to do (in one example, for vulnerable hydrogeological areas). Those EPA guidelines, however, help the states only as to where not to site, not where or how to site new facilities.

Before Love Canal, only three states had statutes covering hazardous waste facility siting. By 1986, that number had jumped to 36, with legislation passed precisely in states where the need to site was most pressing.[15] No two state laws were alike, but they do fall into a few basic patterns, which reflect fundamental assumptions about the nature of the "problem."

Preemption

Historically, within policy areas such as roads and utility lines, the coordination provided by regional or state (and sometimes federal) planning and administrative control is necessary to keep the whole system from degenerating quickly into a hodgepodge of too-small segments and redundant costs. Faced with these results in the past, states eventually were able to preempt siting authority from local jurisdictions. Exercise of eminent-domain powers became typical. To some extent, municipal solid waste (garbage) issues took on that infrastructure character.

Traditionally, hazardous waste facilities have had the character neither of a natural monopoly nor of an inherently integrated system that could justify the preemption of local siting authority. Nevertheless, in the fallout of political storms over hazardous waste management during the early 1980s, post–Love Canal, nine states adopted legislation to preempt local authority to select appropriate hazardous waste sites; four even included provisions for possible state ownership and operation of hazardous waste disposal facilities.[16]

Statutes are not in themselves policy, however, and these efforts at state preemption have proved futile so far. The most futile and understandably frustrating example as yet is the extraordinary effort by New Jersey, where the need for new treatment capacity was keenly felt, the formal powers granted the state were unequivocal, and the commitment of state officials to the siting effort was substantial. But even after several years of study, litigation, public protest, and old-fashioned politicking, when it came down to actual siting and construction of facilities, local opponents have prevailed.[17]

Minnesota provides another case in point, different in most ways from New Jersey except it too began the decade with a strong state siting statute. Minnesota's 1980 law called for the state to designate "preferred areas" for locating treatment facilities, leaving the rest of the decisionmaking on site characteristics and facility operations to private applicants and local governments to negotiate. The Minnesota law also called for the state to identify specific sites for a hazardous waste disposal facility.

Six years later, after numerous false starts attempting to identify a site where strong local opposition to such a facility could be overcome, the state legislature gave in to the political realities of local self-determination. In 1986, it passed a new siting law covering hazardous waste disposal facilities that effectively banned any new facility from being sited anywhere in the state. Minnesota will now site, at most, a modern residuals repository, only for treated wastes.[18]

Mediation and Negotiation

The evident failure of conventional state-directed legislative and regulatory approaches to solving siting controversies led to a concerted effort to find alternative, less adversarial mechanisms for resolving these disputes.[19] It was hoped that introducing neutral third-party mediators and facilitators into the siting process would go a long way toward bridging the obvious gap in understanding, perspective, and trust between siting proponents and opponents and, presumably, appreciably enhance acceptance of the needed facilities.

The relative degree of success uncovered by Gail Bingham in her comprehensive study of mediation in environmental disputes suggests its value in general.[20] But all issues do not lend themselves to mediation and dispute resolution, especially not those raising fundamental policy questions or involving the siting of major new hazardous waste landfills or treatment facilities. Nevertheless, 19 states incorporated into their statutes some form of negotiated siting procedures; among these states were California, Connecticut, Illinois, Massachusetts, Minnesota, North Carolina, New Hampshire, Rhode Island, Texas, Virginia, Washington, and Wisconsin.[21]

The Wisconsin approach offers a good illustration. In 1981, the state adopted a negotiated siting process after the courts rejected the state's preemption effort. The comprehensive Wisconsin law covers both hazardous waste and municipal solid waste facilities and includes explicit mediation provisions. Negotiations between developers and local communities take place concurrently with the permitting process, considerably reducing the applicant's time factor. Incentives were built in to encourage all sides to negotiate successfully all outstanding issues.

However, even after seven years, this carefully crafted systematic procedure had not resulted in the siting of a single new offsite commercial hazardous waste treatment facility, though there have been successful sitings of several new onsite facilities.[22] It may still be too early to judge, but the assumption has not generally been borne out that local communities would accept new hazardous waste facilities if only those localities were given greater leverage over builders and operators through direct negotiation.

Offsetting Compensation

Many traditional politicians (and economists) believed siting problems could be boiled down to "compensation." If local residents were most perturbed because the true costs to them of accepting a hazardous waste facility in their midst exceeded its benefits, the solution was to offset community costs with more benefits. These could include additional public services or tax revenues derived from the facility, or whatever other material issues either government or facility owners could offer. This approach assumes, of course, that citizens or community leaders will behave as rational economic actors and respond positively to an attractive financial package.

Consequently, the emphasis becomes less one of reducing potential harm from a facility than of offering benefits until in the minds of the local residents these outweigh the perceived risk.[23] This approach assumes that a benefits package of sufficient magnitude will offset resistance and induce local residents finally to accept the proposed facility.

That theory was tested in Massachusetts, where mechanisms to seek offsetting compensation were an integral part of state-mandated siting negotiations with local communities. Still, after several failed attempts with that process to work out an acceptable siting accommodation between facility proponents and local communities, it became clear that when the debate was about hazardous wastes, conventional compensation simply was not enough.

To find out why, Kent Portney studied several Massachusetts communities where compensation failed. He discovered residents were not unmoved by promises of economic benefits, but they so feared the potential risks they associated with hazardous wastes that "virtually no reasonable amount of compensation, by itself, can have much impact."[24] In other words, local residents' fears (rational or not) were so strong that their support for a proposed facility could not be bought at any reasonable price.

On a more hopeful note, it seems that if project proponents are willing to give more emphasis to mitigating potential risks from their facilities instead of simply seeking to "buy" community support, and if they satisfactorily address safety concerns, community members are less apprehensive and are willing to entertain proposals that include offsetting compensation.[25]

Public Participation

Traditionally, the public was notified that a new hazardous waste facility was being planned for its community only after most of the key decisions had been made. Usually, this occurred after a site had been chosen by the private developer and approved in principle by the appropriate governing bodies.

By the late 1970s, hazardous waste facilities had become far too controversial for customary behind-the-scenes administrative processes to suffice as an acceptable means of decisionmaking. One of the reasons often given was it excluded the public from the decision process—the implication being that bringing citizens in early and allowing them a meaningful voice in the siting process would lead to successful siting. At a minimum, the principle is clearly in keeping with the promise of American democracy.

The idea caught on quickly, and some form of citizen participation is now a required component of nearly every state siting law. EPA's regulations under RCRA and SARA also call for citizen participation in virtually every major aspect of toxics activities; developing guidelines for hazardous waste facilities is obviously one such element.

To date, there is no evidence that simply expanding the opportunity for citizens to speak and be heard or even be involved more intimately in the siting process has appreciably changed outcomes. If anything, the result is to the contrary. A 1987 study by the New York legislature found that in none of the states ranked highest in public participation and maximal citizen involvement in siting had any new hazardous waste facilities been sited.[26] The numbers of cases are few, but at best the data suggest no discernible relationship between siting success and the degree of participation.   Although it may be sensible to argue that public participation is a necessary part of the siting process, it is clearly not sufficient.

One reason for this may be the mismatch between form and context that has emerged in nearly every attempt at siting.   When there is fundamental consensus on goals and only technical issues must be decided, the traditional administrative process, which emphasizes scientific and technical criteria, seems acceptable to most parties. Then only minimal citizen involvement is typically needed or requested. However, when siting disputes involve basic values and interests, as with proposed hazardous waste facilities, they cannot be accommodated in a normal administrative process; thus, the issues move into the more adversarial and political arenas: legislatures, media, courts, elections, and public protest.

Merely opening the administrative process to all antagonists in the name of democracy is likelier to undermine administrative decisionmaking than to bring about harmony and consensus.   Even worse, it appears that because of the mismatch of form and context, widening the decision process in hazardous waste facility siting has not only resulted in few successes but has produced even more public frustration and deepened public distrust of government.[27]

A FRAMEWORK FOR SUCCESSFUL SITING

The harsh siting lessons of the first toxics decade cannot be easily dismissed.   To the extent citizens perceive that (1) hazardous waste facilities are simply too risky (true or not) to admit into their communities, regardless of any economic advantages, (2) their communities are being singled out to bear a disproportionate share of the burdens of society's hazardous wastes, or (3) that their political and business leaders cannot be trusted, it is difficult to imagine many new commercial hazardous waste treatment and disposal facilities ever being sited. Notwithstanding all the efforts made to get around this fact of contemporary American life, that is the unavoidable message of the first toxics decade.[28] Such a result leaves HSWA's land disposal phaseout program in limbo—with most of SARA's permanent remedies parked right next to it.

Successful siting, if it is to occur at all, must come through a process that addresses the genuine need for these new facilities, safety, equity among communities, and benefits and costs. The process must also give communities genuine control over their own destinies. In short, it must accommodate both the technical dimensions of the proponents and the social dimensions of the host community. Experience to date suggests that successful siting is quite unlikely to be accomplished on a site-by-site basis alone. The most promising approaches to siting new hazardous waste facilities are in more comprehensive designs that apportion waste treatment needs and facilities on a statewide or regional basis. California has taken the lead in developing such approaches and offers an instructive example of their potential and problems.

YIMBY as an Alternative to NIMBY

In the early 1980s in southern California, the concept of YIMBY (yes in many backyards) was introduced as a guiding principle for distributing unwanted hazardous waste facilities among all the counties participating in the Southern California Hazardous Waste Management Project, which later was restructured into a joint powers authority.

The YIMBY philosophy asked each county to take responsibility for its fair share of the waste problem, though not necessarily to manage all of its own wastes. A heavily populated industrialized community with large volumes of hazardous wastes might accept siting of a set of treatment facilities designed to accommodate not only its own wastes but some wastes from less-developed surrounding areas as well. In exchange, a less-developed area might accept a residuals repository for permanent storage of treated wastes from the entire region. If such an arrangement made good economic sense, under YIMBY most communities might agree to accept facilities adequate to handle primarily their own waste streams. Modular transportable hazardous waste treatment systems might make sense, located first in one community, then in the next on an agreed-upon schedule.[29]

Under an equity-based YIMBY philosophy, waste management problems are addressed at a comprehensive regional level, with the search for solutions guided by principles of equity and justice among communities rather than pure market forces or raw political power (preemption). Within a YIMBY framework, it is possible to imagine that costs associated with establishing the full range of needed treatment facilities across a region might be shared on the basis of equity, calculated by a mutually acceptable formula.[30]

The YIMBY approach was a direct outgrowth of local community concerns over equity and justice in facility siting. Under this philosophy, each community formally accepts that it is part of the problem (because local businesses generate hazardous wastes) and thus has some responsibility for solving the problem (that is, no community can simply ship its wastes elsewhere). At the same time, no community is asked to accept more than its fair share of waste treatment and management responsibilities, though a few may volunteer to do that willingly in exchange for explicit advantages. Thus, the onus for facility development rests mainly on the larger waste-generating areas, not the remote periphery that has been the target of most past siting proposals.

Intercounty agreements called for by the YIMBY approach do not ban flows of hazardous wastes across county lines (an approach neither practical nor constitutional). Quite the contrary. Generators are free to send their wastes to any licensed facility designed to accept them, wherever that facility may be. Prices for treatment and disposal (and for transportation to a facility) remain the primary determinants of waste flows.

Under YIMBY, the intercounty agreements focus on land use issues: the scale of new facilities to be built in particular locations and siting approval procedures. Counties agree under these plans to accept new facilities of a type and on a scale appropriate to their needs and those of other counties in the regional agreement. Thus, these new facilities meet both equity and economy-of-scale criteria. Because the facilities are located close to local generators, transportation costs are lower, and most local generators will find it economically attractive to use them. Local political officials can defend their YIMBY-based approval of such a facility against local NIMBY criticisms by pointing out that the facility indeed serves mainly local needs and that their community is not being exploited merely to meet the needs of outsiders.

The initiative for proposing new facilities still derives mostly from the private hazardous waste management industry. Now, however, siting proponents can be more confident their proposals will meet with local acceptance provided the proposals are consistent with local efforts.

This approach allows for economies of scale and lets business judgment determine the actual locations for facilities as long as each facility meets the agreed YIMBY formula. In southern California, besides brokering the YIMBY agreement among the communities of its region, the Southern California Hazardous Waste Management Authority (SCHWMA) stands ready to mediate between local communities and private companies during facility siting and permitting.[31]

YIMBY is based on the implicit belief that spreading a handful of facilities across a region is far more feasible politically than trying to locate a few larger, more centralized facilities, often in less-populous or poorer communities. Regionwide, some level of understanding is needed on waste generation, source reduction, and the numbers and types of facilities before individual communities can be convinced they are in fact being asked to accept their "fair share."

Clearly, YIMBY can play an important role in overcoming the natural local resistance to siting hazardous waste facilities. However, the experience of SCHWMA suggests that alone YIMBY too is not enough. The counties in the region were the first in the nation formally to adopt the fair-share principle for siting new hazardous waste facilities, but even they could not agree on just how many facilities of what kind were going to be equitably shared.

Agreement on the concept has proved far easier than agreement on specifics. Political pressures against defining numbers and types of facilities in particular jurisdictions overwhelmed the already agreed-upon YIMBY philosophy. Instead, SCHWMA decided to leave it up to private industry to propose the number and types of facilities that would come into the region, as has traditionally been the case.

A few environmental and other activists agreed with this deferral to expediency, but for very different reasons. They sought to keep the number of new hazardous waste facilities at a minimum in order to maximize the pressure on business to reduce generation of hazardous wastes in the first place.

SCHWMA was unable to overcome that impasse, and soon its efforts were eclipsed by a statewide effort to join siting with source reduction, waste minimization, and overall hazardous materials safety issues. That new statewide process, in turn, was itself overwhelmed by intensifying local-state tensions over YIMBY and fair-share principles. The scope of the problem had to widen even further before it could be narrowed back down to siting.

Programs of Comprehensive Waste Management

By the mid-1980s, controversies in California over land disposal, siting new hazardous waste treatment facilities, cleaning up federal and state Superfund sites, and administrative ineptitude in the state's hazardous waste and hazardous materials programs, as well as confrontations between business and environmental interests, had at last reached the crisis stage.

The circumstances were roughly as follows: The business community decried closure of its landfills, claiming new ones (far more safely designed) were imperative for the state's economic survival. But no one could say how many new landfills were needed, nor would industry talk much about what the future waste load in the state would really be. The primary business strategy for overcoming local self-determination on siting was to demand state preemption to "guarantee" siting of those facilities in accord with industry's self-perceived needs. However, not even the most probusiness state politicians were eager to assume that responsibility in view of the public's ire on the topics of toxics and siting.

State experts were calling for initiating the nation's first phaseout of land disposal, with waste treatment replacing it. Meanwhile, environmental and health activists were demanding that industry drastically reduce waste generation rather than just seek new dump sites.

More radical activists even began to call for "zero" discharge of hazardous wastes—as impossible as that might be—and for a full ban on toxics in agricultural and industrial production wherever human harm might result.[32] Environmental and health interests were not willing to limit their focus simply to hazardous wastes. They saw the issue much more broadly as one of use and management of hazardous materials throughout society and the adverse effects of these substances on health and the natural environment.

As the toxics controversy heated up in 1982, an extraordinary dialogue was initiated in which all the leading interests in toxics policy in California eventually were able to agree on several important points and principles. That accord formed the foundation of a comprehensive new approach to dealing with the state's hazardous waste management problems. Consensus took several years to emerge, and implementation of policy has been characterized by ongoing superfailure. Nevertheless, the process does suggest some important lessons for America's second toxics decade:

1. Debate must be conducted free of speculation. Participants in the California program agreed conjecture seemed to be the basis for almost everything being said about the need for a network of hazardous waste facilities for the state, toxics safeguards in industry and for communities, projections of future hazardous waste loads, waste minimization possibilities, and almost everything else relevant to the toxics debate. Further, they agreed that debate in such an atmosphere was counterproductive. It was misleading, prone to creating antagonisms between contending parties, and hardly conducive to achieving good public policy.

2. Discussion must be based on facts and scientific analysis. An informed and intelligent discussion of toxics issues requires sound information about current patterns of hazardous waste generation, waste treatment and waste minimization technologies, cost data, and so on. Moreover, all facts need to be assembled openly and professionally, with contributions made by all interested parties.

3. Informed, open dialogue among relevant policy experts is the route to good policy. With solid information in hand, it should be possible to

conduct a sophisticated and rational policy discourse, which would include business, government, environmental, healthcare, and technological experts. Given the widespread fear of toxics and the ingrained resistance to anything remotely associated with them, that discourse should take place at the state level as well as in those communities and regions across the state most directly affected, where responsibility would ultimately rest for the safe management of hazardous wastes and hazardous materials.

4. Planning should be guided by broad policy goals, including recognition of the need for some new facilities. Policy for the state must recognize the importance of safety considerations and the need to change dramatically waste generation and waste management practices. No matter how successful waste minimization might become, however, all parties involved would have to reconcile themselves to the need for many new treatment facilities and one or more residuals repositories to be sited and constructed throughout the state.

5. Planning must be rational, comprehensive, and professional. The process requires rational, comprehensive planning guided by professionals, albeit with considerable community and interest-group consultation, and must be kept as much as possible outside the conventional partisan political arena.

It took two years to arrive at agreement on these principles, through the state-chartered bipartisan Hazardous Waste Management Council. Three more years were needed to persuade a conservative new governor—skeptical of the land disposal bans and risk assessment initiated by his predecessor—finally to sign the enabling legislation, after vetoing it twice. The new statewide planning and siting bill called upon each of California's 58 counties voluntarily to develop a hazardous waste plan within two years. All 58 did. Failure to develop a plan would have left the area particularly vulnerable to the later actions of a new statewide siting appeals board.

County plans included these key elements:

- an analysis of the hazardous waste stream generated in the county by types of waste, estimated through 1994 with overall figures projected through 2000;
- a description of existing hazardous waste facilities that treat, handle, recycle, and dispose of the county's hazardous waste, including the aggregate capacity to manage waste generated in that area by facilities in the county;
- an analysis of the potential in the county to recycle and minimize the volume of hazardous waste at the source of generation;

- consideration of strategies for managing hazardous waste from small-quantity generators and households;
- the need in the county for additional hazardous waste facilities to manage properly its current and future waste loads;
- specific siting criteria to locate needed facilities and identification of generally suitable sites within the county;
- a statement of overall county goals and objectives for hazardous waste management through 2000 and an implementation plan including specific time lines.

To carry out this enormous planning effort, the legislation provided $10 million to be parceled out to the counties by the Department of Health Services (DHS)—the state's regulatory agency for hazardous wastes. A great deal of local consultation was called for, with each county's elected board of supervisors asked to appoint an advisory committee including at least one representative each from industry, an environmental organization, and the public; at least three representatives from cities; and where possible, other members expert in hazardous waste management from the engineering, geological, and water quality viewpoints.

DHS was given responsibility for developing guidelines to assist county planning, reviewing and approving plans, and, ultimately, assembling from the county plans an overall state plan called for by companion legislation.

There was little illusion that the most comprehensive, rational, and agreed-upon plans by themselves would necessarily overcome all local resistance to new hazardous waste siting proposals. Nor did participants believe that the counties would voluntarily prepare their plans unless strong future sanctions (besides planning money) were available. Therefore, the legislation established a new state board with authority upon appeal to review and, if need be, to override any local facility-siting decision (either a NIMBY-style rejection of a proposed facility or a siting approval).

This appeal board was composed of seven persons: three state agency directors (the heads of Health Services, the Air Resources Board, and the Water Resources Control Board) and four local elected officials (one county supervisor serving at-large statewide and another selected from the affected county's board of supervisors, plus a city council member serving at-large and a council member from the city most directly affected). Simply put, it was the board's role to rule, upon appeal, in favor of good facilities—facilities with sound engineering and design, locally needed, and in technically adequate locations. The board's primary criterion was the consistency of the proposed facility with an approved county plan.

The Results of County-Based Planning: Progress and State-Local Tensions

Draft plans were completed by all 58 California counties, from Alpine with 20,000 residents to Los Angeles with 8.6 million. They reveal an impressive record of accomplishment in this complex policy arena.

Equally noteworthy are the substantially different interpretations of the basic goals of toxics planning evidenced by the counties and by the state. The earlier state-local consensus disintegrated substantially over the issue of fair share. Most counties strongly endorsed the YIMBY philosophy developed earlier in southern California; the state explicitly did not.

If nothing else, the planning exercise forced Californians to put into concrete terms the scope of hazardous wastes used in the state, from city and county levels upward. Requiring each county to reconcile its hazardous waste load, now and into the future, with its capacity to manage those wastes safely in light of upcoming state and federal bans on land disposal and stringent restrictions on sewering served to convert almost everyone to the virtues of source reduction and waste minimization.

The relative size of the numbers and their projected growth by 2000—unless industry radically changes its waste management practices before then—are themselves sobering. This is clearly seen in the waste loads from and treatment needs of the eight counties comprising southern California, from Santa Barbara in the north to San Diego along the border with Mexico (see Box 7.1).

Confronted with the larger and ever-growing waste loads, which parallel what all counties believe will be California's continually expanding economy, along with the attendant need for new treatment facilities and thus for difficult siting decisions, the counties largely declared source reduction to be a major (if not primary) policy strategy. Their goals range from 30 percent reductions in San Diego County to 75 percent in Santa Barbara County by 2000. Other counties have simply included strong language about their commitment to maximum feasible waste reduction. With the counties committed to these goals, the pressures already mounting on industry to reduce at the source will become even more intense.

The data gathered by the counties on wastes and on existing treatment facilities can be used to determine the type, number, and capacity of treatment facilities needed by each county through 2000. Statewide,

BOX 7.1 Current (1986) and Projected (2000) Hazardous Waste Generation in the Southern California Region and By County

Treatment Facility Needs in Region

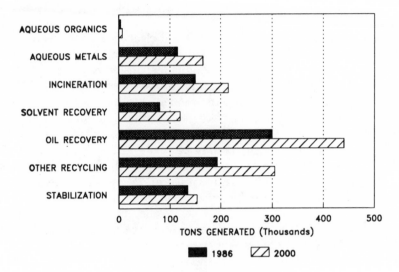

Hazardous Waste Generation by County

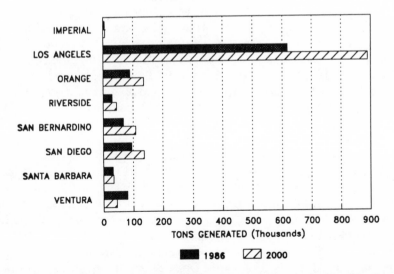

Source: Southern California Hazardous Waste Management Authority, "Southern California Hazardous Waste Management Plan—Regional Plan, Part One." Los Angeles: The Authority (January 26, 1989), 22, 23.

offsite treatment capacity shortfalls are most pronounced in incineration and recycling (except for waste oils and stabilization). At this time, the more difficult task is to specify where these facilities could be located, an issue going to the very heart of the most serious state-county controversy over hazardous waste management planning: equity and "fair share."

The language of the new law makes it clear its authors were hoping to achieve county-level recognition of the hazardous waste problem and, in turn, acceptance by each county of its responsibility to resolve its own facility-siting problems. The more hazardous wastes generated locally, the more responsibility to site the modern facilities needed to manage those wastes safely. Counties were given both responsibility and power, which can be seen in the requirements that data be collected on a county basis, that decisions for the county be made in the county, and that a broad consensus be developed around the plan throughout the county.

On these points, the law is unequivocal. Moreover, drawing on the several years of failure of every other approach to siting and on the evolving experience in southern California, the legislature carefully adopted the YIMBY principle of equity; each county would take responsibility for its own waste stream.

The law also reflected pragmatic vote-counting in the legislature and the consensus developed earlier in the Hazardous Waste Management Council. Local government interests had supported the initial bill because it explicitly protected them, especially the smaller and more rural counties, from being encroached upon by the larger, industrialized, more politically powerful areas. With that in place, both the County Supervisors Association of California (CSAC) and the League of California Cities had supported the legislation. Once locally based plans were in place and approved, facility developers could not use their political muscle to override local land-use decisions.

Therefore, it came as a serious setback when the state's guidelines published in late 1987 called for each county to identify feasible sites for all types of new hazardous waste facilities, regardless of that county's size and waste management requirements. County plans for facility siting were to be based solely, the state decreed, on a specific list of environmental, health, and other technical considerations. Equity was no longer part of the equation. It was as though the process were no more than a conventional exercise in land-use designation. Alpine County was to plan conceivably for as many facilities as Los Angeles County, without regard to local needs. The state's Department of Health Services (DHS) refused to approve county plans not in accord with its approach.

If adhered to, of course, this approach would open the door to unlimited siting of hazardous waste management facilities in any and all counties, wherever such facilities happened to be proposed by private proponents, based solely on technical considerations. That was an extraordinary departure not only from the promises made to counties, cities, and community groups during the legislative deliberations on the law but also from the specific language in it.

The perverse result was that counties following these state guidelines strictly and obtaining plan approval would be even more vulnerable to having their decisions overriden by the appeals board (because to be approved under the state guidelines a county plan had to accommodate any and all new facilities) than was the existing case when there was no approved plan. Clearly, the YIMBY of legislative compromise had been rejected by the mandates of the state executive branch—under the governor who had twice previously vetoed the legislation before finally signing it in 1986 (an election year). The state's preemptive approach would encourage the same local-based opposition that had inspired the siting compromise process in the first place.

Despite vociferous county objections, DHS refused to abide by the fair-share principle or the regional YIMBY compact. In the words of a top DHS official, reliance on county-by-county planning was "wrong-headed"; therefore the agency could not be bound by the letter of the law.[33]

The law had given DHS authority to develop the state guidelines each county was obliged to follow if it wanted DHS approval. The agency had used that provision to redefine the goals to its liking. It has argued since that a county-based, county-specific siting approach is neither economically feasible nor in keeping with a free-market approach to facility siting.

Most counties simply refused to go along with the state, though the state and counties continued to negotiate over the meaning of "fair share." In effect, the planning and siting process reached an impasse. To date, only Los Angeles County (which in any event needs all kinds of facilities, of all sizes) and two much smaller counties acceded to the state requirements to plan for more than their own wastes; several others engaged in litigation; most awaited further developments. That does not mean the counties were oblivious to the considerations of economies of scale and market forces in facility siting. However, their solution was not to negate the fair-share principle but to supplement it with intercounty compacts and bilateral negotiations with other counties.

The concept developed by the eight southern California counties (before the advent of the statewide planning process) recognized that not every county in the region would need to site a residuals repository, neutralization facility, incinerator, or other such operation. These facilities were to be sited based on the region's needs rather than the county's needs.

The solution the counties came to was to enter into binding intercounty compacts stipulating that if county A sited one type of facility larger than it needed, county B would agree to do likewise for another type. By this method, public officials could agree on the overall distribution of these facilities, on a process for siting, and on a scheme to ensure the agreement could be enforceable. As long as aggregate treatment capacity meets the region's hazardous waste treatment needs, the system will be in accord with the fair-share principle while providing adequate economies of scale and efficiency criteria.[34] The southern California counties currently have that equity-based system in place, though actual siting of facilities has stalled in the face of broader state-local tensions.

The state agency simply refused to recognize as acceptable the dimensions of a county's plan either on the principle of fair share or the use of intercounty compacts. Apparently, DHS and the business interests that had the ear of the state administration during that period felt the county-based approach would overly restrict the waste management business, which desired to site large facilities, at times in less-populous locations.

For some time to come, it will not be clear whether the state agency and the California counties can overcome their differences. One attempted reconciliation is suggestive, however. Faced by the prospect of rejecting almost all the draft county plans because they included provisions either for fair-share or intercounty agreements, DHS proposed a compromise that under certain circumstances would allow both principles.[35]

At the same time, DHS rejected several draft county plans that failed to provide the enforceable siting guarantees it had been demanding. If negotiations between the counties and the state finally result in a decision recognizing the fair-share and YIMBY principles, presumably all 58 California counties will be able to move to final approval of their plans. Meanwhile, the legislature continues to postpone the deadlines for final approval, hoping for some kind of resolution.

This new type of political compact for dealing with hazardous waste management through county plans requires industry to make significant strides toward source reduction as a condition of receiving local permits and approvals for new (or modified) hazardous waste treatment and disposal facilities. These facilities will allow an area to meet its capacity goals and thereby contribute to implementing the transition away from land disposal.

In turn, the county and its cities will accept the responsibility both for defending their plan before local constituencies (in the face of typical NIMBY attitudes) and for approving siting of those facilities actually called for in their plan. If siting permission is refused for a proposal that meets all the needed requirements and is consistent with that county's plan, its applicant can then appeal that rejection to the statewide review board on the strong presumption that the local rejection will indeed be overturned.

The viability of California's comprehensive county hazardous waste management plans has yet to be tested. Nevertheless, they provide striking evidence of a dramatic turnabout, perhaps most notably by many business and local government officials, in people's thinking about the proper course of hazardous waste policy and the future of toxic materials use in industry and commerce in the state. The focus on source reduction, safe hazardous waste management, and systematic planning and management signifies an important (even if only implicit for some) embrace of the new environmental ethic.

All that is only a first step, of course. If the county plans and overall decisionmaking process are going to provide a working blueprint for hazardous waste management and source reduction to 2000 and beyond, those plans will need to receive state approval and be updated and revised on a continuing basis.

Comprehensive Planning Nationwide Under SARA

In 1986, Congress indirectly pressured the states to face up to their needs for siting hazardous waste management facilities. It added to SARA an amendment offered by Senator John Chafee of Rhode Island under which the states were given three years to submit plans to EPA showing how their hazardous wastes would be managed over the next 20 years within the strictures of RCRA, Superfund, and any other applicable federal laws.

Failure to provide this "capacity assurance" would result in the withholding of future federal Superfund monies. Chafee and others assumed states that could not show the needed capacity would face unavoidable pressure to site new treatment facilities rather than lose their cleanup funding.

In fact, the states responded to the Chafee provision less by promising to site new facilities than by adopting a California-like comprehensive approach to siting. This approach, designed in large measure by the National Governors Association (NGA), was endorsed by EPA with a single major exception: EPA placed much weaker emphasis on interstate agreements than NGA had proposed. Interstate versions of California's intercounty agreements emerged as a very important issue.

Many states joined together in regional agreements to share available waste treatment and disposal facilities. These agreements were based largely on existing capacities within the group of states taken as an aggregate. Attention also was given to source reduction (again, as in the county-level plans in California) to reduce the need to develop more treatment capacity.

Although state capacity assurance plans have been criticized for lacking enforceable provisions and detailed source reduction commitments, for the first time all 50 state documents make it quite clear that from now on, siting decisions throughout the United States will need to be made within the context of a comprehensive approach—in terms of geography, politics, waste management technology, and source reduction.

After a decade of toxics policymaking and implementation efforts, clearly the issue has come full circle, right back to facility siting. Once again, superfailure has intervened to halt effective implementation of improved toxics management policies. It is now painfully clear there has been a great deal of community and marketplace resistance to siting needed new facilities. The bitter legacy of past hazardous wastes mismanagement and the often exaggerated claims about the need for new facilities have left all concerned considerably more cautious, if not downright skeptical.

However, if the vitally needed revolution in toxics management is to be realized, new facilities must be sited. In the early 1990s, the YIMBY principle and California's statewide process suggest in part how this might be accomplished.

NOTES

1. Legislative Commission on Toxic Substances and Hazardous Waste, "Waste Facility Siting: A National Survey," report to the New York State Legislature (June 1987), 11 [cited hereafter as New York Legislature].

2. The CCHW was started by Lois Gibbs, a leader of the grassroots citizens group at Love Canal, who moved to Washington, D.C., to form a nationwide citizen action group. The NTC was started by John O'Connor, working out of his home in Boston, as the result of his efforts to gain greater citizen involvement in the Superfund cleanup process. Both groups have risen to become major players in the siting process and toxics policy process. See Dick Russell, "The Rise of the Grass-Roots Toxics Movement," *The Amicus Journal* 12 (Winter 1990), 17–21.

3. David Morell and Christopher Magorian, *Siting Hazardous Waste Facilities: Local Opposition and the Myth of Preemption* (Cambridge, Mass.: Ballinger,

1982), ch. 2.

4. Michael Kraft and Bruce Clary, "Citizen Participation and the Nimby Syndrome: Public Response to Radioactive Waste Disposal," *Western Political Science Quarterly* 44 (June 1991), 299-328.

5. B. A. Payne, S. Jay Olshansky, and T. E. Segel, "The Effects on Property Values of Proximity to a Site Contaminated with Radioactive Waste," *Natural Resources Journal* 27 (1987), 579-590.

6. A parallel could be drawn to the 1970 Clean Air Act, which proclaimed clean air by 1975, with a possible extension to 1977. Now, two decades later, smog and acid rain are still prevalent. Why would congressionally mandated land disposal phaseout deadlines for hazardous waste management fare any better?

7. The growing appreciation of the multifaceted nature of risk perception and how we might bridge both the technical and social dimensions of the issue are the themes of two recent books by leaders in the risk communications field: Sheldon Krimsky and Alonzo Plough, *Environmental Hazards: Communicating Risks as a Social Process* (Dover, Mass.: Auburn House, 1988); Committee on Risk Perception and Communication, National Research Council, *Improving Risk Communications* (Washington, D.C.: National Academy Press, 1989). Elected officials' perceptions are addressed in William R. Potapchuk, "New Approaches to Citizen Participation: Building Consent," *National Civic Review* (Spring 1991), 158-168.

8. Susan G. Hadden, "Public Perception of Hazardous Waste," *Risk Analysis* 11 (March 1991), 49.

9. Hadden, "Public Perception," 49.

10. Andrew Baum, "Disasters, Natural and Otherwise," Psychology Today (April 1988), 57-60.

11. Harry Otway and Detlof von Winterfeldt, "Beyond Acceptable Risk: On the Social Acceptability of Technologies," *Policy Sciences* 14 (1982), 247-256.

12. Seymour Martin Lipset and William Schneider, *The Confidence Gap: Business, Labor, and Government in the Public Mind*, rev. ed. (Baltimore: Johns Hopkins University, 1987); Kraft and Clary, "Citizen Participation."

13. Winner/Wagner and Associates, Inc., "Hazardous Waste Materials and Waste Assessment Project: Public Opinion Survey" (Sacramento, Calif.: California Council for Environmental and Economic Balance, 1987).

14. Richard Andrews, "Hazardous Waste Facility Siting: State Approaches," in Charles Davis and James Lester, eds., *Dimensions of Hazardous Waste Politics and Policy* (New York: Greenwood Press, 1988), 117.

15. New York Legislature, 9.

16. Andrews, "Hazardous Waste Facility Siting," 119.

17. The failure of pioneering New Jersey to shift siting powers to the state is told in Morell and Magorian, *Myth of Preemption*.

18. Peter M. Sandman and Emilie Schmeidler, "Getting to Maybe: Decisions on the Road to Negotiation in Hazardous Waste Facility Siting," Environmental Education Fund, Rutgers University (January 1988), 292-304.

19. William Ury, Jeanne Brett, and Stephen Goldberg, *Getting Disputes Resolved: Designing Systems to Cut the Costs of Conflict* (San Francisco: Jossey-Bass, 1988); Lawrence Bacow and Michael Wheeler, *Environmental Dispute Resolution* (New York: Plenum, 1984).

20. Gail Bingham, *Resolving Environmental Disputes: A Decade of Experience* (Washington, D.C.: Conservation Foundation, 1986).

21. New York Legislature, 16–17.

22. Andrews, "Hazardous Waste Facility Siting," 124; Gail Bingham and Timothy Mealey, "Overview: Negotiating Hazardous Waste Facility Siting and Permitting Agreements," in Gail Bingham and Timothy Mealey, eds., *Negotiating Hazardous Waste Facility Siting and Permitting Agreements* (Washington, D.C.: Conservation Foundation, 1988).

23. Michael O'Hare, Lawrence Bacow, and Debra Sanderson, *Facility Siting and Public Opposition* (New York: Van Nostrand Reinhold Co., 1983).

24. Kent Portney, "The Role of Economic Factors in Lay Perceptions of Risk," in Davis and Lester, *Dimensions of Hazardous Waste Politics*, 60.

25. Hadden, "Public Perception," 52.

26. New York Legislature, 19–20.

27. Albert Matheny and Bruce Williams, "Rethinking Participation: Assessing Florida's Strategy for Siting Hazardous Waste Disposal Facilities," in Davis and Lester, *Dimensions of Hazardous Waste Politics*, 37–52.

28. On this point there is near consensus. See Hadden, "Public Perception of Hazardous Waste"; Krimsky and Plough, *Environmental Hazards;* and Committee on Risk Perception and Communications, *Improving Risk Communications.*

29. David Morell, "Transportable Modular Incinerators: Effectiveness and Community Acceptance in Different Uses," paper presented at the Annual Meeting of the Air and Waste Management Association (Anaheim, Calif., June 1989).

30. David Morell, "Siting and the Politics of Equity," *Hazardous Waste* 1 (1984), 555–571.

31. In the single most important instance of this collaborative effort, Kaiser Fontana seemed to have found a viable public-private partnership approach to siting. That effort was prematurely terminated, however, by Kaiser's bankruptcy, an event that once again illustrated the nesting of siting/public opposition concerns within the broader context of economics and marketplace uncertainty.

32. This is a frequent call from environmentalists in California, where fully one quarter of all pesticides applied in the world are being used.

33. Paraphrase of comments by C. David Willis, DHS, conference on "The Tanner [Hazardous Waste Management Planning] Process: One Year Later" (January 7, 1988).

34. The southern California counties developed the model for intercounty (or other interjurisdiction) agreements on facility siting. See "Breaking Political Gridlock: Experiment in Public-Private Cooperation for Hazardous Waste Policy," California Institute of Public Affairs (1988).

35. Letter from Kenneth W. Kizer, director, DHS (October 6, 1989), on behalf of the DHS negotiating team to all lead agencies responsible for preparing county hazardous waste management plans.

CHAPTER EIGHT

Looking Forward: An Effective Toxics Policy Agenda for the 1990s

For nearly every shortcoming of America's toxics policy, proposed solutions abound to cope with the problems: the old hazardous waste sites, the continuing stream of hazardous wastes being generated, and more than ever before the management of hazardous materials throughout industry and the home environment.

Some voices call for more and tighter federal, state, and local control; others demand "market solutions." "Make the polluter pay" is heard, as is "rely on economic incentives" both for firms and individuals. A few would ban the most toxic of materials from any use at all. A cafeteria list of strategies has been suggested—and as noted in Chapter Seven, a few have even been tested—to solve the conundrum of siting new hazardous waste facilities. Almost everyone agrees facilities are needed, but so far no one wants one in his or her backyard.

This final chapter addresses that panoply of policy suggestions and presents others we have developed. To begin with, we are convinced that the status quo is surely undesirable. More of the same is not an acceptable political, economic, or ecological choice. More superfailure cannot be allowed; basic changes in toxics policy and implementation are a must.

We are also convinced that the role of government—especially the Environmental Protection Agency at the federal level but states and locals too—should be fixed at the level of macropolicy, not micromanagement.[1] Toxics management policies should be guided to the greatest extent possible by broad principles laid down by elected representatives of the American people, but implementation of these policies—to encourage source reduction and waste minimization and possibly to shift the burden of proof about the safety of hazardous materials back to the producers and commercial users—ought to be driven by the major forces of market incentives, decentralized decisions, and individual choices. Incentives for positive action must replace today's bizarre situation with its clear preference for harmful inertia.

Likewise, the more that local communities can participate in determining their own destinies, the better. While it may be unrealistic to permit unequivocal local vetoes over all decisions on facility siting, some mechanisms need to be adopted that—when properly used—encourage the greatest possible exercise of local will and thereby gain sincere local assent to facility-siting imperatives.

Finally, from the broadest choices about toxics policy right down to the specifics in a community or at a designated facility, actions must be guided by a set of consistent social and moral principles. Five guideposts of *equity* and *justice* in this modern era of toxics management defined by Roger Kasperson can serve as useful reminders:

1. The general well-being of society demands that some individuals will have to bear risks on behalf of others.
2. Whenever reasonable, those risks should be avoided rather than acknowledged through compensation alone.
3. Unavoidable risks should be shared among the entire population of beneficiaries, not just concentrated among a few.
4. Unavoidable reasonable risks should be accompanied by compensatory benefits.
5. Risk bearing should be made as voluntary as reasonably possible within the constraints of deploying facilities in a timely way. The burden of proof for site suitability should fall on the developer, not on the proposed community.[2]

It is unlikely that all these principles as they apply to toxics management can be met within a strict market framework assigning unfettered power to narrow private interests. Equally, they cannot be achieved by a top-down, command-and-control government. And surely the needs are not being met by the ineffective, fragmented regulatory regimes that have evolved piecemeal during America's first toxics decade. The challenge is to devise approaches incorporating all five principles yet be sensitive to the complex political, economic, technical, and social contexts of modern American society.

Michael E. Porter argues that environmental protection and economic competitiveness can be made mutually reinforcing:

> Strict environmental regulations do not inevitably hinder competitive advantage against foreign rivals; indeed, they often enhance it. Tough standards trigger innovation and upgrading. . . . Turning environmental concern into competitive advantage demands that we establish the right kind of regulations. They must stress pollution prevention rather than merely abatement or cleanup. They must not constrain the technology

used to achieve them, or else innovation will be stifled. And standards must be sensitive to the costs involved and use market incentives to contain them.[3]

Keeping these considerations in mind, we turn to policy alternatives for the second toxics decade. In the first section, we consider how several of the broad strategies that have been suggested for better control over environmental pollution in air, water, and other arenas might apply to toxics; these strategies include information gathering, hazardous materials banning, privatization, taxation, fee-and-rebate systems, and no-fault insurance systems. In the remainder of the chapter, we consider proposals directed at the siting and management of specific facilities and analyze the political and social framework within which hazardous wastes and toxics policy must be set.

BROAD STRATEGIES TO DIRECT
DECISIONS OF INDIVIDUAL FIRMS

"Sunshine" Disclosures and Information Systems

One of the major stumbling blocks to an effective toxics policy has been the absence of good information on the extent of hazardous wastes and toxic materials in need of better management throughout society. As has been learned in other environmental arenas and as common sense would suggest, developing an appropriate information base is an important first step toward an effective toxics policy. Frequently, simply shedding light on the subject and the attention this brings can be by far the least expensive way to achieve better toxics management. The need is obvious, though the process of developing the data bases has been slow to evolve and is an area in need of major improvement.

New Jersey pioneered in requiring mandatory site assessment as a provision of deed exchanges for all industrial and commercial property.[4] Far more so than have any of that state's command-and-control regulatory schemes, that single provision has energized banks, engineering consultants, and especially property owners to pay close attention to possible hazardous waste contamination of their properties and to safe management of all hazardous materials onsite. The extent of past hazardous waste mismanagement problems no longer remains hidden in New Jersey; this is not the case in other areas.

On the industrial processing front, information is essential to effective policy implementation by thousands of individual firms, whatever their size. Source reduction and waste minimization will be driven primarily by detailed knowledge of a firm's particular process streams: Where and how are various hazardous wastes being generated? That information allows the facility owner to modify existing operations, to introduce appropriate new techniques and technologies, and thus to reduce hazardous waste generation.

Some local governments have also encouraged businesses to carry out detailed waste reduction audits: Ventura County and the City of Los Angeles are two California leaders. Several state laws have also required firms to carry out waste audits.[5] RCRA now requires all waste generators to certify they are pursuing waste reduction strategies; the 1990 Pollution Prevention Act goes much further (see Chapters Four and Six). Enforcement still lags well behind such statutory mandates, but the obvious hope is that individual firms will use available waste audit information to pinpoint specific cost-saving measures for themselves, responding to direct economic incentives to proceed with implementation.

Compliance with the vast maze of toxics regulations is predicated on availability of clear, concise information on what exactly is being demanded by all the federal, state, and local regulatory agencies responsible for implementing many different laws. Comprehension is prerequisite to compliance.

To make firms aware of all the different laws that apply to them, a number of innovative information systems have emerged. These materials can make compliance with permit and other requirements a reality. For example, a large wall chart ("Hazardous Materials Program Matrix") is commercially available in twelve states—California, Florida, Illinois, Massachusetts, Michigan, New Jersey, New York, North Carolina, Ohio, Pennsylvania, Texas, and Washington. The chart and an accompanying loose-leaf service (*Hazardous Materials Program Commentary*) present summary information on all relevant federal and state laws. All these documents are updated frequently and are available on an annual subscription basis (see Box 8.1). Another loose-leaf resource (*Environmental Compliance in California: The Simplified Guide*), newly available in 1991, provides users with clear checklists in easy-to-follow question-and-answer format.[6] In addition, companies often develop their own compliance manuals for individual facilities to provide details on deadlines, requirements, reports, training, and other assignments.

Through modern computer technology, a range of automated compliance-information systems is available. Some focus on specific regulatory requirements. Others provide comprehensive information interweaving regulatory and operational details on hazardous materials purchases, use, and storage; hazardous waste generation, treatment, and disposal; and personnel training and capability. Regulatory information centers being considered in several areas can provide local small businesses with appropriate and timely data on regulations, on technologies, and even on financing options.

Bans on Selected Activities or Products

At first glance, bans on unwanted behavior seem a straightforward way to stop it. In the toxics arena, two types of bans have actually occurred. Continued use of a number of substances that beyond question are harmful to human health and to the environment have been prohibited in whole or in part. Good examples are lead additives in paint and gasoline, DDT as a pesticide, and more recently chlorofluorocarbons (CFCs). Sweden's comprehensive ban on products using or containing cadmium, including their import, is a striking example from Europe. An even broader approach to banning is being considered by the members of the Organization for Economic Cooperation and Development as part of its multinational campaign against products that detract from sustainable development.[7]

A second type of ban has prohibited entire categories of hazardous wastes—halogenated solvents, cyanides, heavy metals—from being deposited in landfills without adequate prior treatment, first in California and later nationwide under the HSWA changes to RCRA. The goal of these rules is to eliminate the adverse effects such wastes can have when dumped untreated onto the land (even into landfills that are more secure today), with the real potential for those contaminants to escape into surrounding soil, the air, and adjacent waterways. Land disposal bans became the centerpiece of national policy governing industry's continuing generation of hazardous wastes, inspiring a more rapid shift toward treatment instead of disposal.

To date, banning selected toxic substances has been adopted in extraordinary situations and on a case-by-case basis. A guru of the environmental movement, Barry Commoner, advocates banning as the most effective hazardous materials management strategy available to society.[8] In retrospect, his case is powerful. Over the past 25 years, banning has probably had the most impact of any action in ridding our air and waterways of certain harmful substances. However, as prospective toxics policy, banning has two huge shortcomings. First, it is not clear what criteria should be applied to review a substance in order to consider its prohibition. In most cases, widespread harm will not yet have been established at the time of public review. Only conjecture about possible harm (and possibly relevant data from animal studies) would be available and such risk assessments are often not very convincing. Second, it is fairly easy for society to cope economically and politically with a minimal list of banned substances. But where does such an

BOX 8.1 *Environmental Compliance in California: The Simplified Guide*

ENVIRONMENTAL

COMPLIANCE IN

CALIFORNIA:

The Simplified

Guide

THE SIMPLIFIED GUIDE

is a new tool to aid California
businesses in addressing
such pressing issues as:

▸ *Hazardous Materials Management*

▸ *Hazardous Waste Management*

▸ *Air and Water Requirements*

This unique and easy-to-use
management tool offers businesses of all
sizes guidance to complex environmental
requirements:

- Waters Bill
- La Follette Bill
- Transportation
- Tanks: UST /AST
- OSHA HCS
- SARA III
- Emergency Response
- Medical Wastes
- Water Quality
- Sewer Discharge of
  Industrial Wastes
- Air Quality
- Air Toxics
- Asbestos
- Pesticides
- Proposition 65
  Small Business Assistance

(continues)

BOX 8.1 *(continued)*

---

*Yes/No question &
answer format makes
effective compliance a
reality, even for
the smallest firm*

Example from Section 1:

Question 1:

Am I subject to Waters Bill
requirements?

YES ___ NO ___

(If you answer "YES" to Questions 1.1,
1.2, AND 1.3, you are subject to Waters
Bill requirements.)

(If you answer "NO" to Questions 1.1,
1.2, OR 1.3, you are not subject to
Waters Bill requirements. Please go on
to another section of this *Simplified
Guide.)*

The Waters Bill's inventory and Business
Plan requirements apply to any **business**
that handles **hazardous materials** above
determined **threshold quantities.**

**This loose-leaf
subscription service
features:**

- *Self-Assessment
  Checklists for All
  Major State &
  Federal
  Environmental
  Compliance
  Requirements*

- *Yes/No Question and
  Answer Format*

- *Quarterly Updates*

- *Tables of Regulations
  and Chemicals*

- *Forms, Charts,
  Organizational
  Materials*

- *Three-Ring Binder*

Prepared by and available from EPICS INTERNATIONAL, 1410 Jackson Street,
Oakland, California 94612   (510) 891-9794.

across-the-board policy begin or end? California's listing of chemicals under Proposition 65 is evolving gradually because users want to avoid liability, not because of any top-down rulings by some toxics-banning czar.

Moreover, the bluntness of outright banning almost always creates serious problems for product users and occasionally produces all-or-nothing political tugs-of-war. If banning ever does become a routine aspect of toxics policy, it would seriously challenge the capacity of American political style.

Without question, prohibition is a comprehensive approach to eliminating unwanted toxic substances from the environment. Selectively, it has proven effective in the past and in extraordinary circumstances can make eminently good sense. As prospective overall policy for coping with the thousands of hazardous substances in use throughout American society, the approach does not seem feasible.

Privatization

Better management of hazardous wastes and hazardous materials can be achieved by converting some of the affected environmental resources into private assets, then relying on individual property owners to protect them. Although this idea emerged first from America's political right, whose adherents usually see environmental problems as associated with government's mismanagement of public resources, it has growing appeal to the left as well.

The "tragedy of the commons" parable used to explain the environmental pollution crisis of modern industrial society asserts that it is in every person's self-interest to overconsume what is held in common—such as air, water, clean land—but to shepherd what is his or hers alone.[9] As a result, common resources soon become despoiled. The solution? Privatize public lands, auction off water and other resource rights, and establish private ownership where it has never before existed, as in the oceans.

Better than any safeguard for the environment, so the argument runs, is "self-interest [which] drives the private property owners to careful management and protection of their resources."[10] When disputes arise or injury results from poor management of private property, such as dumping liquid hazardous wastes where they can leak into someone else's underground drinking-water aquifer, anyone who is affected can then rely on private claims and tort law instead of government regulators to win appropriate relief.

Moreover, government policy all too commonly is determined by the lobbying efforts of organized interests rather than notions of the common good. Business advocates on one side and environmentalists on the other expend enormous resources on the political battle rather than directly on environmental protection. Rather than find ways of bargaining and working together to actually solve problems, as the parties would be compelled to do if all resources were held in private, the competing forces engage in a constant and nonproductive political tug-of-war.[11]

The privatization theme has also been taken up of late by the more populist-oriented left, but for different reasons. These advocates are interested in a "citizens' bill of rights" that would hold all polluters accountable for environmental and health protection. If a clean and healthful environment were everyone's constitutional right, then anyone who polluted could be brought to account through private litigation.

California's Proposition 65 goes a step in this direction by declaring that no one has the right to contaminate the state's underground aquifers (see Chapter Six). That approach shifted onto waste generators and hazardous materials users the full burden of proof for the safety of their actions. Violators can be pursued by ordinary individuals in protection of their rights as citizens. Indeed, anyone who brings suit may share in any fines that may result if a district attorney should subsequently join the case on behalf of the public.

Privatization—assigning environmental rights and calling upon market mechanisms—has an important role to play in toxics policy. This is especially true in moving those who generate pollution to internalize the true costs to society of managing their pollution, thus avoiding the need for the government to employ the legions of bureaucrats who will otherwise be needed to police the regulatory schemes evolving under RCRA and, as pointed out in Chapter Six, the Clean Air Act as well. As will be shown, even with respect to the siting of an individual hazardous waste facility, for example, a privatized solution by way of an enforceable contract between the community and the facility owner/operator is a promising idea.

Yet privatization does not work in a vacuum. For instance, would a "clean environment bill of rights" mean that a person or business could not generate any pollutants, ever? Would not that force all productive activities to stop altogether? If not, what pollution generation would be allowable in each case? These are questions government regulatory agencies still need to resolve, which takes resolution of the issues out of the marketplace and back into the political/regulatory arena.

In effect, market forces are critical to motivating the hundreds of thousands of hazardous wastes generators and handlers. This can be accomplished, however, only within the framework of a nationwide toxics policy.

Finally, under the theory of pure privatization, use of natural resources would inevitably be weighted in favor of those with the most financial resources, not in favor of public health, the environment, or individual citizens. Environmentalists have banded together in the past and to some extent offset the concentrated wealth of corporations and businesses to secure the nonuse or nonpollution of a resource, but financial parity is not likely to be achieved anytime soon. Thus, polluters might pay, but they would still be able to pollute.[12]

Waste-Based Taxes

Ask an economist for the best way to manage hazardous wastes and he or she will tell you to tax them, not ban them. A cogent case for this possibility was made by David Carol and Kenneth Rubin of the Congressional Budget Office, as a means to accomplish the hazardous waste minimization goals RCRA calls for, but is unlikely to achieve.[13] Their approach assumes that taxing disposal of wastes onto land makes businesses incur a dollar cost for continuing conventional hazardous waste disposal practices (e.g., land disposal, deep-well injection) on a par with or greater than the cost of converting to the preferred safer management approaches prescribed under RCRA.

Faced with added costs for improved waste management, many firms would invest in less-expensive waste management strategies, such as instituting onsite treatment, reusing and recycling hazardous materials, substituting nonhazardous materials, and changing in-plant processes to reduce hazardous waste by-products in the first place. Waste-based taxes are a powerful incentive to minimize, to substitute, and to treat. Most important, each business will respond to the taxes by adopting the most efficient—for it—method of waste management. Consequently, the need is greatly reduced for government monitoring and prescription of specific hazardous waste management practices.

Tax revenues can also provide funds to clean up abandoned sites and can pay to operate the government's monitoring and related toxics programs.   Taxes also can be used to encourage waste reduction practices. A proposal before the New Jersey legislature to increase the annual percentage rates for state corporate income tax requires the state environmental agency to define specific waste reduction guidelines and to allow firms to petition the state agency for rebates on added taxes upon proof of their conformance with state standards.[14]

Taxation can discourage use of hazardous materials as feedstocks in business and industry, set at whatever level is required to discourage use of a targeted material. For example, if the state's goal is to remove 70 percent of substance X from commerce, the tax would be set at a level that will drive users to substitute or simply to cease producing a product with X in it, leaving only 30 percent of X in use by those who have no substitute at the given price or maybe no substitute at all, so they will continue to purchase X even with the tax added. This approach would deal effectively with our unwillingness to prohibit a material when its use is vital yet damaging; the potential harm to the environment is internalized in the cost of the material at the feedstock level.

Because it operates through the market, a waste-based tax system is a powerful way to produce efficient responses from many different types of firms. Each company selects the mix of specific actions that maximizes its profitability. Thus, this kind of tax encourages both waste minimization and the adoption of waste treatment technologies most appropriate to any firm's unique characteristics and needs. Simultaneously, these taxes use monetary incentives instead of command-and-control regulations, which channel too-scarce EPA and state resources primarily into standard-setting, monitoring, and enforcement.

Any taxation scheme engenders some (potentially serious) public concerns that those with money, especially large corporations, can simply purchase the right to pollute—and in a noncompetitive market simply pass on their increased costs to consumers. In that context, the "polluter pays" principle takes on new meaning. Moreover, designating the appropriate agency to set taxes at particular levels and by what criteria will unavoidably become hot political issues.

Without question, taxes play an important role as economic incentives in moving American business (and individual consumers) toward safer hazardous waste management practices and toward source reduction and waste minimization. The trick is to set the tax rate, be it on feedstocks or hazardous wastes or waste streams, so as to accomplish the goals of toxics policy without undermining the integrity of the businesses affected.

Fee and Rebate (Deposit and Return)

The diversity and scope of the hazardous waste problem are beyond the capacity of government to track and monitor in detail. The problem is most evident in the fact that more than 250,000 small-quantity generators have yet to be made part of the national drive for safe management of hazardous wastes. Especially troubling is that these small generators face disproportionately high costs of waste management (compared with larger firms in the same industries),[15] while detection of their possible illegal disposal methods is almost nonexistent.

Given these circumstances, a fee-and-rebate system may offer especially attractive opportunities for effective hazardous waste management. Senators Timothy Wirth of Colorado and the late John

Heinz of Pennsylvania proposed a deposit-and-return system to address these problems for containerized ("lab pack") wastes.[16] They proposed a front-end tax or deposit, with a refund payable when quantities of the substance involved are returned after use to an authorized recycler or disposer. With that economic incentive, set at an appropriate level, the thousands of managers of small firms would have good reason to collect and return much of their containerized hazardous wastes, which would otherwise most likely "evaporate" (literally and figuratively!). Effective hazardous waste management would be more attractive for these firms than illegal dumping (which, of course, poses risk of fines, not return of a cash deposit). Whereas a waste-based tax is an indirect pricing signal to a firm (the firm decides whether to pay the tax or change waste-generating practices), a fee-and-rebate system provides less latitude to the firm but ensures that the wastes involved are collected and treated properly.

Fee-and-rebate programs are being proposed in several states for lead-acid batteries and motor vehicle tires, items that pose worthwhile experiments for this approach.[17] A variation on this concept was also proposed in Congress, though not adopted, in 1989 to ensure safe management of automotive lubricating oil, mainly through recycling and reuse. Introduced by Representative Esteban Torres, Democrat from the Los Angeles area, a system would be mandated whereby major oil refinery operators would be responsible for retrieving and reprocessing spent lubricating oil or, alternatively, for purchasing an equivalent number of coupons obtained from EPA by refiners and recyclers who had. The amount of recycling required would increase yearly, based on a refinery's production of lubricating oil. The approach called for increasing the extent of mandatory recycling by 2 percent a year for 10 years, thereby expanding the aggregate level of recycling from the current level of about 30 percent up to 50 percent.

The attractive features of this approach included its modest scope: The goal was not complete recycling but a gradual yet significant increase over 10 years. The scheme left to the marketplace, not the government, determination of the coupon values. When the value of recycled lubricant fell relative to virgin lubricating oil, the redemption value of the coupon would rise; likewise, when the value of recycled oil rose, the value of a coupon would fall. The proposal had the virtue of minimal government administration because the system would function among a small number of refineries. Although transportation and transfer records would have been required of suppliers (e.g., gas stations) and transporters, the paperwork was to be minimal and short-term. Finally, the approach envisioned a mechanism for collecting and reusing lubricating oil that might otherwise end up on the ground or untreated in sewers and waterways. Thus, fee-and-rebate systems have potential for harnessing public purpose to private incentives and may become as common as bottle and can deposit-and-return approaches today in many communities for solid waste recycling.

No-Fault Cleanup

The causes of Superfund's miserable implementation are many, as spelled out in Chapter Two. Of the many recommended changes holding out the promise of expediting Superfund,[18] few have received as much attention as has the proposal to move from the polluter-pays principle to a no-fault system and to create a national environmental trust fund to pay for cleanups of old and abandoned hazardous waste sites. Not surprisingly, the proposal is being promoted by the insurance industry, which finds itself paying both the extensive legal fees generated by the current liability system and then the eventual cleanup costs. The proposal, which is being advertised widely in a multiyear campaign to change public views about who should pay for Superfund cleanups, and how, was initiated by the New York–based American International Group, Inc. (see Box 2.4). Their case is persuasive.

The past decade shows that the effort to assign responsibility at each Superfund site has resulted in little more than acrimony and delay as lawyers fought over who is responsible and to what extent for the depositing of hazardous wastes in landfills 10, 20, and even more years ago. Because under strict joint and several liability, anyone involved can be held accountable for the entire cleanup costs, businesses (and most recently municipalities) have devoted an enormous amount of energy to fighting EPA and one another through the legal system rather than contributing to the cleanup task.

It is estimated that the legal costs to private businesses in sorting out liability and responsibility is running $1–2 million per "potentially responsible party" (PRP), or $10–20 million per major Superfund site.[19] The result has been little more than a misallocation of resources, a distortion of incentives, inequity, and an emphasis on liability sacrificing cooperation.[20]

A no-fault system has its drawbacks. It would take the pressure off of businesses to police each of their transactions to avoid becoming ensnared in a web of Superfund liability. And business could become less diligent in ferreting out as yet undiscovered old or abandoned hazardous waste sites. Also, Congress and the public would have to forego pinpointing responsibility and assigning blame and costs for the sins of past hazardous waste management practices.

Yet on the whole, no-fault would probably be worth the price if it actually resulted in directing attention to the science, technology, and community needs of the cleanup process, without all the wrangling over who did it and who is going to pay.

POSITIVE-ACTION PERMITTING, COMPLIANCE, AND CLEANUP

Positive-Action Permitting

Revisions to today's cumbersome—indeed nightmarish—permitting system are needed to accelerate significantly the transition away from landfilling to new treatment and source reduction and generally to facilitate environmental control technology development. Before the demands for sound new environmental control technologies can be translated into reality, federal and state permitting regimes need drastic surgery. Some changes in permitting are under way already, but at best they represent only the faintest glimmers of a dawning new era.

The scope of needed change includes not only the entire approach to RCRA permitting but also a legion of air, water, and other regulatory permits. It includes approvals to use remediation technologies to achieve permanent remedies at federal Superfund and other state and local cleanups. The focus must shift to what we term *positive-action permitting*: use of positive incentives to encourage accelerated, simplified permit approvals.

Positive-action permitting will certainly stimulate development of new and improved hazardous waste treatment technologies, but its most important function will be to facilitate the introduction and widespread use throughout industry of environmentally desirable technologies already proven to work well under defined conditions. To achieve our toxics policy objectives, RCRA in particular and other related statutes and regulations must become aggressively technology-diffusing rather than just naively technology-forcing.

Potential users of environmental management technologies must be sure that they actually can use them; thus they must be confident that they can obtain all the necessary permits, at a reasonable cost, within a reasonable period of time. In the absence of such assurances—the situation today—users will refuse to purchase and install these technologies. In turn, the companies planning to devise and sell such technologies will fail to obtain the investment capital they need to fund their development business plans. From that perspective alone, accelerated permitting that allows deployment of new environmental control technologies is a prerequisite to improved research and development of those technologies from their inception. All of this activity, of course, is a prerequisite to widespread availability of increased hazardous waste treatment capacity, both onsite at a generator's facilities and offsite at commercial treatment facilities.

EPA's National Advisory Committee for Environmental Policy and Technology (NACEPT) in January 1991 called for massive improvements in the federal permitting system as it affects development and use of environmental technologies. The title of the NACEPT report is illustrative of the approach taken by this high-level advisory body: "Permitting and Compliance Policy: Barriers to U.S. Environmental Technology Innovation." Box 8.2 summarizes this group's basic recommendations.

BOX 8.2 Principal Recommendations of EPA's Focus Group on Environmental Permitting

- Modify environmental permitting and compliance systems to aid in the development, testing, and demonstration of innovative technologies for environmental purposes

- Implement permitting processes that aid the commercial introduction of innovative technologies for environmental purposes

- Use compliance programs to encourage use of innovative technologies to solve environmental problems

- Support regulators and other involved communities to maximize the effectiveness of improvements recommended in permitting and compliance systems

- Identify and remove regulatory obstacles that create unnecessary inflexibility and uncertainty or otherwise inhibit technology innovation for environmental purposes

- Make changes needed to the environmental regulatory system to create incentives to encourage the environmental technology innovation process

Source: U.S. Environmental Protection Agency, "Permitting and Compliance Policy: Barriers to U.S. Environmental Technological Innovations" (Washington, D.C.: EPA, January 1991).

Permit-by-rule systems offer an attractive way to accelerate permitting of environmentally sound hazardous waste treatment technologies. Such systems, already available in some states, applied initially to permits needed to use certain transportable treatment units (TTUs) and have now been applied to selected onsite treatment modes as well. The technique also applies to selected air and water quality permits.

Under this technique for positive-action permitting, the regulatory agency defines the basic envelope of desired performance for the treatment unit: the types of wastes it can process, its maximum capacity, permissible emissions and effluents (types and amounts), disposal methods required for any sludges created by the treatment, and (for a transportable unit) the maximum duration it would be allowed to operate at any particular generator's site. These performance criteria need to be spelled out in considerable technical detail, yet communicated clearly both to thousands of individual hazardous waste generators and to the owners (or potential developers) of treatment units that would qualify for permits to operate under these rules.

Facility owners whose waste generation situation and needs meet these basic preconditions and satisfy the permit rules can self-certify their ability to operate either a fixed treatment unit or a TTU at their site. Firms with qualified treatment units would notify potential users (the waste generators) of the availability and price of their services, emphasizing that they are qualified for easy commencement of operations under the permit-by-rule approach. For these many waste generators and technology operators, permitting would no longer be the dominant constraint to use of appropriate hazardous waste treatment techniques.

EPA in the mid-1980s created a federal permit-by-rule regulation that allows transportable incinerators to destroy PCBs at different locations throughout the country. In addition, aspects of both the new source performance standards (NSPSs) under the Clean Air Act (devised as early as 1970) and the industrial wastewater effluent guidelines under the Clean Water Act (devised as early as 1972) define the acceptable levels of technical performance needed to gain permit approval.

The Texas Air Control Board's new source review program has used 122 standard exemptions that define the types of changes that a facility can make without undergoing public notice and extended review. The standard exemptions were covered in an initial statewide public hearing process. The facility simply notifies the state that it is following approved standard requirements and can then proceed to make the changes.

Under both RCRA and Superfund, however, EPA has adamantly refused to allow any permit-by-rule approaches to accelerate the complex permit approval process. As a result, the state permitting innovations apply solely to those few waste streams classified as hazardous under the state's law but not considered hazardous under RCRA. To treat any RCRA-defined hazardous wastes, firms must still pursue the nightmare of Part B permit approval (even though the Part B permit would be issued by the state regulatory agency under delegated federal authority).

The permit-by-rule concept has great potential as the heart of a system of positive-action permitting. It could certainly be applied more broadly to a range of new environmental control technologies and approaches deemed significant by EPA or by a state environmental agency. Rules could be established to accelerate greatly permit issuance for both fixed and transportable treatment units, for use both onsite and offsite. After technical performance standards have been established, users could then readily acquire, install, and operate new technologies without further regulatory hassles simply by informing the appropriate environmental regulatory agency they had done so, then obtain their permits (by rule). Burden of proof would rest upon the user of a technology to demonstrate later, if required, that the technology actually did meet its defined performance characteristics. Penalties for failure to comply would be severe.

Then, rather than spending countless hours reviewing permit applications—a present manifestation of superfailure—EPA and state regulatory agencies could spend much more time on development of appropriate technical standards and on enforcement, making sure the technologies actually in operation were really consistent with agency rules and that holders of permits-by-rule were not abusing their privilege. Regulatory agencies could also spend more time organizing permit-by-rule procedures.

Accelerated positive-action permitting would considerably improve operations under both RCRA and Superfund as well as their state statutory equivalents. But just how difficult would it be for EPA or selected states to set performance conditions for particular hazardous waste treatment technologies? At one extreme, of course, this is a highly complex technical challenge, calling for broad-based knowledge of multiple technologies and their applications. From another perspective, however, incremental conditions could well be established for selected technologies and their environmentally (and economically) desirable applications.

Treatment of hazardous waste liquids could be included in the initial accelerated permitting system, for example, because this technology is well understood. Thermal destruction could be added later as more is learned about this technology. Incinerating some organics could be covered under positive-action permitting, though chlorinated solvents would not qualify. Stabilization systems could be allowed for certain inorganics but not others.

EPA's efforts to define treatment standards for the HSWA land disposal bans should help develop new approaches to accelerated permitting. EPA approaches to stormwater permittings under the Clean Water Act, and forthcoming EPA maximum achievable control technology (MACT) standards for air toxics under the Clean Air Act, provide examples of the possibilities available under RCRA (and CERCLA).

Positive-Action Compliance

Similarly, new approaches to positive-action compliance offer the best hope for achieving universal compliance with the maze of complicated toxics rules and regulations. Today, complexity and confusion are so widespread that most hazardous waste generators and hazardous materials users simply ignore many applicable rules. Conceivably, no operating facility is in total compliance with all the rules, no matter how well intentioned its managers. Furthermore, no traditional command-and-control regulatory enforcement system will ever have enough resources to change that situation completely for the nation's many thousands of firms that use hazardous materials and generate hazardous wastes.

Only one reasonable alternative exists. We must rely on individual businesses to comply fully (or almost fully) on their own, deploying the government's scarce enforcement resources as carefully and selectively as possible to achieve that result. (As President Ronald Reagan said when he paraphrased a Russian proverb in negotiating an arms control agreement with Mikhail Gorbachev: "Trust, but verify.") This process we call positive-action compliance; it is patterned after positive-action permitting.

As the first step in such a process, firms large and small would receive clear, concise information on their specific compliance responsibilities. (As previously noted, comprehension must always precede compliance.) Generators of hazardous waste and users of hazardous materials would receive clear, easy-to-use checklists and guidelines to allow them to carry out various self-audits: of their waste generation patterns, their hazardous waste management and storage practices, and their air toxics controls. Metal finishers, graphic arts facilities, auto body shops, and so on would each receive different forms—until the full range of industry categories had been covered.

These self-auditing forms and procedures would identify typical measures taken by firms in each industry category to achieve cost-effective, workable compliance. Checklists would also reveal which activities and associated regulatory requirements fell outside the norm, thereby necessitating special attention. In those cases, users would be encouraged to obtain expert assistance (from specialists available as consultants in their local areas, perhaps).

To encourage positive-action compliance, regulatory agencies would provide training on use of the compliance forms. They would also provide loan guarantees or other forms of financial assistance so that smaller firms in particular could afford to install effective environmental control technologies.

Under positive-action compliance, individual firms would have to certify in writing—yearly, most likely—that they were aware of their specific compliance responsibilities; had completed appropriate compliance checklists and self-audit forms; and had tried their best to comply fully with regulatory mandates. (The 1990 Clean Air Act amendments include extensive reporting requirements of this kind, as part of the new federal air quality permit program.)

New guidance issued by the Department of Justice in mid-1991 "represents a serious new attempt to promote environmental self-policing." One senior-level observer suggested that "audit procedures adopted by companies should be regularized, should allow comprehensive evaluation of all media and sources, and should have an adequate resource commitment that is commensurate with the size of the operation. . . . Response to audit results should be immediate, should go beyond compliance, should use adequate resources, and should include post-violation compliance commitments."[21] Many of the required documents could simply be kept on file as part of each firm's required recordkeeping procedures; some reports would go to government regulatory agencies.

Federal, state, and local regulatory agencies would target their inspection and enforcement resources accordingly, exacting strong penalties not only for compliance failures but also for failure to keep adequate records or file necessary reports and—especially—for fraudulent responses on the annual self-certification forms.

Some firms would be selected at random for onsite inspections; others would be targeted because of size, complexity, extent of toxics emissions, or history of noncompliance. Those guilty of infractions would become visible examples for others, thereby further encouraging widespread compliance. Positive-action compliance would become the central feature of environmental management, allowing both regulatory agencies and regulated firms to apply available resources effectively.

Positive-Action Cleanup

Although the attention of toxics policy in the second toxics decade is moving toward the management overall of hazardous materials used in commerce and industry and their release into the environment, the cleanup problems posed by past hazardous waste management practices remain unresolved. Indeed, addressing the cleanup needs at Superfund sites proved to be especially frustrating throughout America's entire first toxics decade. With few sites decontaminated and with the cleanup process being dragged out literally over decades—possibly to the middle of the next century—nothing less than a dramatic overhaul of the approach taken in the 1980s is required.

A few of the features of the Superfund regulatory scheme are worth retaining, but in most respects the system as a whole has engendered unnecessary procrastination, expensive litigation, and endless bickering. Our recommendation is for procedures designed to induce positive-action cleanup akin to positive-action permitting and positive-action compliance, with emphasis placed on completing the job expeditiously. These procedures include incentives to clean up now rather than later; shifting the burden of proof regarding cleanup techniques, levels, and costs; special roles for both environmental arbitrators (to avoid litigation) and an accelerated judicial process (when it proves unavoidable); an emphasis on cleanup fees rather than penalties imposed as financial punishment; and scientifically assessed, risk-based cleanups. This approach applies not only to federal Superfund sites but also to the many more sites requiring cleanup under state and local lead.

To begin with, the financial burden of a Superfund site cleanup should be absorbed primarily by the existing base of industry and population in the area of contamination. This is a matter of equity and the best way to use pricing signals to direct the behavior of business. The approach places the first line of responsibility for the cleanup strategy and costs with those who stand to gain most from the resultant cleaner environment. To facilitate this locally motivated and funded cleanup process on a national scale, the unit of government responsible should be the county—a region typically large enough for meaningful economies of scale while small enough for hazardous waste and cleanup sites to receive serious attention and action.

The needed revenue could be generated in one of two ways. Funds could be raised through annual charges levied on each type and size of industrial firm in the county (based on standard codes of industry type), combined with a local relatively modest surcharge on residents' water rates (because so many cleanups are associated with the remediation of drinking-water contamination). Alternatively, a levy could be assessed on all firms based on their present use of hazardous materials of all kinds or on their total toxics emissions, both of which are routinely reported to EPA under SARA Title III (see Chapter Six).

The revenues would be used for accelerated cleanup activities at all identified contamination sites within the county, from national Superfund sites to underground fuel tank leaks at a local gas station. The locally raised revenues would be required to cover 80 percent of the costs at a national Superfund site located in a county, with 10 percent coming from EPA's cleanup fund and 10 percent from the state. To clean up state Superfund sites in a county, local revenues would cover 90 percent of the costs, with the remainder coming from the state. The county would pay for 100 percent of the cleanup costs of locally identified sites. The federal and the state shares of costs would be doubled in those instances when the potentially responsible parties (PRPs) had successfully negotiated a mutually binding cleanup procedure along the lines suggested later.

We do not propose to shift funding responsibility totally away from those who actually caused the contamination, however. The intent is to provide a positive focus for accelerated cleanup, to be followed later as appropriate by cost allocation or punitive action. But the thrust would be to raise sufficient funds to clean up the sites, by methods selected largely by those who must live with the consequences of their actions, and only after that to seek out reimbursement from PRPs.

For the cleanup to accelerate will also require altering the liability scheme established under CERCLA to avoid some of the legal bickering under the current system (see Chapter Four). CERCLA liability should be modified as follows:

- Retain the provisions for joint and several liability.
- Modify the provisions for strict liability so that EPA still would not have to show negligence but would need to show probable causality: "quasi–strict liability." A responsible party would thus be one who was actually responsible for the contamination in some way, even if not negligent. Innocent landowners would be excluded by this provision; original waste generators would be excluded if their wastes had been passed on to another (a transporter, for example) without incident. However, the burden of proof to assert one's innocence would rest with the PRP, not with EPA; this too would accelerate the cleanup process.
- Allow EPA to seek full reimbursement of a federal Superfund site cleanup costs from PRPs defined in this manner. Funds actually collected would go first to reimburse the federal Superfund's share (10 or 20 percent). Money remaining would go next to reimburse the state's share; then into a special statewide fund to provide financial assistance (grants, loans, information outreach) to small business for environmental compliance, hazardous waste source reduction, and so on.
- Absolve those PRPs who had proceeded to complete a negotiated cleanup of these sites from any further cleanup costs or Superfund

liability. This would encourage cooperation in the cleanup by the PRPs in exchange for relief from additional legal claims by either EPA or other PRPs.

Similar provisions could be adopted by states and counties to accelerate cleanup of the sites under their jurisdiction.

More is needed, however, than simply new funding mechanisms and some liability relief if we are to replace superfailure with positive-action cleanup. The overall process needs to shift away from the normal court process, with its potential for endless delay. To accomplish this, three additional innovations are needed: procedures to greatly increase negotiated, voluntary cleanups; vastly expanded use of mandatory environmental arbitration when negotiations break down; and special court access (or a special court) when judicial involvement is unavoidable.

CERCLA needs to be amended so that the PRPs and local communities (the county) near Superfund sites are encouraged to negotiate an acceptable cleanup directly, with a minimal role for EPA (and its engineers and consultants). EPA and the affected state agencies would need to approve the negotiated cleanup, but its scope, content, and timing would emerge from direct PRP-community negotiations.

How can we encourage this to happen? First, as just noted, absolve PRPs from any further CERCLA liability for those sites on which they can achieve an agreeable negotiated settlement. Second, provide sufficient Superfund money to enable local communities to hire expert consultants and thereby engage in equal negotiations with the PRPs (this is an extension of the program of grants up to $50,000 already included in SARA in 1986). Third, double the federal and state funding available for those sites which achieve negotiated settlements. And fourth, set strict time deadlines for cleanup negotiations to be completed before bringing the parties into mandatory arbitration (at which point, doubled outside funding for the cleanup would no longer be available).

Both to encourage numerous voluntary agreements and to speed the initiation of cleanups when agreement cannot be reached, mandatory environmental arbitration must be given a much greater role in the process. This will put the emphasis on the "action" in positive-action cleanup.

America already has an impressive stable of environmental mediators, and there is a growing tradition of arbitration more generally as a supplement to the formal judicial process. The revised CERCLA should define limits to the voluntary negotiations process, triggering thereafter mandatory arbitration guided by specified procedures.

The idea is that all the parties interested in a particular cleanup (PRPs, local communities, and EPA and state environmental agencies) would present their case to the arbitrator. Briefs would be presented in writing, accompanied by the inescapable consultant reports; oral arguments would be made. Then the arbitrator would make a decision (again, within a specified period of time) that would be binding on all these parties. After that point, a court-issued temporary restraining order or permanent injunction would be required to stop the cleanup process from proceeding. Action would be under way.

Parties would retain their inalienable rights to pursue litigation after having exhausted available administrative remedies. It may be appropriate to grant special court access for such ultimate appeals or to establish a special panel to hear nothing but Superfund appeals. However, given the several steps outlined, it would only be the truly exceptional case that reached the conventional judicial arena. Therefore, we believe the scheme will in practice greatly accelerate the cleanup process.

But how clean would these cleanups need to be? Here several of our central themes come together. In all instances, permanent remedies are essential. Thus, to start with, the practice of excavation and redisposal as a method of site cleanup must be prohibited by Congress by a ban against the disposal without proper treatment of any contaminated soil or remediation materials. All such materials must be treated by an appropriate technique instead.

To encourage the use of new treatment technologies, it is important that the innovation introduced in SARA of lessening permit requirements for onsite remedies at Superfund sites needs to be strengthened further. First, the law should make clear that it applies to all federal, state, and regional and local regulatory permits: (air, water, and so on) required to operate at these Superfund sites, not just those permits issued formally by the federal EPA. Second, the concept needs to be extended beyond federal Superfund sites to encompass all other state and local cleanups as well.

Cleanups must also focus on reduction of defined public health risk (and environmental harm), not on punitive action based on outrage and anger. The cleanup strategy must be appropriate to the task, though this balance is not always easy to accomplish. For example, when the public learns that an underground aquifer is contaminated with toxic substances, the demand is usually for a total cleanup of the aquifer, which can involve an extremely lengthy process and expensive pumping and aerating systems. Yet treating the water at the wellhead as the water is drawn out of the ground for consumption is both cost-effective and possibly, when the implications of primary and secondary effects on air, water, and land are considered, the most effective method of treatment. The point is that when the decision about cleanup approach is made at the local level and is balanced between costs and health effects, the more appropriate cleanup strategy is far more likely to be chosen than when costs are borne by someone else (the federal government or PRPs) and the community members are not included as equal participants in the decisionmaking (and funding) process.

A promising example of positive-action thinking in cleanup appeared in a bill introduced in Congress in May 1991 by Representative Esteban Torres to move from the conundrum of Superfund delay to positive action in groundwater cleanup in the San Gabriel Valley aquifer of greater Los Angeles. The 195 square miles covered by the aquifer is the home of 2 million people who rely on groundwater as their primary source of drinking water and of hundreds of industrial facilities that have contributed to its pollution for over three decades by their disposal of hazardous wastes in lagoons and ponds and their spills of hazardous materials onto the ground. The aquifer is now the most heavily contaminated potable groundwater basin in the United States; a quarter of the drinking-water wells in the valley are closed. The basin is divided into four huge segments, each listed separately on the federal Superfund list.

The bill proposed by Torres for addressing this problem has several key features designed to end the debates over the appropriate treatment strategy and over who pays and instead to facilitate cleanup. The bill calls for treating water at the wellhead to remove contaminants as needed at the area's 275 public water wells. The cost involved is estimated at $30 million, in contrast to the $800 million estimated by EPA for a full Superfund cleanup of the aquifer. The treatment system would be funded 80 percent from a proportionate tax on all participating industries in the valley, with the remainder to be paid for by EPA. In exchange, the PRPs who participate are exempted from any further Superfund liability or obligations for the cleanup of the aquifer. Those industries not participating voluntarily would remain ensnared in the regular Superfund process. In Torres' view, "a public-private partnership can solve the environmental problems in the valley at the least cost to society. The San Gabriel Basin Demonstration Project would clean up the San Gabriel aquifer much faster than the EPA is capable of moving."[22]

Although the bill is not a perfect solution, it is clearly a vital first step in this direction and an indication of what may lie ahead as elected officials, community leaders, and businesses increasingly try to fashion effective ways of circumventing Superfund roadblocks in order to move forward with hazardous wastes cleanups.

A COMMUNITY CONTRACT FOR SITING
A SINGLE FACILITY

For positive action to occur—in permitting, compliance, cleanup, and the introduction of new treatment facilities and environmental control technologies—more than a revision of the philosophy and structure of CERCLA and RCRA will be needed. It will require finding new methods of involving the affected community more intimately in the decisionmaking process, from the level of broad policy setting down to the siting and oversight of individual facilities. That is one of the clearest lessons of the 1980s and an issue we turn to now.

A potentially successful method for siting a new facility to manage hazardous wastes or use hazardous materials is suggested in the quasi-experimental work of Michael Elliott, who has systematically probed the motivations underlying people's concerns and fears in situations of facility siting.[23] We believe that his work points the way toward a means of resolving siting controversies.

Elliott finds that most project proponents and their designers spend considerable time attempting scientifically to predict possible problems with equipment and operations of a plant and to design technical preventive mechanisms; their mindset is primarily of the technical-rationality type (see Chapter Seven). By contrast, the surrounding community is more worried about detecting hazardous conditions that may actually develop at the plant and about developing mitigating measures to lessen or reverse possible dangers. Residents worry about whether response measures will be applied speedily enough if a problem should actually arise rather than about the virtues of exotic, technically advanced equipment; these citizens fall into the cultural-rationality category in their perception of risk.

As already noted, these differing perspectives between facility sponsors and local residents are often the most volatile fuel for an area's NIMBY tendencies. Elliott finds that if required to choose, community members, consistent with their attitudes, prefer a more understandable, less technically sophisticated facility provided that its operators place more emphasis on early and rapid detection of any problems and on effective and speedy mitigation of problems detected. Given the concern of community members with their immediate health and safety and their apprehension of both government and business leaders, especially those located outside their community, it is easy to see why locals would emphasize safety and emergency responsiveness over technical sophistication and promises of governmental oversight. Elliott concluded the only realistic way to convince an ever-wary community that the facility's operators were committed to detection and mitigation was to open the operations of the plant to close community scrutiny and to subject the safety practices to intense and frequent local citizen review.

The case is a compelling one. To encourage successful siting of suitable facilities in suitable locations, long-term oversight arrangements may have to be formalized between a facility and its host community. Conceivably, that could be accomplished with an enforceable contract between the facility owner or operator and the local people. With a facility siting and operations contract in place, a facility's neighbors would no longer need to rely only on government permitting and enforcement activities, which were so notoriously ineffective during the 1980s. The power to act would rest with the local people as well, who would be able to mount a court action under breach of contract.

The specific terms of each contract would be negotiated during the facility-siting process. Many contracts might contain only those operational provisions already proposed to be included in the facility's regulatory permits. If so, what reason would the facility developer have to resist signing the contract—other than skepticism that the regulatory agencies would really not enforce the permit conditions? That is the same skepticism, of course, that motivates NIMBY actions. The agreement might also embody a facility owner's further commitments: to accelerated source reduction or to limit the types of wastes to be handled or hours and scale of operation. These commitments might be elicited in exchange for the community's begrudging approval of siting the facility. Each party would compromise on some points during the negotiations that lead up to signing of the siting and operations contract.

In effect, the contract would establish legally enforceable rights and responsibilities between the negotiating parties, provisions that would remove the perverse incentive to confront and block inherent in the conventional regulatory framework. The contract approach would provide incentives instead to reveal true preferences, to bargain in good faith, and ultimately to cooperate and move forward together.[24]

Violation of contract terms could be enforced directly by the community through traditional breach-of-contract judicial proceedings. A court could even be asked to issue a temporary restraining order requiring the facility to cease operations until it could again meet its contractual obligations. A court master might be appointed at that point to ensure that the facility did so. With an oversight committee of community members in place at the facility, such legal action should not be necessary, however.

The option of contract enforcement may well be the price a community in the 1990s will demand in exchange for local siting approval. No contract, no approval. The mechanism can guarantee stability over the full term of future facility operations.

Inviting community participation in facility oversight may seem a radical departure from past practices. Yet it is clearly an inclusive, community-based—and in that sense, democratic—process. It provides an extremely promising mechanism for achieving the sense of risk sharing—in this instance, between the facility operator and the community—and volunteerism essential to Kasperson's principles.

If Elliott is correct that the public does not so much fear technology and chemical substances as fear how they will be managed, then the contract approach may go a long way toward overcoming concerns and allowing needed facilities to be built and operated in good locations. Most importantly, the contract approach may be the key to solving the puzzle of successful community-based siting of new hazardous waste management facilities.

A PUBLIC UTILITY MODEL FOR SITING, PERMITTING, AND MANAGEMENT

Many of the facilities rejected by local communities during America's first toxics decade were intended to manage hazardous wastes through recycling, neutralization, detoxification, incineration, or storage; land disposal was not the sole option. In Europe, similar facility-siting rejections have occured far less often, chiefly because hazardous waste management has been widely assumed as a national responsibility akin to highway building and sewage treatment.

Bruce Piasecki and Gary Davis have proposed for the United States a variation on this European approach, making the case that the nation could follow the regulated public utility model of close public-private cooperation and thus move more rapidly from conventional land disposal practices toward a closed system that recycles, treats, stores, and protects hazardous wastes. Akin to regulated gas and electric utilities, these new institutions would be operated independently and managed as profit-making corporations. Closely watched and regulated by state public utility commissions, they would receive liability waivers, charge regulated prices, and operate exclusively within set geographic or functional boundaries.

These new publicly regulated private corporations would handle wastes from small generators; provide hazardous waste management information services analogous to services provided by agricultural extension services; operate as transfer stations for bulking and blending; and perhaps carry out the full range of needed offsite hazardous waste management functions. Piasecki and Davis note:

In exchange for treating all of the waste generated in an area, including hard-to-treat waste and household toxics, at set prices and using specified technologies, the private firm would have no competition in its service area and would receive a guaranteed return on its investment in treatment facilities.[25]

The best example of such an operation in the United States is the Gulf Coast Waste Disposal Authority in Houston, Texas, which operates as an independent, quasi-governmental, nonprofit corporation to plan and operate waste facilities. It can issue tax-exempt bonds for financing and can condemn land to site its facilities. A joint study sponsored by a coalition of business and municipal agencies in Los Angeles County, California, found a good deal of support for a public-private utility model approach to the region's hazardous waste management needs. The idea is especially attractive to the region's hazardous waste generators who have been unable to move forward on their own in establishing an integrated system of new transfer, storage, and disposal facilities.[26]

Because it offers a comprehensive system of modern treatment facilities, the public utilities approach has much to recommend it and may prove to be a vital element of America's strategy for hazardous waste and materials management in the 1990s. It could be particularly valuable for siting needed new facilities if the assumption is correct that local governments and citizens would be more receptive to those facilities knowing they would be operated by a utility that is under close public scrutiny, has the goal of safe waste management practices, and at the same time operates with the efficiency of a private business.

If lack of progress continues as a result of the contentious conflicts between facility proponents and their opponents today—with little or no movement toward successful siting, continuing NIMBY-ism, and ongoing gridlock—the public utility model for hazardous waste management may become a necessary approach for the 1990s. However, many of the weaknesses of today's regulated electric and gas utilities could be anticipated. For one thing, winning public assent for siting would not be automatic under this model. Moreover, dealing with hazardous wastes is only one component, albeit an important one, of hazardous materials use and of the overall siting dilemma society faces.

REGIONAL COMPACTS
AND MANAGEMENT STRATEGIES

As spelled out in detail in the previous chapter, an unusual effort is currently unfolding in California that in many ways adopts some of the best features of both the model for siting an individual facility and the public utility approach. There, a hazardous waste planning and siting process was initiated in response to the state's facility-siting gridlock. Its objective is to enable every county to map its own hazardous waste and hazardous materials future and to accept local responsibility for toxics management.

Even though the process was not mandatory, every one of California's 58 counties decided to participate. Each county has developed a profile of existing waste streams and projected growth and source reduction through 2000. County plans call for compiling inventories of existing and needed new treatment facilities, stipulating criteria for siting new facilities, and identifying acceptable general locations within the county. Counties also may enter intercounty compacts.

The countywide plans are being prepared with the involvement of cities, industry, environmental and health groups, and the general public. All of these parties have a formal right to participate in the process and have strong vested interests in its outcome. If successful, California will be unique in the nation for having in place locally determined, community-based plans for hazardous waste management.

The California law created a new state siting appeals board with the power in selected cases to overturn local facility-siting decisions, whether to approve or reject the proposed facility. Facility developers can appeal to the new state board requesting an override of a local rejection. If their siting proposals were consistent with the approved county plan and met all technical and procedural requirements for siting, but were still turned down by local authorities (under NIMBY-style pressures, for example), state override is probable. Thus, local vetoes of good facilities in appropriate locations may no longer hold up in California.

Given the realities facing local communities and the diverse business, environmental, and other interests that are negotiating, bargaining, and cooperating through this new process, there is some hope this approach may break the impasse over facility siting in California and serve as a model for other areas. Before agreeing to new facilities, local communities and environmental groups can be expected to press business for maximum waste minimization and source reduction, because this decreases the area's need to host new facilities. SARA's capacity-assurance planning process has introduced many of these principles into all 50 states. Equity-based fair-share formulas and regional compacts have become imperatives in the dynamics of successful facility siting.

COMPREHENSIVE WASTE MANAGEMENT THROUGH AUCTIONS

A virtue common to the two models just described—the public utility model of the sort developed in Europe or the model evolving in

California of extensive local and regional planning with private implementation—is that they engage fully both the public and private sectors in the management of hazardous wastes and hazardous materials. We would like to suggest a third approach, one that calls upon government to set broad goals for the safe management of hazardous wastes but that relies on the marketplace to implement those goals in a dynamic, cost-effective, and technology-inducing manner.

The proposal brings together several of the ideas previously discussed: regional comprehensiveness, government standards-setting, a deposit-and-return system to ensure the compliance of the thousands of individual hazardous waste generators involved, and strong incentives to promote source reduction, recycling, and development of more efficient production processes. The goal is to allocate proportionately (thus equitably) the costs of managing hazardous wastes among all generators as well as to internalize these costs as an important consideration within their normal operations. The approach is best suited to a regional-level microeconomy: a state, a major metropolitan region, or a cluster of smaller states (e.g., New England). For purposes of this discussion, we use a state.

The plan works this way: Every three years the state auctions off the right to collect and treat all the hazardous wastes being generated within its boundaries. Separate auctions are held for each of the approximately 70 categories of industrial facilities, which account collectively for nearly all the wastes generated today. (Industry categories—manufacturing steel pipes and tubes, oil refining, and the like—can be defined in terms of four-digit standard industrial codes or SICs). For ease of administration, the 70 or so auctions can be staggered over a three-year cycle, with a third of the state's industrial groupings covered every year. Bids would be structured on a cost-per-ton basis to manage different types of wastes from particular industry categories.

Before assuming responsibility for collecting and managing all wastes from an industry category, the lowest qualified bidder for that category would be given up to 24 months to prepare operations. State certification of that firm's qualifications for managing the wastes would depend on the winner's ability to recycle, neutralize, incinerate, and safely store them.

Allowing waste generators to pay the waste management firm directly might encourage generators to dispose of their wastes illegally instead of declaring them and paying the fee. Therefore, the state should serve as the intermediary, collecting necessary fees from all generators within each particular industry grouping and in turn contracting with and paying the waste management firm(s).

Just as waste management firms base their bids on industrial categories, the state collects fees from waste generators on that basis, which will greatly simplify setting fee schedules for the numbers of individual businesses involved. To set these fees, the volume and types of waste from each industrial category and the amounts generated by each business or industry would be estimated as closely as possible. Estimates of these amounts developed by EPA, the Congressional Budget Office, and other sources can be adapted to the particular set of business and industry categories and operations by the designated state agency or commission.[27]

Under this plan, the state regulates closely only the selected waste management firms, which undoubtedly will be few in number. An important aspect of the approach is that once the fee is paid to the state by the waste generator, the generator no longer has any incentive to manage hazardous wastes poorly or dispose of them illegally. The generators will be charged the standard fee for their industry category. Meanwhile, the costs of waste management are borne by all generators in approximate proportion to the actual costs of managing properly the wastes they produce.

Another important feature of this plan is that it fully exploits competition among waste management firms to keep the price of waste management as low as possible, thus enabling firms to remain efficient players in the marketplace. Although the approach does not ask government to manage wastes, the state is responsible for establishing basic guidelines for hazardous waste management, including banning traditional landfilling practices and prescribing safety and cleanup standards that waste managers must meet as a condition of obtaining and keeping a state waste management franchise.

Many businesses may discover they can safely manage their own wastes less expensively onsite than if they pay state fees to have their waste managed by a third party. The system should allow firms to do so. Larger firms, especially, already rely on onsite hazardous waste management techniques. Further, more transportable treatment units available for onsite use are coming into the market. This focus on onsite waste management also provides incentives for intensified source reduction and waste minimization.

Under comprehensive waste management, firms would be encouraged to use onsite techniques. A fee reduction procedure would be established by the state's fee collection agency to meet the needs of waste generators whose production processes deliver fewer wastes than the average for their industry category. Such an approach is not only fair, it rewards businesses that have minimized waste generation. Moreover, the burden of proof is on individual firms; they must show they have indeed generated fewer wastes than their industry norm. State enforcement will be needed to avoid illegal dumping.

To operate onsite treatment systems, a firm must have formal written permission from the overseeing state agency. Onsite systems must meet the same standards of treatment performance and state monitoring and certification established for all contracted offsite hazardous waste management. To keep the system financially equitable, any firm managing wastes onsite would pay reduced fees and would be credited with (or repaid) an amount equal to the lowest price paid to the third-party waste management firm for the volume of wastes the generator chooses to manage onsite.

In that way, successful firms could actually profit from treating their wastes onsite, because the credit they received from the state could exceed their costs for onsite waste management. Moreover, treating wastes onsite eliminates transportation mishaps. Letting generators use onsite treatment systems to compete with third-party waste managers also stimulates new managerial techniques, especially through source reduction, and further inspires greater efficiency in the waste management marketplace.

Finally, there is good reason to believe that after all hazardous waste generators are required to pay the full costs of waste recycling, neutralization, incineration, and long-term storage, many of them will find it less expensive to change their production processes and minimize their waste generation. Firms minimizing in this way would be entitled to proportionate reductions in their fees as a way to reward this form of effective waste management.

An additional issue remains: how to dispose of the 10 to 20 percent of the waste volume remaining as treatment residuals after all feasible recycling, neutralization, incineration, and other treatment efforts have been completed, both onsite and offsite. At that point, the dewatered and far more manageable material must be stored in one of a handful of moisture-free warehouses (residuals repositories) located throughout the state.

Because of the risk of monopoly-like behavior by one (or at most a few) residuals repository owner as well as the public's extreme sensitivity to locating such land disposal facilities—even modern ones—within their communities, these facilities would be public entities (though operated perhaps by private parties under contract to the state, as in the public utilities model). This approach allows for strict government supervision over these few but vital operations, including control over their prices to all users, yet takes advantage of private-sector incentives for efficient facility management.

Although this plan does not resolve all the problems associated with hazardous waste management, it provides a workable approach that overcomes the paradox of current thinking by spelling out a minimal role for government and relying on market dynamics to provide the most efficient means of achieving waste minimization, recycling, neutralization, incineration, treatment, and residuals storage. Most important, costs are borne proportionately by all waste generators, large and small. Finally, generators would have every incentive to help solve the state's overall hazardous waste management problem.

Although this scheme deals comprehensively with waste management, it does not respond to the harsher realities of siting. It relies more on market-based incentives than does the public utilities model, which is somewhat more "public"-oriented from an administrative standpoint.

DEMOCRATIC DISCOURSE AND TOXICS POLICY

Approaches for better management of hazardous wastes and hazardous materials for America's second toxics decade fall into two broad categories. The first requires government to deal more or less directly with the behavior of individual firms (through taxes, bans, positive-action permitting and compliance, and so on). The second involves the need for areawide discussion, planning, and decisionmaking about the siting of new hazardous waste and hazardous materials facilities needed to accelerate industry's transformation in hazardous wastes and materials management.

Few of these ideas will be implemented, especially those involving siting of new facilities, without the consent of members of the communities affected and of the organized environmental and health groups who have taken a keen interest in toxics policy. Therefore, the manner in which new programs and policies are introduced and implemented is critical to their success. This was the hard lesson of the first toxics decade. In a positive vein, it was also the lesson of the Clean Sites approach to negotiating workable Superfund cleanup strategies; the hazardous waste planning process in California; Elliott's research; and the growing body of experience on how to work through these issues at the community level, information coming out of the field of risk communications.[28]

As for the development of needed treatment capacity, local opposition to new facilities symbolized the broad failure of America's democratic discourse in the 1970s and 1980s. Despite the judgment of experts that the benefits of many proposed new facilities clearly outweigh their costs (at least as conventionally understood) or that potential risks of these facilities are smaller than continuing present hazardous waste disposal practices, new projects have been adamantly opposed.

It is understandable that local residents and facility sponsors would fail to arrive at common understandings and agreements on siting because they have focused on different aspects of the issue—technical capabilities of a facility versus the potential harm to an individual member of the community, for example—and talked past one another. At the root of the problem is a lack of shared understanding, perceived mutual interests, and trust. Still excluded from most decisions that lead to initiating proposed new facilities, people today can and do just say "no." The resulting gridlock inhibits commencement of any serious improvement in toxics policy.

That situation will not change overnight, but some potent harbingers are becoming evident as the second toxics decade begins.

Public-private partnerships are beginning to emerge because both sides recognize the futility of following the slippery path leading only to more superfailure.[29] Facility-siting contracts can include long-term community oversight of facility operations and can provide a focus for effective mitigation and compensation measures as well as siting/source reduction compromises. The local emergency planning committees (LEPCs) mandated under SARA Title III for involving industry, government, and diverse citizen groups in hazardous materials emergency response planning can offer forums for communitywide discussion of toxics policy where no similar outlets presently exist.[30]

Most significant, regional and statewide siting efforts based explicitly on the politics of equity offer the best hope for melding successfully the interests of those who would identify either with those who bear the costs or those who benefit from conventional facility-siting disputes. Equity principles can be combined with new, smaller, often transportable technologies to allow siting the right facilities in the right locations; this balancing may begin to encourage communities to say "yes." If siting is guided by fundamental ethical principles, the YIMBY response may then replace NIMBY as the hallmark of siting in the 1990s.

The crucial issue of achieving safer overall use and management of hazardous wastes and hazardous materials is an issue for which the most attractive approaches simply do not lend themselves to regulatory postures. Instead, the needed changes go to the heart of industrial production practices and thence to the consumption choices of individual Americans in the 1990s and beyond. They therefore require a mix of publicly set goals, market-based incentives for action, minimal administrative interference, and the rapid introduction of new hazardous waste management technologies and of production technologies that are less waste generating and polluting to begin with.

We have summarized a number of the approaches being discussed at the outset of America's second toxics decade and suggested several of our own. There is no single best answer. Instead, we favor the use of several complementary approaches. We are especially persuaded, however, that use of a system combining fees and rebates with auctions is essential to bringing about appropriate hazardous wastes management by the literally thousands of smaller firms across the nation. In addition, positive action is needed in permitting, compliance, and cleanup, and this will require dramatically changing the philosophy and structure of both RCRA and CERCLA. Finally, and equally important, comprehensive planning with respect to hazardous wastes and hazardous materials and full public participation are required in the thousands of community settings across the land as the only enduring strategy for the United States in gaining control over its toxics destiny.

NOTES

1. Daniel A. Mazmanian and David L. Morell, "EPA: Coping with the New Political Economic Order," *Environmental Law* 21 (1991), 1477-1491.

2. Roger E. Kasperson, "Hazardous Waste Facility Siting: Community, Firm, and Governmental Perspectives," in National Academy of Engineering, *Hazards: Technology and Fairness* (Washington, D.C.: National Academy Press, 1986), 139.

3. Michael E. Porter, "America's Green Strategy," *Scientific American* 265 (April 1991), 168.

4. New Jersey Environmental Cleanup Responsibility Act (ECRA), N.J. Statutes Annotated, 13:1K-6 *et seq.*; the regulations are in N.J. Administrative Code, 7:26B.

5. California's S.B. 14, for example: the California Hazardous Waste Source Reduction and Management Review Act of 1989, California Health and Safety Code, 25244.12 *et seq.*

6. These documents are prepared and updated by EPICS International (Environmental Programs Information and Compliance Services), Oakland, California, and published by Specialty Technical Publishers, Inc., Vancouver, B.C., Canada.

7. Jeffery A. Foran, "The Sunset Chemical Proposal," *International Environmental Affairs*, 2 (Fall 1990), 303–308.

8. The case for adopting an aggressive policy of banning potentially harmful substances for use in society is presented by Commoner in "The Environment," *New Yorker* (June 15, 1987), 46-71.

9. Garrett Hardin, "The Tragedy of the Commons," *Science* 162 (December 13, 1968), 1243–1248.

10. Robert J. Smith, "Privatizing the Environment," *Policy Review* (Spring 1982), 43.

11. Terry L. Anderson and Donald R. Leal, *Free Market Environmentalism* (Boulder, Colo.: Westview, 1991), esp. ch. 2.

12. That polluters would pay is central to achieving the socially "optimal" level of pollution for the privatization paradigm, and the idea is therefore applauded by its proponents. The environmental paradigm, in contrast, frames the issue in terms of pollution elimination. Its advocates typically resist schemes that allow impersonal, nonscientific, nonecological "market forces" to determine the level of pollution that will be accepted within society.

13. Congressional Budget Office (CBO), U.S. Congress, "Hazardous Waste Management: Recent Changes and Policy Alternatives," (May 1985). David Carol and Kenneth Rubin are named as authors in the preface to this report.

14. Senator William Gormley has proposed this approach to the New Jersey Senate, one explicitly designed to encourage firms to intensify source-reduction practices.

15. CBO, "Hazardous Waste Management," 78–79.

16. "Project 88—Harnessing Market Forces to Protect Our Environment: Initiatives for the New President," public policy study sponsored by Senator Timothy E. Wirth, Colorado, and Senator John Heinz, Pennsylvania (Washington, D.C.: December 1988), 74–76.

17. A battery-recycling bill has been introduced in California. This overall approach was recommended in Seymour I. Schwartz, Wendy Pratt Cuckovich, Nancy Steffenson-Ostrom, and Cecilia F. Cox, "Managing Hazardous Wastes Produced by Small Quantity Generators," Senate Office of Research, California Legislature (April 1987).

18. Clean Sites, "Making Superfund Work: Recommendations to Improve Program Implementation" (Clean Sites, Inc., January 1989); William K. Reilly (EPA Administrator), *A Management Review of the Superfund Program* (Washington, D.C.: June 1989).

19. Gene A. Lucero, "Cleanup of Old Waste: Some Thoughts on Rethinking the Fundamentals of Superfund," *Risk Analysis* 11 (March 1991), 66.

20. Dennis Connolly, "Comments on 'Cleanup of Old Wastes: Some Thoughts on Rethinking the Fundamentals of Superfund,'" *Risk Analysis* 11 (March 1991), 69.

21. "Environmental Audits May Improve Compliance, but Beware of Disclosure, Attorneys Caution," *Environment Reporter* (August 30, 1991), 1195–1196. The Justice Department document referenced is "Factors in Decisions on Criminal Prosecutions for Environmental Violations in the Context of Significant Voluntary Compliance or Disclosure Efforts by the Violator" (July 1, 1991).

22. Esteban E. Torres, "Perspective on Pollution; It's Do-It-Ourselves Time," *Los Angeles Times* (October 28, 1991), B5.

23. Michael L. Poirier Elliott, "Improving Community Acceptance of Hazardous Waste Facilities Through Alternative Systems of Mitigating and Managing Risk," *Hazardous Waste* 1 (1984), 397–410.

24. For the general theoretical underpinning of this property rights approach, see Anderson and Leal, *Free Market Environmentalism*, 82–84.

25. Bruce W. Piasecki and Gary A. Davis, *America's Future in Toxic Waste Management: Lessons from Europe* (New York: Quorum Books, 1987), 229.

26. Economic Impacts Analysis Project, "Hazardous Waste Treatment Facility Funding and Use in Los Angeles County," a joint venture by the County of Los Angeles Department of Public Works, County Sanitation Districts of Los Angeles County, and Southern California Coalition for Hazardous Materials Management (June 1988).

27. See CBO, "Hazardous Waste Management," ch. 2, and the technical documents accompanying this report.

28. This literature is expanding quite rapidly. See John D. Graham, Laura C. Green, and Marc J. Roberts, *In Search of Safety: Chemicals and Cancer Risk* (Cambridge, Mass.: Harvard University Press, 1988), esp. ch. 7; Sheldon Krimsky and Alonzo Plough, *Environmental Hazards: Communicating Risks as a Social Process* (Dover, Mass.: Auburn House, 1988); Committee on Risk Perception and Communication, National Research Council, *Improving Risk Communications* (Washington, D.C.: National Academy Press, 1989); "Risk," *Daedalus* 119 (Fall 1990), entire symposium issue.

29. Carl E. Van Horn, "Breaking the Environmental Gridlock: The Report on a National Conference" (New Brunswick, N.J.: Eagleton Institute of Politics, 1988).

30. Susan G. Hadden, "Public Perception of Hazardous Waste," *Risk Analysis* 11 (March 1991), 54–55.

Glossary

Acid
A large class of substances that form solutions having a low pH. Stronger acids are corrosive to metals and other materials. Acids may be neutralized by being mixed with bases or alkalis to form salts.

Acid waste
A waste with a pH less than 7. (The pH scale shows increasing acidity as numbers decrease from 7 toward zero. Anything above 7 is alkaline or "basic.") An acid waste is hazardous when its pH is 2.0 or less. See "pH."

Activated sludge treatment
Exposing wastes to microorganisms and air. A portion of the organic matter is oxidized to carbon dioxide and water; the remainder is synthesized into new microbial cells.

Acute
Type of effects manifested soon after exposure to a hazardous material.

Adsorption
Gathering a gas, liquid, or dissolved substance on a surface (e.g., when charcoal adsorbs gases). Can be used to remove low concentrations of organic materials from gaseous and watery waste streams.

Aerobic
Occuring in the presence of free oxygen.

Alkaline waste
A waste with a pH between 7 and 14. An alkaline waste is hazardous when its pH is 12.5 or greater.

Ambient
Reference to existing conditions of air, water, and other media at a particular time.

Anaerobic digestion
Process used to break down organic wastes through biological activity in the absence of oxygen.

Aqueous
Of, relating to, or resembling water.

Aquifer
A porous geologic formation capable of yielding a significant amount of groundwater to wells or springs.

Base
A substance that forms a salt when it reacts with an acid. Bases have a pH greater than 7.

Berm
A concrete curb built around liquid storage tanks that acts as a catchment basin in the event of spills or leaks.

Binding arbitration
A process for the resolution of disputes. Decisions are made by impartial arbitrators. The decisions of the arbitrators are final, and acceptance of these decisions must be agreed to in advance by the parties.

Bioaccumulation
Process by which substances increase in concentration in living organisms (that are not readily metabolized or excreted) as they breathe contaminated air, drink contaminated water, or eat contaminated food.

Blending (waste streams)
Mixing two or more waste streams.

Boiler
A pressure vessel designed to produce vapor from liquid by the application of heat.

Buffer zone
An area of land that surrounds a facility handling hazardous materials and on which certain land uses are restricted in order to provide partial protection of public health and the environment from the migration of hazardous constituents.

Cap
A layer of clay or other highly impermeable material installed over the top of a closed landfill to prevent entry of rainwater and thus minimize production of leachate.

Carcinogen
A chemical strongly suspected of causing cancer by various means of exposure.

Catalyst
A substance, usually present in small amounts relative to the reactants, that increases the rate of a chemical reaction without being consumed in the process.

Caustics (bases, alkalis)
A large class of substances that form solutions having a high pH. Stronger caustics are corrosive to many materials. Caustics react with acids to form salts.

Cell
A portion of compacted wastes in a landfill that is enclosed by natural soil or cover materials.

Cement-kiln incineration
Burning organic wastes as a supplementary fuel at very high temperatures during the production of cement.

"Characteristics" of hazardous waste
A method of identifying which substances are hazardous waste by their physical/chemical properties. EPA has established four "characteristics" that can be determined by tests:

Ignitability: the ability to catch fire.
Corrosivity: the ability to wear away or destroy other materials, including human tissue.
Reactivity: the ability to enter into a violent chemical reaction that may involve explosion or fumes.
Toxicity: the ability to release certain toxic constituents when leached with a mild acid.

Chemical oxidation
Adding strongly oxidizing chemicals to waste streams to effect a reaction that can produce less-toxic substances and may reduce quantities of such substances. (Cyanide can be detoxified by the addition of hypochlorite or some other oxidizing agent.)

Chemical reduction
The addition of chemicals to wastes to cause partial or complete decomposition of particular waste components into their basic nontoxic parts.

Chronic
Type of effects that continue over time.

Clay lining/clay cap
A landfill enclosure made from heavy clays of very low porosity.

Compensation
Payments awarded either through the courts or a government-administered fund to cover injury or damage caused by exposure to hazardous substances.

Composting
Allowing microbial action to break down solid waste mixed with soil in a landfill.

Conditional use permit (CUP)
A discretionary permit, issued by cities and counties, that is required for certain projects allowable by special permit only. A conditional use permit imposes conditions on a project that are designed to ensure that the project is compatible with the local general plan and zoning ordinances and that impacts to neighboring land uses are minimized.

Containment
Any process of immobilizing hazardous wastes, usually in the ground, that prevents their migration offsite.

Criteria pollutant   An air pollutant for which there is considered to be a safe level of exposure and for which standards have been set. Current criteria pollutants are sulfur oxides, particulate matter, carbon monoxide, nitrogen oxides, ozone, and lead.

Dechlorination   Using chemical reactions to detoxify wastes by removing chlorine from chlorinated compounds.

Deep-well injection   Disposal of wastes by injecting them into geological formations deep in the ground, sometimes after treatment to prevent solidification.

Developer   A person, government unit, or company that proposes to build a hazardous waste treatment, storage, or disposal facility.

Dilution   To thin down or weaken by mixing with another substance or substances (e.g., to dilute with water).

Discretionary project or permit   A project or permit that requires the use of judgment or deliberation when the public agency or body decides to approve or disapprove a particular activity, as distinguished from situations in which the public agency or body merely has to determine whether there has been conformity with applicable statutes, ordinances, or regulations (compare "ministerial").

Disposal   Abandoning, depositing, interring, or otherwise discarding waste as a final action after use has been achieved or a use is no longer intended.

Disposal site   The location where any final depositing of hazardous waste occurs.

Dissolution   Dissolving a substance in water or organic solvent.

Distillation   Separating a mixture of liquids with different boiling points by heating the mixture, separately boiling off and retrieving the different components in the process of recondensation.

Drum decantation   Pouring only the liquid material from a drum, leaving settled solids in the drum.

Effluent   Any liquid flowing out of some process or container; usually describes the discharge of a liquid pollutant.

Electrostatic precipitators	Devices that remove particles from a gas stream by passing the gas through an electric field to charge the particles. The particles stick to the oppositely charged plate and are removed mechanically.
Eminent domain	The right of a government to appropriate private property for necessary public use, with compensation paid to the landowner.
Encapsulation	Complete enclosure of wastes with some nonreactive material.
Environmental impact report or statement	A report describing and analyzing the significant environmental effects of a project and discussing ways to mitigate or avoid the effects.
Environmental impairment liability (EIL) insurance	A relatively new form of liability insurance which extends the general liability insurance that nearly all businesses purchase; also known as gradual pollution liability insurance.
Epidemiology	The study of prevalent diseases in humans.
Evaporation	A process for concentrating nonvolatile solids in solution by vaporizing the liquid portion, usually water. Solar evaporation utilizes uncovered ponds.
Excavation	Removal of earth; usually denotes the transfer of substantial amounts of contaminated soil to another site or treatment location.
Exposure	Contact with a hazardous material, commonly by skin contact, breathing, or taking by mouth.
Feedstock	Any chemicals or other raw materials used to manufacture another end product.
Filtration	Separating liquids and solids by passing suspensions through various porous materials.
Fixation	Process by which waste is made unchangeable and/or stationary.
Flammable	Capable of burning below 140 degrees Fahrenheit, either spontaneously or through handling, as a result of coming into contact with already flaming material.

Flocculation	Physical or chemical process that causes particles to aggregate into a mass that may be easier to handle or to treat.
Fluidized-bed incineration	Injecting wastes into agitated beds of inert granular material and burning them. Suitable for sludges and liquid wastes; solid waste may need grinding.
Generator	The person or facility who, by virtue of ownership, management, or control, is responsible for causing or allowing to be caused the creation of hazardous waste.
Groundwater	Water found in saturated underground strata; also feeds wells and springs.
Halogenated	Existence in the structure of substance of chlorine, bromine, fluorine, or iodine atom.
Hazard ranking system (HRS)	Federal EPA ranking system used for preliminary estimation of the degree of contamination in suspected hazardous waste sites. Sites receiving a score of 28.5 or more are included on the federal Superfund list. Also called the MITRE model.
Hazardous material	Any substance that is toxic, corrosive, flammable, reactive, an irritant, or a strong sensitizer and that therefore pose a threat to human health and the environment. Hazardous materials that spill onto roadways or other surfaces automatically become hazardous wastes.
Hazardous waste	Waste or a combination of wastes that may either (1) cause or significantly contribute to an increase in mortality, or in serious illness that is irreversible or reversible but with continuing incapacitation or (2) pose a substantial present or potential hazard to human health or the environment when improperly treated, stored, transported, disposed of, or otherwise managed.
Hazardous waste facility	A facility that handles, stores, treats, or disposes of a hazardous waste. Does not include facilities oil producers use to biologically neutralize oil and water mixtures so that resulting liquid can be safely disposed of in sewers.
Hazardous waste manifest	Form that contains a description by chemical content and weight of materials being transported as well as their origin and destination.

Heavy metals   Toxic, high-density, metallic elements such as lead, silver, mercury, and arsenic.

Herbicide   A chemical used to kill plants.

High-priority wastes   Wastes that have properties particularly hazardous to human health (toxicity), that can accumulate in living organisms (bioaccumulation), and that remain hazardous for a long time (persistence); or that pose increased potential for air emissions because of their volatility, and for groundwater contamination because of seepage through soil (mobility). Examples include wastes that contain pesticides, PCBs, cyanides, toxic metals, halogenated organics, or nonhalogenated volatile organics.

Hydrogeology   The geology of groundwater, with particular emphasis on the chemical composition and movement of the water.

Incentives   (1) Measures that provide benefits to communities above and beyond the costs associated with hazardous waste management facilities. Incentives are intended to make a community better off than it would be without a hazardous waste management facility. (2) Also refers to certain measures (low-interest loans, tax breaks) taken by government to stimulate the development and implementation of improved technologies for managing hazardous waste.

Incineration   Combustion of wastes in any form at very high temperature (1,500–2,200 degrees F). Used to destroy particularly dangerous materials (e.g., PCBs) that are difficult to handle or to neutralize by chemical or other means. Produces a less-hazardous or nonhazardous residual ash that is often landfilled or stored in a residuals repository.

Inert   Exhibiting no chemical activity; totally unreactive.

Injunction   A court order to do or refrain from doing a particular activity.

Inorganics   Chemicals or mineral-containing materials that do not contain carbon. Inorganic wastes are thus rarely associated with pesticides or solvents; rather, they often contain toxic heavy metals, cyanide compounds, or sulfur.

Ions   Chemical constituents of a solution having a positive or
                                negative electrical charge.

Irritant   Substances that are not corrosive but can injure or inflame
                                living tissue.

Judicial review   Legal evaluations courts made of administrative agency
                                decisions and actions.

Lab-pack wastes   Small, containerized waste packages; often placed into
                                drums containing absorbent packing material.

Lagoons /   Lined or unlined pits used for storage or evaporation of
evaporating ponds   hazardous wastes.

Land application   Hazardous waste disposal method, now in limited use,
                                involving spreading waste onto the ground and allowing
                                the sunlight to evaporate the water contained in it.

Land disposal   Disposal, storage, or treatment of hazardous waste on or
                                into the land, including but not limited to landfilling,
                                surface impoundment, waste piles, deep-well injection,
                                land spreading, and coburial with municipal garbage.

Landfill   Large excavated pit used to dispose of wastes. It may be
                                lined with clay or plastic or unlined.

Liability

   Apportioned   Liability is assigned proportionally to all responsible
                                parties according to their degree of fault.

   Contingent /   Future or continuing strict liability is limited to the extent
   channelled   of actual possession of hazardous substances, provided a
                                responsible party has conformed to specific allowable
                                practices while handling those materials.

   Joint and several   Any party responsible at any point for specific wastes is
                                liable for all damages, but may compel any other
                                responsible parties to share in indemnities.

   Strict   A party is responsible for damages attributable to
                                hazardous substances under the party's control, no matter
                                how long ago or what management practices were
                                followed. Retroactive strict liability is the application of
                                strict liability even when the action causing damage was

not in violation of laws in effect at the time the action occurred.

Mediation A voluntary negotiation process in which a neutral mediator assists the parties in a dispute to reach a mutual agreement.

Microbial action Process by which microbes destroy or transform compounds such as toxics.

Microorganism In the context of biological treatment of wastes, microscopic bacteria, protozoa, fungi, and other living matter that degrade organic wastes.

Migration Movement of a substance from one place to another through natural processes.

Ministerial project or permit Governmental decision involving little or no personal judgment by the public official as to the wisdom or manner of carrying out a project. The public official merely applies the law to the facts as presented and uses fixed standards or objective measurements, but exercises no special discretion in reaching a decision. Common examples of ministerial permits include automobile registrations, dog licenses, and marriage licenses

Monitoring well A well, drilled near a hazardous waste management facility, to allow groundwater to be sampled and analyzed for contamination.

Mutagenic Description for a substance that causes alterations in the structure of the genetic material of living things.

Negligence Breach of a recognized duty of care that causes damage.

Negotiation A process through which tradeoffs are made by parties in a dispute to reach an agreement satisfying them all.

Neutralization Chemical treatment that inactivates the hazardous aspect of a substance.

New source Within the context of air pollution control, a new facility or a modification of an existing facility that is a source of air pollution. Applicable regulations may cause restrictions on the development of some hazardous waste facilities.

Nonattainment area   Area having ambient air levels of pollutants that exceed federal or state standards. It may be difficult to obtain approval for certain kinds of hazardous waste facilities, such as incinerators, in nonattainment areas.

Nonhalogenated   Absence in a substance of a halogen (chlorine, bromine, fluorine, iodine); such substances evaporate at relatively low temperatures.

Offsite hazardous waste facility   An operation involving handling, treatment, storage, or disposal of a hazardous waste in one or more of the following situations:

   (1) The hazardous waste is transported via a commercial railroad, a public road or public waters, the land adjacent to which is not owned by or leased to the producer of the waste.
   (2) The hazardous waste is at a site not owned by or leased to the producer of the waste.
   (3) The hazardous waste is at a site that receives hazardous waste from more than one producer.

Offsite treatment   Treatment of a waste at a site physically separate from the site where the waste was generated.

Onsite hazardous waste facility   An operation involving handling, treatment, storage, or disposal of hazardous waste on land owned by or leased to a waste producer and that receives only that producer's hazardous waste.

Onsite treatment   Treatment of a waste on the site where it was originally generated (e.g., within an industrial plant or on the premises).

Operator   A person, government unit, or company that conducts treatment, storage, or disposal. The operator may or may not be the developer.

Organics   Carbon–containing compounds. Some of the most toxic substances are organic chemicals like PCBs, DDT, and many solvents.

Orphan site   A site for which no responsible party can be identified, located, or compelled to pay for cleanup.

Osmosis   Process that separates materials by passing them through a semipermeable membrane.

Oxidized by-products   By-products generated by oxidation (combining with oxygen).

PCB   Polychlorinated biphenyl, any of a group of chlorinated compounds used in industrial processes in the form of colorless, odorless, viscous liquid and discharged in industrial wastes.

Permeable   Ability of a substance to allow passage of liquids or gas throughout the material.

Permit   (Noun)—A document issued by a government unit that allows specific activities to proceed under specified conditions. (Verb)—To grant a permit.

Pesticide   A chemical used to kill destructive insects, such as fleas.

pH   A measure of the acidity or alkalinity of a liquid. The scale indicates neutrality at 7; acidity is indicated by numbers below 7 down to zero. Alkalinity is indicated by numbers above 7 up to 14.

Pickling liquors   Corrosive liquids used for removing impurities (scale, oxides) from the surfaces of metals.

Plastic lining   Relatively impermeable plastic sheeting used to line a landfill, thereby preventing water and other liquids from seeping into or out of the fill.

Ponding   The process of holding water in ponds to encourage the water to evaporate or pass downward through the soil.

Postclosure   The time period following closure (shutdown) of a facility.

Precipitation   The changing of a substance held in solution by adding a chemical to cause the substance to change into a solid form, thus allowing the solids to be gathered and removed from the liquids.

Prevention   Taking measures to minimize the release of wastes to the environment.

Process substitution   Substituting one industrial or production process for another, usually in order to reduce the amount of toxic or unwanted material used or produced.

Pyrolysis   Heating toxic materials in an enclosed space, in an
                                 oxygen-deficient situation, to create a residual material of
                                 lowered toxicity.

Recharge zone   A land area where rainwater infiltration from surface
                                 streams, impoundment areas, or other sources soaks into
                                 the ground and enters an aquifer.

Recycling   The reuse of a material that prevents its disposal into the
                                 environment.

Remediation/   The restoration of a degraded site to some specified
remedial cleanup   standard of cleanliness or to a lower degree of potential
                                 harm.

Residuals repository   A waste disposal and storage landfill facility designed to
                                 protect against any infiltration of liquids (covered at all
                                 times) and to permit retrieval of residuals for further
                                 reclamation or treatment in the future.

Residue   Material remaining after treatment processes. Residues
                                 may be less hazardous or, at least, less voluminous and
                                 easier to handle than the original wastes.

Resource recovery   The salvage of discarded hazardous materials or their
                                 conversion into a reusable, salable, or valuable form.
                                 Salvaged or converted materials are not considered waste.

Responsible party   Federal law (CERCLA) defines persons responsible (or
                                 liable) for hazardous waste site cleanups as the owner or
                                 operator of a hazardous waste vessel, facility, or disposal
                                 facility; persons who arranged for disposal, treatment, or
                                 transportation of hazardous waste; and persons who
                                 transported or disposed of hazardous waste.

Risk   A measure of the likelihood and severity of injury.

Rodenticide   A class of pesticide that kills, repels, or controls rodents
                                 (rats, mice, rabbits, squirrels, gophers).

Rotary-kiln   The burning of liquid or solid wastes in large inclined
incineration   cylinders lined with firebrick and rotated to improve the
                                 movement of solids through the incinerator. Virtually any
                                 kind of waste, in any form, can be incinerated in rotary
                                 kilns.

Sensitizers   Substances that produce allergic reactions.

Sludge   Wastes that are concentrated in a semiliquid, semisolid suspension.

Slurry   An aqueous mixture of insoluble materials.

Solidification   A treatment process for limiting the solubility of or detoxifying hazardous waste by producing blocks of treated waste with high structural integrity.

Solid waste   All solid and semisolid wastes (e.g., garbage, rubbish, paper, ashes, industrial wastes, demolition and construction wastes, abandoned vehicles and parts, discarded home and industrial appliances, vegetable or animal solid and semisolid wastes, manure, and other discharged solid and semisolid wastes). Also includes liquids disposed of in conjunction with solid wastes at solid waste transfer/processing stations or disposal sites but excludes (1) sewage collected and treated in a municipal or regional sewerage system and (2) material or substances of commercial value salvaged for reuse, recycling, or resale.

Solvent   A liquid having chemical properties that allow it to dissolve a solid.

Solvent extraction   Treating a solid or liquid waste to extract hazardous substances so that the bulk of the waste stream may be discarded as nonhazardous.

Source reduction   Any manufacturing process change that results in significantly lower initial demands for the use of hazardous materials as feedstock.

Stabilization   A treatment process to limit the solubility of hazardous wastes, or to detoxify them, by adding materials that ensure maintenance of the hazardous constituents in their least soluble and/or toxic form.

Superfund   The short name for CERCLA (1980). This act is "Superfund" because it relies on a tax on petroleum and chemical feedstocks as a means of financing cleanup of dangerous hazardous waste disposal sites around the United States.

Surface impoundment	A hazardous waste facility devised from a natural topographic depression, manmade excavation, or diked area, designed to hold an accumulation of liquid wastes or wastes containing free liquids, usually in order to treat the wastes.
Synergism	The action of two materials together to produce an effect that is greater than the sum of their individual actions.
Toxic	Capable of producing injury, illness, or damage to humans, domestic livestock, or wildlife by being ingested, inhaled, or absorbed through any body surface.
Toxic air contaminant	An air pollutant that may cause or contribute to an increase in serious illness or that may pose a present or potential hazard to human health.
Toxicity	Relative degree of being poisonous.
Toxicology	The science of toxic substances, including their effects and antidotes.
Transfer station	Any facility where hazardous wastes are transferred from one vehicle to another or where hazardous wastes are stored or consolidated before being transported elsewhere.
Treatment	Any process that renders a hazardous waste less harmful, inert, or reduced in amount.
Biological	Treating liquid hazardous wastes with microorganisms capable of digesting the wastes and converting them to other forms. The five principle techniques include activated sludge, aerated lagoons, trickling filters, waste stabilization ponds, and anaerobic digestion.
Chemical	Treating wastes chemically to reduce concentrations of hazardous wastes or to render them less dangerous. Principal techniques include neutralization, precipitation, ion exchange, chemical dechlorination, and chemical oxidation/reduction.
Physical	Separating, by physical means, water or other liquids from hazardous wastes.
Thermal	Using elevated temperatures as the primary means of changing the chemical, physical, or biological character of

the waste; the most common type of thermal treatment is incineration.

Treatment facility   Any facility at which hazardous waste is subjected to treatment or where a resource is recovered from a hazardous waste.

Ultrahazardous activity   Activity involving substantial risk of injury, damage, or death that even the utmost care cannot eliminate.

Waste   Any material that has no intended use or reuse and that is to be discarded.

Waste exchange   Clearinghouse approach to transferring treated and untreated hazardous wastes to an industrial user for use as raw material.

Waste minimization   Either (1) reducing the generation of waste or (2) reducing the waste that is generated; definition differs by agency.

Waste streams   All waste coming into, through, or out of a facility. Sometimes used to refer collectively to all wastes.

About the Book and Authors

Despite numerous small success stories, the big picture of America's toxics programs is one of overall failure. Superfund has failed to clean up America's worst dump sites; policies to regulate generation of new hazardous waste have foundered; standards have been set for only eight of several hundred air toxics; transportation spills and industrial accidents continue unabated. In part, this "superfailure" reflects problems of bureaucratic implementation, but more importantly, it points to a failing of democratic discourse, technical risk assessment, and ultimately, the political process. Mazmanian and Morell address these issues and others in proposing a new approach to toxics policymaking for the 1990s and beyond.

Skillfully employing case studies and examples from all over America and abroad, the authors chronicle the history of toxics disasters and success stories and then recommend basic changes in the way the U.S. should handle environmental problems of all types in the future. Chief among these prescriptions is a new emphasis on community-based discussion and decisionmaking, in combination with federal macro-level policy guidelines and industry-initiated policy innovations. The authors set forth detailed suggestions for ways to replace today's policy inertia with initiatives they characterize as "positive action compliance, positive action permitting, and positive action cleanup."

Engaging and thoroughly accessible, *Beyond Superfailure* will be of interest to students and practitioners of environmental policy as well as to activists and citizens who want to improve both the environment and the democratic process. Extensively illustrated with charts, checklists, and diagrams, the book should be useful and provocative in presenting a case for positive policy change.

Daniel Mazmanian is a professor of political science and public policy at the Claremont Graduate School. **David Morell** is founder and president of EPICS International, an independent consulting firm specializing in regulatory information and compliance assistance. Both authors are recognized for their numerous books and articles on environmental policy and hazardous waste management.

Index

monitoring, 61. *See also* Monitoring
regulating, 16–17, 19, 61, 151–161,
167–169. *See also* Regulations and
source control, 131–132. *See also*
Source reduction
state regulation of, 147–151
threat from, 145–147, 174
and toxics populism, 169–174
transporting, 166–167. *See also*
Transporting
and underground storage tanks,
161–166. *See also* Underground
storage tanks
See also Toxics policy
*Hazardous Materials Program
Commentary*, 212
Hazardous Materials Transportation
Act (HMTA), 89, 166–167
Hazardous Substances Response Trust
Fund, 33–34
Hazardous waste
defining, 80–83, 98, 113(n37)
exporting, 88
household, 82, 84–85(box), 137,
138–139(box)
substance bans, 213
volumes, 83, 96–97, 99, 175, 199(box)
See also Cleanup; Land disposal;
Toxics policy; Treatment
Hazardous Waste Management
Council (California), 196, 200
Hazardous waste sites
cleanup liability issues, 33–37,
49–50(box)
cleanup process for, 30–31, 32(box),
52(n11)
cleanup settlements, 37–39, 46(box),
53(n22), 54(n28)
effectiveness of cleanup, 57–58
health effects, 33
intergovernmental cooperation in
cleanup of, 39–42
Lipari Superfund site, 58–75
remedial choices for, 42–45, 47–48
and volume of wastes, 112(n13)
See also Cleanup; Superfund
Hazard ranking system (HRS), 31
Health
and hazardous materials, 2, 33, 60, 83
and Lipari site, 64–65, 71–73
and Love Canal, 3–4
See also Risk(s), health versus costs

Health groups
and democratic discourse, 241
and siting issues, 180, 181, 195
Heavy metals
disposal of, 15, 213
treatment of, 122
Heinz, John, 219–220
Hirschhorn, Joel, 68
HMTA. *See* Hazardous Materials
Transportation Act
Hooker Chemical Company, 45
Household hazardous waste, 82,
84–85(box)
collecting, 137, 138–139(box)
HRS. *See* Hazard ranking system
HSWA. *See* Hazardous and Solid
Waste Amendments
Hughes, William, 67, 69
Hunter Environmental Services, 125
Hydroxides, 118

IBM, 53(n22)
Illegal dumping, 9, 220
and enforcement, 240
and land disposal phaseout, 107
and RCRA, 86, 89
Illinois, 14, 39, 93, 109
Incentives
for delaying RCRA implementation,
105–106
and Denmark, 137
economic, and waste management,
217
fee-and-rebate system, 219–221
for good-faith bargaining, 234
for hosting treatment facilities, 185
for positive action, 209, 222–232
for source reduction, 102, 158, 212,
237, 239–240, 244(n14)
waste-based tax, 109, 218–219
Incineration, 15, 119, 123–124
capacity shortfalls in, 200
costs, 128–129(box)
permits for, 108, 114(n51), 225
and public attitudes, 13
and TTUs, 126
Indiana, 37
Industry
and cleanup costs, 221, 228. *See also*
Cleanup
and cleanup liability, 36–37. *See also*
Liability